SLEEP
ON IT

and change your life !

Acknowledgements

I am deeply indebted to the volunteer dreamers who stepped forward and offered to share their dreams, experiences and innermost thoughts through joining the Dream Survey. Without their help, this book would not exist. I also extend my thanks to the hundreds of others who have consulted me about their dreams, in person, through the mail and over the airwaves. You have all contributed.

I wish to thank ABC Brisbane's 612 4QR radio station for courageously introducing dream awareness through my weekly dream talkback segment on Paul Lineham's afternoon show. A special appreciation goes to Paul, whose early cynicism kept me on my toes while he grew to witness the importance of dreams in the lives of his audience. His promotion of dream talkback fired both my own enthusiasm for doing this research and the hearts of many of its listeners who have responded to the survey with such generosity.

Thank you friends, colleagues, family and neighbours for provocative discussion and terrific support during this research work and writing period.

May your dream lights shine.

Dedication

This book is dedicated to Glenn, my husband and
my own private magician. Thank you for unwavering
support and encouragement and for many beautiful dreams
come true. I love you too.

And to Rowan, my daughter, and Euan, my son,
in thanks for their love, faith and understanding
which stretches beyond their years.
May you grow to truly comprehend the enormity
of the power of your dreams and may they
all be as beautiful as you.

CONTENTS

PART THREE
PHYSIOLOGY, PSYCHOLOGY AND PHILOSOPHY
Dreaming the Holy Grail

INTRODUCTION

Just a Dream?

'Don't worry, dear, it's only a dream,' comforts the father, whose distressed child has just woken from a nightmare. 'What a vivid imagination!' laughs the proud mother, 'You'll make a good storyteller one day!' unwittingly belittling her child's dream experience. Her son grows to forget his dreams as he is taught that his outer world, his career, even his vivid imagination are far more important than the world within.

As adults we wonder why we forget our dreams or even why we seem not to dream at all. Surely this is no surprise if we have been conditioned to believe our dreams are confused mumbo jumbo, or the brain's electrical filing system sorting through the previous day's events and chucking out the old useless memories. Why would we respect, recall or take a second glance at what we are programmed to believe is mere night-time garbage?

In these decades of changing economic times and spiritual evolution, the focus is on 'how to' and self-reliance, yet people everywhere emerge from their nightly sleep with little comprehension of the power their dreams hold to give clear direction and to change their lives. Why waste what the night brings?

Dream amnesia commonly sets in when our dreams deal with issues we'd rather not face. Who would want to spoil the delicate balance of their daily life even though that balance may be as tricky to maintain as walking along a knife edge? If we can get to the end of each day without putting a foot wrong, without too much pain, who would want to risk jeopardising this by peering over the edge into their dreams? I would! I'd much rather look at the underlying causes of my life's patterns, the ways I react and behave in different circumstances and gain new understanding that can convert that stomach churning knife edge into a pair of wings! All it takes is the willingness to open yourself to your dreams, their meanings and their ability to provide you with the means to change your life. This requires an open mind and the courage to look right in the eyes of whatever comes up. Are *you* ready to take that journey?

This book is based on the Dream Survey which researched the dreaming and waking lives of 160 people from a variety of backgrounds. The results bring a clearer understanding of the meaning and practical application of our dreams to our lives. The research from the study reveals how to improve your dream recall, how to open yourself up to more dream experiences and, most importantly, how to take actions based on them!

Reuniting with your true self through your dreams means getting back in touch with a long-lost language: the language of symbol and intuition. Deep inside you have a perfect knowledge of this universal and ancient tongue. It simply needs to be rekindled and brought back into your conscious awareness where it can serve you best and awaken your full power to create the life you deserve. This book reconnects you with this dream language by teaching you up-to-date, practical, tried and tested methods for interpreting and understanding your dreams. This is made easier with the 'Tree of Discovery' in Chapter 22 which guides you though this process.

Once we see our dreams as vehicles of meaningful information or guidance which can help us to transform our lives, we must question the source of this nightly wisdom. Where do our dreams come from?

Does our religion or our spirituality influence our dreams? Do we see the face of God we are raised to expect? Do we meet angels, saints, Buddha, light beings, spiritual guides or Hindu deities? Or do our dreams confront us, challenge our spiritual beliefs and cause major changes in our outlook on life? Do we write off religious or spiritual dreams as conditioned symbology, as reflections of our subconscious worlds, or do they inspire us to greater purpose and fulfilment?

How do you feel when you suddenly find yourself reliving a dream in waking reality? You suddenly realise that you have glimpsed the future in a dream and now it is taking place in front of your eyes. How does this experience affect your understanding of life? Does deja vu inspire understanding of alternate realities? Many people experience time travelling in their dreams. Can we use this phenomenon to make better decisions or to alter the situation when it plays out before us? How do we cope with living through a bad experience that we have pre-seen, either in a dream, or in a misty, long-lost sense of having 'been through this before'?

Do we carry our unresolved problems into our sleep, and, if so, do our dreams take over and work on the solutions that our conscious minds have ignored, or found too hard? Do worriers dream more about their problems than people who positively set about solving their difficulties? Can dreaming provide fresh insight, or more creative answers than our more logical daytime problem solving techniques? Can we use dreaming to our advantage, and hand over our weightier challenges and decisions to our dreaming selves? Is there good cause to snuff out the late night candle, close the account books and burn the midnight oil in your dreams instead, getting a good night's sleep into the bargain? Or is it better to address your problems, clear your head, and settle for a stress free rewarding night of pleasant dreams? Is there good advice in the well-worn phrase 'Sleep on it', or is going to bed with matters unsettled a cop-out?

People you know, used to know, who are dead, hardly know, or just plain strangers all enter your dreams. Who are they and why are they there? You may dream of places you used to live in, or of times that feel like past lives. How can you tell the difference between time travelling and symbolic settings? How can you use these experiences to make your waking life easier or more successful?

How does writing down your dreams, thinking about them or taking part in the dream survey affect your dreams? Does diet, exercise, your sleeping and waking routine, and other aspects of your lifestyle affect the quality or quantity of dreams you remember? Does interpreting, understanding and acting upon your dreams change or influence your dreaming life? Do future dreams confirm or comment on the actions you have taken?

How does daydreaming or meditating affect your dreams? Is it possible to resolve unfinished dreams or go back into a dream to fish for lost details? Why do some people have recurring dreams and nightmares? Can these be stopped?

Apart from speech, which other senses pervade our dreams? Some people dream in colour, or in intense colour quite unlike waking life. Others dream in black and white. Taste, touch, telepathy, out-of-the-body sensations and other psychic senses add detail to our dreams. Our hearts beat faster, our bodies may feel paralysed and some people, particularly women, report orgasms. Are these dream sensations real or symbolic?

What do we mean when we question the 'real' and the 'symbolic' in our dreams? What is our measure of reality? Is reality what happens to us when we are awake? Are dreams illusions because we are asleep when they occur? We see rainbows and mirages when awake. Are they real or illusions? When we are awake, we know that we dream, but in the middle of a dream, unless we are lucid (consciously aware that we are dreaming while we are in the dream), we have no idea that we have another life: a waking life. In the midst of a dream, we have only one reality and that is our dreaming life. The things we experience and the emotions we feel are, at that moment, real. We carry these dream feelings over into our waking lives, often with as much conviction as a daytime, conscious experience.

We can and do bring back different points of view, spiritual insights, details of future events, medical diagnoses, lotto numbers, chemical formulae, mathematical theories, winning horses and accurate information about those close to us. When our dreaming worlds expand and explode into detail, we experience a 'reality' far greater than our waking consciousness and finally begin to glimpse new dimensions. As we learn to remember these dream details, to bring back more of our dream life, we find increased practical application in our waking life. We begin to break the bonds of our own restrictions and manifest our true potential.

The survey roams the far reaches of night-time experience, from symbolism to precognitive dreaming, from word play to time travel and from mental housekeeping to conversations with God. But where are the borderlines? When all is said and done, what is the difference between dream reality and waking reality? Should we look for dream signs and symbols in waking life too? Can we align both worlds to gain a deeper yet practical understanding of our overall reality and the actions we can take to change it?

Physiology, psychology, philosophy and metaphysics meet and mingle in this book to give an overall, practical perspective on the realities of dreaming and waking life, and how to fine tune yourself to benefit from travelling in both worlds.

Enjoy the journey!

SLEEP ON IT … AND CHANGE YOUR LIFE is presented in three parts.

PART ONE invites you to complete the Dream Survey Questionnaires, to meet the survey dreamers and to compare *your* answers with *theirs*. The research is summarised to show how our waking and dreaming lives interplay. Finally, Part One ties together the survey findings in the 'Guide to Good Dreaming' which gives practical suggestions on how to improve your dream recall and experience.

PART TWO takes an in-depth look at how to interpret your dreams and take action on them, as well as a considered approach to questioning other aspects of our dream experiences, such as time travel and other forms of psychic dreaming. It teaches you how to become 'The Magician on the Astral Plane'

Introduction

and bring back the magic of insight, practical application and food for spiritual thought from your dreaming life.

PART THREE looks at dreaming though the eyes of science, psychology and philosophy. In my language, that roughly translates as the body, mind and soul of dreaming. This section reviews it all and offers an all embracing theory of dreams. It takes you into the realm of merging your dreaming and waking lives and a step closer towards 'Dreaming the Holy Grail': discovering the meaning of life.

PART ONE

THE DREAM SURVEY

I Had This Dream

I Had This Dream

Waking
A whisper of morning
Calling him.
Sieved light,
A moment to flicker
To consider ...
but no
Not yet. Let go to fade.

Dreaming back to the seashore
close warmth of jade waves
Calm, serene, liberated.
The blood splattered shells
Her severed hand
Still cradling
Her newborn child.
The deep let go.
Bliss.

Waking
Harsher light ...
His wife's red hair:
'Morning! How did you sleep?'
she asks.
'I Had This Dream ...'
words slowed.
Red hair like blood
'Oh yes?', she reaches for her watch.
Like blood.
'It was nothing,' he smiled
At peace.

CHAPTER 1

The Dream Survey

Tomato Soup: A New Journey

I sat in the audience watching a rather dull, preschool play when a messenger squeezed between the ordered rows of hard backed chairs to hand me an envelope. His sudden attention broke my reverie, for my mind had been far from the stage, resting instead upon the tall yachts shimmering on the horizon. I opened the envelope and read 'Follow the Tomato Soup'. Nothing could be clearer, since this was a dream, and what seems bizarre to the waking mind makes perfect sense to the dreaming self. I stood up, left the dutiful audience and set out on my quest.

Upon waking I was left with the sense of pioneering, of seeking out a new direction with great purpose. Later that day I was browsing through a new dream dictionary and casually looked up 'soup' to find 'something to satisfy your hunger'. 'Tomato' was listed as 'a fruit representing passion'. This cut and dried approach to dream interpretation is far from my method, but the coincidence (or synchronicity as I now prefer to call it) was begging me to listen. The message now became 'Follow your passions to satisfy your hunger.' My passion, at that time, was writing, dream work and the media. I promptly dropped my other career pursuits and contacted a couple of radio stations to propose a dream talkback segment. Within a few weeks I had a half-hour live talkback spot on Queensland's ABC radio.

I was a bit slow on the writing idea. Although I had much experience in writing short pieces and newspaper columns, I

3

wanted to do more. I'd like to say a dream gave me guidance here, but it didn't. In fact I was so close to the trees that I couldn't see the woods. After three radio programs I had received many phone calls at home from listeners who were intrigued at my approach to dreams. Many were relieved to be able to talk about their dream experiences without the fear of being labelled weird and being rushed off to the nearest psychiatric ward. Many more asked where they could buy my book. It took another week before the penny finally dropped! I committed myself with a passion the next time I was on air, much to the surprise of my husband who watched from the other side of the glass. I asked for volunteers interested in sharing their dreams and their ideas on dreaming to contact me and contribute towards my research for my new book on dreaming. And here it is!

A year and what seems another lifetime later, I completed the research and fell asleep. My publishing contract had been signed on the basis of projected chapter headings and the pioneering nature of the research, well before anyone knew what the survey results would show. As I entered my dream world, I took with me my concerns of how to present my findings in the best way. That was last night and only the second time in my life that I remember dreaming of tomatoes!

This time I was having difficulty breathing and two nurses were curing me with a scalpel by slicing into the nail bed of the little finger on my right hand. The pain was intense. They then placed tomato circles into the little cuts, leaving my finger looking much like a triple decker tomato sandwich. The little boy who was watching asked what they were doing. The nurses replied: 'We have to inject through the tomato so that she can breathe again.'

After that painful process they gave me pure oxygen from a gas cylinder. Since, in my understanding of our long-lost intuitive language, the fingers represent our creativity and how we handle things, while the right hand relates to our outer world (don't worry, this will be second nature to you by the end of the book), I knew this dream was commenting on how I should express my writing. Yes, you've got it: with passion and a breath of fresh air. I only hope I can live up to that excellent advice. I fear, as I must lapse into numbers and data from time to time, that your passion may cool, or that the air may become harder to breathe, or the details harder to take in. I hope you will ride the roller-coaster with me and finally agree, as you turn the last page, that the journey into our dreaming life was well worth the ride.

The Researcher and the Reason

My formal academic background is in science, where I gained an Honours degree from the University of Glasgow, specialising in the biology of embryonic development. I entered the world of scientific research and narrowed my interests to the world of the developing nervous system. Intellectually I was excited by the intricacies and wonder of how embryonic or regenerating nerves find their way to the brain to make the appropriate connections which produce a fully functional, totally alive being. Little was known, so we could sit and muse upon imagined concepts and come up with the most bizarre ideas for later testing. My curiosity took me into the deep recesses of the brain until I felt I had stood in the shoes of the strictest reductionist (one who believes that life is merely the sum of its parts, and no more, like a computer made up of electronic bits and pieces).

Yet this was not the answer. I found it difficult to make contact with anyone in those mid-seventies days of science who was open minded enough to tip their hat in respect of an alternative, more holistic view of life. Now, some twenty years later, scientists and non-scientists alike have an inkling that quantum physics must inevitably change our understanding of life, and question the more stoic nature of our old scientific attitudes.

For myself, my quest for understanding life became more passionate the day I walked away from the National Institute for Medical Research in London, where I had enrolled to do my

PhD, because I could no longer see any relationship between life and the anaesthetised, eyeless green goldfish left on a lab bench simply because it was time for lunch. I took my scientific knowledge and my questions out into the world and worked at communicating with people.

My career has taken me through teaching, writing, the media, counselling and motivating, while family life challenged my adaptability and understanding of the world and its people through time spent living in tropical Africa and the Andean peaks of South America. This background, my constant and fantastic dreams since childhood, my children, my divorce, my remarriage, my private reading on dreams and my experience as a dream counsellor constitute my qualifications for embarking on this research.

So, let's turn the spotlight away from me and direct it to its rightful place: the dream survey.

Setting Up the Survey and Collecting the Data

This research is not based on a random sample. In the first instance, a random sample would have generated a large number of blank responses since many people have difficulty recalling their dreams to the extent demanded by this survey. Secondly, I wanted to sample what is happening for the strongly motivated dreamers; those who have a place of honour for their dreams, or those who had the burden of years of silence to release, who wanted to 'come out of the closet' with their dreams without fear of retribution from their family or friends. This was to be a book about what people are really dreaming about, where their thoughts and feelings about their dreaming lives have led them, and what possibilities their insights can offer you, the reader. My task was to find these strong and willing dreamers and then persuade them to spend hours thinking, recalling and filling out my lengthy Dream Survey Questionnaire. I was astounded at the ease with which this was achieved.

The survey dreamers came forward through my appeals on

radio, through newspapers, magazines, television interviews and word of mouth. I also asked key people in various geographical areas to spread the word, which proved a viable source of excellent volunteers. This brought a good response because, I was later informed, merely contemplating the questionnaire and filling it in was good therapy in itself. Since each person was asked not to show the questionnaire to anyone else, the material itself became 'hot stuff' and the survey population was rapidly built. The popularity of the questionnaire as a tool to focus on one's dreaming life made me realise that it should be included in this book, so that you, the reader, might start from the survey dreamer's point of view, by completing the questionnaire at the end of this chapter before reading further.

Some 260 people contacted me to join the survey, although not everyone returned the questionnaires. I guess they either found the therapy of filling in the survey pages enlightening enough, or they found it all too hard, too intimidating or too personally revealing. I finally centred on 160 complete questionnaires as the basis for this research, and yes, their confidentiality has been guarded. Each has chosen a dream name for use in the book, and, where necessary, other names and places mentioned in their dreams have been changed to confer anonymity.

Many open ends were built into the questionnaire, partly to place less emphasis on the type of information I was particularly seeking, and partly to motivate the participant to write additional pages. Most people did this, and frequently followed through with several letters over the following months.

At the end of the data collection phase of the research, I invited 25 of the strongest (mostly precognitive) dreamers who lived within a five hour drive of my home, to a Saturday afternoon discussion. That day was a fascinating opportunity to meet and talk with other dreamers, especially for those people who had felt some degree of isolation from those who share their waking lives but who have no compassion for their night-time world. Two hours of that afternoon discussion were taped, and, with the dreamers' permission, later transcribed for use in this book.

At the end of the six month survey period, I sent a short 'End of Dream Survey Questionnaire' (reprinted here, along with the original questionnaire, at the end of this chapter) to investigate dreaming progress since the start of the survey. This was kept extremely brief in mindfulness of the amount of time and effort that everyone had already donated and in the hope that they would be swiftly completed and returned.

Analysing the Data and the Dreams

The data and the dreams have been analysed and handled on many levels. In line with my holistic approach, especially given the often illogical nature of the world of dreams, I have presented the research from both statistical and anecdotal viewpoints.

As a scientist I see great value in examining the hard data as a whole, while as a dreamer I give equal credence to the experience of each individual in his or her own dreaming life. No statistic can ever touch the pure emotional impact of a vivid dream, a sleeping experience which has the potential to change a person's life, and often does. Neither is any statistic required to argue or prove to another the validity of a dream experience which is intuitively understood on a personal level. Our dreams and our dreaming worlds are our own and need no comparison to another, because they speak for themselves—once you recall their language, that is. In the meantime, we must relearn the language of dreams and discover how to get back in touch with this vital part of our being.

The more scientific handling of some of the data in this book is aimed at uncovering the road to that rediscovery. The data also serve to satisfy the hunger our rational brain has been trained, through our present educational system, to seek. Data analysis methods are summarised below*, but will not be discussed elsewhere at any length in deference to maintaining the flow of the text, and I trust this approach shall meet with the reader's approval.

Last, but far from least, the data, as much as the individual experiences and quotes, serve to tell the story as it is, to show that those dream experiences we may deny are shared by a wide range of people and backgrounds, and are more common than we may have previously realised.

*Data was assessed and correlated according to basic statistical methods including comparison of observed results for different groups to the results expected by analysis of the overall survey results, bearing the group (sample) sizes in mind. Data was also compared through the preparation of Ranking Lists which aimed to rank the impact of different variables to assess their relative importance. Hard data is presented in terms of averages, percentages and so on, while emphasis was also placed on novel presentation of the data through examining the 'top' dreamers of different categories of dreaming and determining which variables were common to each. This approach was used to compile the individual 'Profiles' illustrated in Chapters 3, 4 and 5 while the more conventional statistical approaches were employed to extract the material discussed in the main text. The 'Ms Survey Dreamer' insights were compiled from the most common (or, occasionally, where it was more appropriate, the mean) responses from the overall survey. (She is a Ms because the survey participants were most commonly female.)

Put Yourself First—the Questionnaires

After completing the Dream Survey Questionnaire, 73.8% of survey dreamers answered 'yes' to the question: Did you feel that you learned something about your dreams simply through spending the time to do this?

Stop right there! Before you go any further, find yourself a quiet corner for an hour★, pick up a pen, and fill in the following Dream Survey Questionnaire, which is an exact copy of that completed by the survey dreamers. You may find that you flow on and start recalling dreams or thoughts, so consider writing these extras down in a journal, or recording them onto an audio tape, as you will find your dreams easier to interpret when you come to Part Two of this book if they are recorded in some way other than free-floating in your head!

★The average time taken for survey participants to complete this questionnaire was 1.7 hours, although 16% took at least 4 hours!

DREAM SURVEY QUESTIONNAIRE

SECTION A: PERSONAL DETAILS

Name: ....

Address: ....

Phone Number: ah: ....bh: ....

Sex: ....

Date of Birth: ....

Nationality: ....

Marital Status: ....

Number of Children: ....

   Living with you: ....

   (How many of these are step children?) ....

   Living with ex: ....

   Left home: ....

Present Occupation: ....

Last Occupation: ....

Highest Educational Level Attained: ....

Religion: ....

Health (please circle): Excellent / Good / Fair / Poor / Very poor

SECTION B: WELLBEING AND LIFESTYLE

1 How often do you exercise each week? .... times per week.

2 What type of exercise do you do? ....

3 Which of the following meditative exercises have you done in
the past three months? (Please circle) Meditation / Yoga / Tai
Chi / Float tank / Massage / Reiki
Other (please state): ....

4 Do you do anything else simply for yourself for peace,
relaxation and solitude? If yes, please list: ....
....

5 What do you usually do when you have a problem on your
mind? ....
....

6 How stressed are you generally? (Please circle):
Extremely stressed / Very stressed / Stressed from time to time
/ Mildly stressed / Rarely stressed / Never stressed

7 Which of the following foods do you eat at least once per week? Please *underline:* Vegetables / Fruit / Bread / Dairy products / Cereals / Red meat / White meat / Eggs / Fish / Junk Food (be honest please!) / Tea / Coffee / Sugar

8 In the above list, which foods do you usually eat every day or every other day? Please circle.

9 How many meals do you eat on an average day? ....

10 How many snacks do you eat on an average day? ....

11 Any other comments on your diet? ....

12 Do you take any dietary supplements (e.g. vitamins, minerals, nutritional drinks, remedies?) If yes, which? ....

13 How many alcoholic drinks do you have in an average week?

14 How many cigarettes do you smoke in an average week? ......

15 Do you take any prescription or over-the-counter drugs regularly? If yes, which? (Please include tranquillisers, sleeping pills, pain killers) ....

16 How many hours of television do you watch in an average week? .... hours per week.

17 Please list your other regular leisure activities: ....
....
....
....

SECTION C: STUDY

1 Are you presently enrolled in a course of study? ....

2 What was the last course of study you completed? ....
....
When was this? ....

3 Do you read or research any personal area of interest without the aid of a formal course? ....
Which subject areas? ....

4 Have you attended a workshop or lecture series recently? ....
What subject? ....

5 Are you considering taking up a course of study within the next twelve months? ....
What subject/course? ....

SECTION D: SLEEP PATTERN

1 How many hours of sleep do you get on an average night? ...
2 How long does it take you to fall asleep, on average? ....
3 How many times do you wake in the night, on average? ....
4 Circle which description suits you best: Deep sleeper /
   Medium sleeper / Light sleeper / Restless sleeper / Insomniac
5 Do you work shifts? ....
   If yes, are these regular or irregular? ....
   How does this shift work affect your sleep? ....
   ....
   ....

SECTION E: WAKING UP PATTERN

1 Which of the following descriptions best indicates how you
   usually wake up on a working day? (Tick as many as you like.)
   Alarm wakes me ☐
   I wake up naturally ☐
   I get up as soon as I wake up ☐
   I lie in bed for a while ☐
   I go back to sleep ☐
   I have great difficulty waking up ☐
   I think about my dreams before getting up ☐
   I plan the day before getting up ☐
   Someone wakes me up gently ☐

SECTION F: DREAMING PATTERN

1 How many times per week, on average, do you:
   Remember your dreams? .... per week.
   Remain aware that you have dreamt, but cannot recall your
   dreams? .... per week.
   Have no dream recall? .... per week.
2 How often, on average, do you:
   Dream in one night? .... per night.
   Wake up in the night remembering a dream? .... per night.
   Write down a dream in the middle of the night? ..... per night.
   Write down your dream later in the daytime? .... per week.
3 Do you keep a journal of your dreams? ....

4 Do you ever talk about your dreams with (please tick):
Your partner ☐
Close friend ☐
Friends ☐
People in general ☐

5 How much do you dream now compared to past years?
(Please circle): More / About the same / Less / Much less

6 Looking back over your life, at what age did you have most
dream recall (dream most)? ....
How would you describe your life during that time? ....
....
....

SECTION G: SENSES IN DREAMS

1 Do you dream in colour? ....
If yes, is colour normal or intense? ....
2 Do you ever dream in black and white? ....
3 Do you ever dream with no visual sense (no pictures, e.g.
sound only)? If yes, describe briefly: ....
....
....

4 Do you hear other sounds apart from speech in your dreams?
If yes, please give examples: ....
....
....

5 Do you dream smells? If yes, please give examples: ....
....
....

6 Can you feel *touch* in a dream? (e.g. textures, hot, cold) If yes,
please give examples: ....
....
....

7 Are you aware of any other senses coming into your dreams?
If yes, please describe: ....
....
....

SECTION H: RECURRING DREAMS AND NIGHTMARES

A *recurring dream* is any dream that you have regularly.

A *nightmare* is a terrifying dream.

For this questionnaire, if you have a recurring dream which is a nightmare, please count it as a nightmare, not a recurring dream.

1 Have you experienced recurring dreams in the *last two years*?

....

2 How many *different* recurring dreams do you have? (Please circle): One / Two / Three / Several / Many

3 Please think about the recurring dream you have experienced most often during the past two years.

How often do you have this dream? ....

What feeling does this dream give you? ....

Is the dream always exactly the same in great detail? ....

Briefly describe the main points of this dream: ....

....

....

4 Have you experienced nightmares in the past two years?

How often? ....

Do you have recurring nightmares? ....

How many different nightmares have you had during the last two years? (Please circle): One / Two / Three / Several / Many

5 Please think about the nightmare you have had most often in the last two years. Briefly describe the main points of this nightmare: ....

....

....

6 Looking back over your life, do you remember a period when your recurring dreams or nightmares were stronger or more repetitive than they are now? ....

If yes, please describe briefly: ....

....

How would you describe your life during that time? ....

....

....

SECTION I: UNUSUAL DREAM EXPERIENCES

1 Have you ever dreamt you were having an out-of-the-body experience? ....
   When was the last time? ....

2 Have you ever had an out-of-the-body experience? ....
   When was the last time? ....

3 Have you ever had a psychic, ESP or prediction dream which came true? ....
   If yes, how often do you have such dreams? ....

4 Have you ever realised, in the middle of a dream, that you were dreaming? ....
   If yes, have you ever decided to change the course of the dream while you're still in it? ....
   If yes, how often have you been able to do this? ....

5 How often do you experience deja vu? ....

6 Have you had any other 'unusual' dream experiences? ....
   If yes, please give a brief outline: (I have received much interest in this area of dreaming and I am keen to collect examples of unusual dream experiences for research. Your comments are much appreciated so please use additional paper if necessary.) ....
   ....

7 Any other comments on this section? ....
   ....

SECTION J: UNDERSTANDING YOUR DREAMS

1 In general, how many of your dreams make sense to you or have some meaning? (Please circle): None / A few / Several / About half / More than half / Most / All

2 Have you ever studied dreams or dream interpretation? ....
   How? (e.g. books, magazines, courses): ....

3 Do you ever take guidance from your dreams? ....

4 Have you ever carried out a decision based on a dream? ......

5 Have you ever made a major lifestyle change based on a dream? ....

6 Where do you believe your dreams come from? ....
   ....

SECTION K: SPIRITUAL BELIEFS

1 Do you believe in life after death? ....

2 Do you believe in reincarnation? ....

SECTION L: TRANSPORT IN DREAMS

(Please note: For all remaining sections, please consider only dreams you have had in the last two years.)

1 Tick transport which regularly appears in your dreams (last two years).(Tick as many as you like):

Bicycle: ☐   Plane: ☐

Car: ☐   Bus: ☐

Motorbike: ☐   Train: ☐

Boat: ☐   None: ☐

Other (please specify): ....
....

2 In the above list, put an 'A' by the most common transport (one item only).

3 Tick which of the following situations most regularly occur in dreams involving transport. (Tick as many as you like):

I reach my destination: ☐

I am chased: ☐

I get lost: ☐

I am chasing someone else: ☐

I miss the bus/whatever: ☐

The ride is slow and difficult: ☐

The transport breaks down: ☐

The ride is fast and easy: ☐

The transport crashes: ☐

I go uphill: ☐

I drive/ride: ☐

I go downhill: ☐

Someone else drives: ☐

I get delayed: ☐

Other (please state): ☐

4 In the above list, put an 'A' beside the most common situation (one only).

SECTION M: BIRTH, MARRIAGE AND DEATH IN DREAMS

1 Tick which of the following events occur regularly in your dreams (last two years). (Tick as many as you like):

Death—serene: ☐   Kissing/cuddling: ☐

Death—accident: ☐   Pregnancy: ☐

Death—murder: ☐   Birth: ☐

Marriage/engagement: ☐   Cradling an infant: ☐

Sexual encounter: ☐   None of these: ☐

2 In the above list, put an 'A' by the most common event (one only).

SECTION N: HOUSES, HOMES AND ROOMS IN DREAMS

1 Tick which of the following regularly appear in your dreams (last two years). (Tick as many as you like):

Your present home: ☐   Cellar/basement: ☐

Home lived in before: ☐   Attic: ☐

Dream home (unknown): ☐   Upstairs: ☐

Holiday house: ☐   Staircase: ☐

Hotel: ☐   Lift: ☐

Lounge room: ☐   Door: ☐

Kitchen: ☐   Window: ☐

Bedroom: ☐   Dining room: ☐

Bathroom: ☐   None of these: ☐

Toilet: ☐   Office/study: ☐

Other (please specify): ....

2 In the above list, put an 'A' by the most common place (one only).

3 Do you often dream of being in a house which looks like the house of someone you know in life? ....
If yes, how closely is this person/are these people related to you? ....
....

4 Any other comments you would like to make? ....
....
....
....
....

18

SECTION O: GETTING AROUND WITHOUT TRANSPORT IN DREAMS

1 Tick the following to show the various ways you usually move in dreams (last two years). (Tick as many as you like):

Walk: ☐   Swim: ☐   Stand still: ☐
Run: ☐   Fly: ☐   Sit still: ☐
Other (please state): ....

2 In the above list, put an 'A' by the most common method (one only).

3 Tick which of the following speeds you commonly move at in your dreams (last two years). (Tick as many as you like):

Fast and easy: ☐   Slow: ☐
Fast but hard work: ☐   Very slow: ☐
Normal (like life): ☐   Stuck/held back: ☐
Fall: ☐   Other (please state): ☐

4 In the above list, put an 'A' by the most common speed (one only).

SECTION P: OUTDOOR LOCATIONS IN DREAMS

1 Tick which of the following outdoor locations regularly feature in your dreams (last two years). (Tick as many as you like):

Your garden: ☐   Cliff: ☐
Dream garden: ☐   Foreign country: ☐
Farm: ☐   City streets: ☐
Forest: ☐   Small town streets: ☐
Plain: ☐   Village streets: ☐
Desert: ☐   Main roads: ☐
Valley: ☐   Back streets: ☐
Mountain: ☐   Highways: ☐
Coast/seashore: ☐   Bridges: ☐
Bus/train stops: ☐   Airports: ☐
Jungles: ☐   Car parks: ☐
Shopping centres: ☐   Parks: ☐
Playgrounds: ☐   Bushland: ☐
Rich areas: ☐   Poor areas: ☐
Other planets: ☐   Sea/afloat: ☐
Other places (please state): ....

2 In the above list, put an 'A' by the most common location (one only).

3 How often do you dream of locations unknown to you in waking life? (Please circle): Never / Occasionally / Sometimes / Often / Most of the time / Always

4 Any other comments you would like to make? ....
....
....
....
....

SECTION Q: WATER DREAMS

1 Tick which of the following regularly occur in your dreams (last two years). (Tick as many as you like):

Deep sea: ☐   Swimming pool: ☐
Edge of sea: ☐   Pond: ☐
River: ☐   Tidal wave: ☐
Stream: ☐   Surf waves: ☐
Waterfall: ☐   Tank: ☐
Lake: ☐   Bath: ☐
None: ☐
Other (please state): ....

2 In the above list, put an 'A' by the most common water scene (one only).

SECTION R: COMMUNICATIONS IN DREAMS

1 Tick which of the following regularly appear in your dreams (last two years).(Tick as many as you like):

Telephone: ☐   Numbers: ☐
Fax: ☐   Television: ☐
Letters: ☐   Radio: ☐
Notes/messages: ☐   None: ☐
Words: ☐
Other (please state): ....

2 In the above list, put an 'A' by the most common and a 'B' by the second most common form of communication (two only).

SECTION S: PEOPLE IN DREAMS

1 Tick which of the following people appear regularly in your
   dreams (last two years). (Tick as many as you like):

   Yourself: ☐   **Strangers, who are:**
   Close relatives: ☐   Dead: ☐
   Other relatives: ☐   Elderly: ☐
   Other people in your life now: ☐   Middle aged: ☐
   Other people from the past: ☐   Young: ☐
   People you know to be dead: ☐   Adolescent: ☐
   Mostly men: ☐   Children: ☐
   Mostly women: ☐   Babies: ☐
   Spirits: ☐   (Please note above
   Extraterrestrials: ☐   list are all strangers)
   Other (please state): ....

2 In the above list, put an 'A', 'B', 'C' and 'D' by the first,
   second, third and fourth most common people or groups of
   people who appear in your dreams.

3 Any other comments about people in your dreams? ....
   ....

SECTION T: EDUCATIONAL INSTITUTIONS IN DREAMS

1 Tick which of the following regularly appear in your dreams
   (last two years). (Tick as many as you like):

   Kindergarten: ☐   Place giving short courses: ☐
   Primary school: ☐   Weekend learning retreat: ☐
   High school: ☐   Library: ☐
   College: ☐   None: ☐
   University: ☐
   Other (please state): ....

2 In the above list, put an 'A' by the most common place (one
   only).

3 Do you ever teach in these places in your dreams?................

4 Are you ever a student in these places in your dreams? ....

5 What do you do mostly in these dreams: *teach* or *learn*? ....

6 Do you appear in other roles in these dreams? ....
   If yes, which:..

SECTION U: ACTION IN DREAMS

1 Tick which of the following actions you commonly take in your dreams (last two years). (Tick as many as you like):
I take part in the action: ☐
I watch and observe the action: ☐
I take control: ☐
I don't take part in the dream: ☐
I make decisions: ☐
I follow others: ☐
I lead others: ☐
I act against my will: ☐

2 In the above list, put an 'A' by the most common action (one only).

SECTION V: FURTHER COMMENTS

Any further comments on matters raised in this questionnaire, or in any other area of dreaming that you feel is important to point out. ....
For my future reference, how long did it take you to complete this questionnaire?...
....
Did you feel, incidentally, that you learned something about your dreams simply through spending the time to do this? ....

END OF DREAM SURVEY QUESTIONNAIRE

Since completing your original Dream Survey Questionnaire:

1 Have you recorded your dreams regularly in your journal? Yes/ No

2 Has your dream recall: Improved/ Stayed the same/ Decreased?

3 In general, how many of your dreams make sense to you or have some meaning? None/ A few/ Several/ About half/ More than half/ Most/ All

4 Have you dreams changed in any other way? ....
If so, please comment below..
....
....

**Compare your
waking life
with the
survey dreamers**

CHAPTER 2

Meet the Survey Dreamers by Day

Now that you've completed your questionnaire, discover how you compare with the survey dreamers.

By the end of this book you will have come to know many of these people through sharing their dreams, but before taking that moonlight walk it is enlightening to glimpse their days. What kind of lives do they lead? To understand how their situations influence their dreams, and how their dreams feed back into their waking days, we first need to meet them in sunlight.

Ms Survey Dreamer (the Composite Dreamer)

Let me introduce Ms Survey Dreamer (for the larger proportion were women, as you will see.) This composite woman was created from the *most common answers* to each section of the questionnaire. Percentages in brackets give the proportion of dreamers who fell into each category★. Occasionally *average* figures have been given when these carry additional enlightenment. Ms Survey Dreamer appears here in *italics*. To meet the other survey participants—see Appendix A.

★Percentages do not always tally to 100% due to incomplete questionnaires.

Age, Education and Occupation

Ms Survey Dreamer is aged 41–50 years (24.4%) although her average age is 39. She (81.9%) finished her formal education during high school (50%), is not presently enrolled in any formal study course (73.1%), but does read or research areas of personal interest (76.9%). She has recently attended a workshop or lecture series of her choice (50%). She is married (40.6%) and is involved in the work force (50.6%).

Spiritual Beliefs and Source of Dreams

Ms Survey Dreamer was raised as a Catholic* (17.5%), and believes in life after death (80%) and in reincarnation (65.6%). She believes her dreams come mostly from her subconscious (46.3%) although does believe that other factors may be operational too.

*24.4% claimed the traditional Western non-Catholic religions of: Anglican, Presbyterian and Protestant.

Diet and Health Supplements

Ms Survey Dreamer eats the following foods at least every other day: vegetables (84.4%), bread (78.8%), dairy products (72.5%), fruit (70.6%), cereals (48.8%) and sugar (43.1%). Equally as frequently she drinks tea (50.6%) and coffee (53.1%).

Less frequently, about once per week, she eats white meat (47.5%), red meat (36.9%), junk food (15%—honest, isn't she!) and eggs (13.8%). She never eats fish (47.5%) and she takes vitamins occasionally (42.5%).

Physical Exercise, Alcohol and Cigarettes

Ms Survey Dreamer takes part in some exercise activity (81.3%) and most commonly exercises 3 times per week (16.9%)*. She mostly walks (55%), although she may include aerobics (16.3%) or swimming (14.4%). Her health is 'good' (55%). She doesn't smoke cigarettes (76.3%), but she does drink alcohol (53.8%), taking an average of 4 alcoholic drinks per week (20% drink 3–7 alcoholic drinks per week).

*31.8% exercise 5 or more times per week.

Stress and Meditative Exercise

Ms Survey Dreamer is 'stressed from time to time' (56.3%) and has practised some kind of meditative exercise in the last 3 months (70.6%). She prefers meditation (55.6%), but includes a second practice (31.9% of total survey), usually massage (27.5% of total survey). For general relaxation, she likes to read (43.1%), listen to music (24.4%) and be outside enjoying nature (15%).

Problem Solving

Ms Survey Dreamer copes with her problems by either thinking them through (35%) or by talking about them (35.6%), but rarely does both (9.4%). She exhibits a split personality when it comes to solving her problems!

Television Habits

Ms Survey Dreamer watches an average 13 hours of television per week, though 28.7% watch 6–10 hours and 28.1% view for 11–20 hours each week.

Sleeping and Waking Routines

Ms Survey Dreamer commonly falls asleep in less than 5 minutes (17.5%) and sleeps 8 hours a night (43.8%). She commonly wakes once during the night (28.1%) and is somewhere between a deep and a light sleeper (46.3%). She wakes up naturally, before the alarm (78.1%), lies in bed (67.5%) and thinks about her dreams (68.1%) before getting up.

Importance Given to Dreams

Ms Survey Dreamer has studied dreams either through books or magazines (54.4%) and most of her dreams make some sense to her (24.4%). She doesn't keep a dream journal (71.3%), but she talks about her dreams to her close friends (67.5%) and her partner (61.3%). She takes guidance from some of her dreams (61.9%) and has carried the guidance through to making a decision (50.6%). She has not made any major lifestyle changes based on her dreams though *(71.3%)*. *She obviously gives some importance to this area of her life since she offered to join the dream survey, and found that by focusing on her dreams when filling out the questionnaire (which took an average of 1.7 hours), she learned more about them (73.8%). She completed a short End of Dream Survey Questionnaire (51.9%).*

Reliving a Dream?

Ms Survey Dreamer experiences deja vu (88.1%) frequently (40.6%).

Moving into the Night ...

As daylight fades it is time to take your knowledge of the survey dreamers' waking lives, and your own, into the world of dreams where all will become much clearer in the darkness of the night. The following chapters which complete Part One of this book enable you to compare your dream experiences (questionnaire answers) to those of Ms Survey Dreamer. These research findings then reveal 'The Guide to Good Dreaming': what you can do, based on the dream survey results, to open your awareness of your dream world.

By the Light of the Moon

CHAPTER 3

Dream Frequency

Science has shown that we all dream, even though many people claim they never dream at all. When people are wired up to dream monitoring equipment which measures brain wave patterns and eye movements, intense bursts of dreaming are observed throughout the night. (See Chapter 23, Physiology: The Body and the Physical Causes of Dreaming.) The question is not so much 'Do you dream?' as 'Do you *recall* your dreams, and, if so, how much do you *remember?*'

Dream frequency (author's terminology) is about *quantity*, not *quality*. How *many* dreams do you recall?

Refer back to your answers in Section F of the questionnaire and compare your dream frequency with Ms Survey Dreamer. (See Chapter 2, Meet the Survey Dreamers by Day, for details of the conglomerate Ms Survey Dreamer.)

Ms Survey Dreamer mostly remembers dreaming on three nights* per week (17.5%), and notices a further two nights of knowing she has dreamed but being unable to recall any details (25.6%). When she does remember her dreams she can recall two a night* (36.3%), and generally remembers one of these when she wakes during the night (51.9%). She recalls about the same amount now as she has done in the past (60%).

* These figures show the most common answers to these questions.
Averaged over the range of the survey the average number of nights of recall was 4.1, while the average number of dreams recalled per night was 2.1. Multiplying the two, this gives an average recall of 8.6 dreams per week.

Top of the list for dream frequency recall were six dream survey dreamers who each generally remember at least 28 dreams per week, compared to the average 8.6. The Profile of a High Frequency Dreamer (below) gives a snapshot picture of these high recall dreamers. How do you compare?

Profile of a High Frequency Dreamer ↗
(Meet the top six for dream frequency recall)

This illustration summarises the similarities between the six survey respondents who recall their dreams every night of the week and who report a minimum of four dreams per night. Each of the following points is true for at least five of the six people.

THEY:
Exercise, but not frequently
Don't drink alcohol
Are stressed from time to time
Read or research areas of personal interest
Are not engaged in formal study
Have seven hours sleep a night
Have dreamed of being out of the body
Do take guidance from their dreams
Don't have recurring nightmares
Wake up naturally
Lie in bed before getting up
Recall dreams seven nights per week
Recall four dreams per night
Have frequent deja vu
Talk to close friends about their dreams

When Are We Most Likely to Recall More Dreams?

The survey dreamers remember more dreams during times of change and transition (15%), either during 'negative' periods (49.5%) such as stress (29.7%) and uncertainty, or when challenged by more 'positive' changes (35.5%) such as adventure and excitement. Times of self-reflection, spiritual awareness or an interest in dreams also rated highly.

Influence of Diet and Lifestyle

Diet and Supplements

Survey dreamers who eat meat at least every other day, particularly white meat, tend to remember more dreams than the average. Minerals and vitamin B also increased dream frequency, as did vitamins generally, but not to such a noticeable extent. Coffee may keep you awake, but it was tea that was linked with night-time wakings and more remembered dreams according to this research.

Stress and Meditative Exercise

The highly stressed groups recalled more dreams than those who described themselves as low stress people.

Tai Chi and Reiki seem to have more effect on dream frequency than meditation and yoga. Both open the body and mind to universal healing energies, whereas meditation and yoga, while also healing, are perhaps more focused exercises.

Physical Exercise

Although five out of six of the top dream frequency profile dreamers exercise regularly, physical exercise did not affect dream frequency across the general survey.

Alcohol and Cigarettes

No effect of either of these drugs was noted. It is common experience that the occasional excess of alcohol leads to restless, broken sleep and often, if the recovery sleep is long enough, some exciting, vivid 'rebound' dreams towards the end of the morning. This survey looked at the long-term effects though, so binges were not noted. Only 2.5% of the survey dreamers admitted to drinking more than 21 alcoholic drinks per week, too small a percentage to draw any conclusions.

Television Viewing

Non-television watchers remembered more dreams than the average television viewer.

Age

People aged 21–30 recalled more dreams than any other age group, while the under 15s remembered the least. In looking at individual dream accounts I expected to see reflections of the predictable age-related traumas and life events: adolescence, mid-life crisis, the search for meaning and so on, but instead I noticed that dream themes crossed all age groups.

Problem Solving

The survey indicated that people who focus specifically on their problems through meditation, or who pray for guidance, tend to recall fewer dreams than those who take a less focused attitude by relaxing and letting go of their worries. It seems that problems inefficiently dealt with do find their way into our dreams for consideration. This idea can be turned around, as described in Chapter 18, Sleep On It—Solving Problems, by releasing yourself from daytime stress and concern and handing your problems over to your wiser, sleeping self to find solutions. Freed from daytime worries, waking life becomes easier to handle. The trick, of course, is in being able to interpret the resultant dreams to understand the solutions—this art will be revealed to you in Part Two.

It was interesting that people on the survey who generally coped with their problems by 'solving them' (indicating a rational course of action), also recalled more dreams than the average, as opposed to the focused meditation or prayer groups. This perhaps questions the efficiency of rational problem solving compared with accessing more intuitive sources through dreams, prayer or meditation. Did our 'solve it' group dream better solutions, presenting as increased dream recall? It is tempting to suggest that a knowledge of interpretation might have given the 'solve it' people better solutions.

Sleeping and Waking Patterns

The dream survey showed that those who slept longer hours did recall more dreams than the average, but then so did many of the short hour sleepers.

According to this research, people who wake four times a night remember more dreams than those who wake only two or three times.

People who get up as soon as they wake up recall few dreams compared to those who start the day at a more leisurely pace. This survey showed the best formula is to lie in bed for a while and focus on the parts of your dreams that you *do* remember. Those who set an alarm, rather than waking up naturally also had better recall, but only if they stayed in bed to ponder their dreams for a while. The chances are high that an alarm will catch you in the middle of a dream. This may not give you a satisfactory dream conclusion, but it does at least give you a beginning until you become more adept at recall.

CHAPTER 4

Dream Detail

So much for quantity, but what about *quality*? One person may recall a dream of walking along the road looking for a bus stop. Period. Another person may recall a similar dream but have far greater recall of the details: the texture and colour of the road, the name of the street, what was displayed in the shop windows and the call of a distant eagle riding a jacaranda scented breeze. The second dreamer clearly recalls more of the quality I have termed 'dream detail'. Science may be sure that we all spend a similar quantity of time dreaming, but do we all experience the same degree of detail? Is detailed dreaming recall simply a matter of good memory, or is it the hallmark of an advanced dreamer: a dream master?

Measure Your Dream Detail Score

To get a measurement of your dream detail, return to the questionnaire and count the ticks you entered in Sections L–T inclusive. This is your dream detail score. You probably dream of many symbols, actions and other details not included in this survey, but that is not the point. The commonly dreamed scenarios represented here give a snapshot view of the amount of detail likely to be present in your dreams, no matter what else your nightly drama may unfold.

The survey's average dream detail score was 46.2. How did your score compare?

The questionnaire asked you to mark with an 'A' your most frequently dreamed symbols in each section. Compare your answers with the most common dream details experienced by Ms Survey Dreamer below. (See Chapter 2 for a description of the conglomerate Ms Survey Dreamer. The following percentages are derived from the most frequently ticked symbols, not only from those marked 'A'.)

Ms Survey Dreamer's water dreams commonly find her by the edge of the sea (55%). When travelling around, she generally takes a car (73.8%), which she drives herself (58.1%) and usually reaches her destination (41.9%). Left to her own devices, she walks (83.8%) or flies (55%), at either a normal speed (77.5%) or fast and easy (46.9%). The most prominent person in her dreams is herself (95%), followed by her close relatives (83.8%). When she dreams of houses, they are dream houses, unknown to her in waking life (60.6%). Inside these houses she most often finds herself in the bedroom (41.3%) or the lounge (33.1%). When outdoors, she is commonly found at the coast (56.3%), in foreign countries (42.5%), or in city streets (41.9%). In the birth, marriage and death stakes she spends most dream time in sexual scenes (56.9%) or kissing someone (48.1%). Means of communication outside normal speech come in the form of words (51.3%), but she doesn't visit educational places in her dreams (49.4%). In the main, she either takes an active part in her dreams (91.9%) or she stands back and watches the action (67.5%).

The *range* of dream detail gathered over this survey is presented in percentage form throughout Part Two of this book.

Top of the list for dream detail score were five people who scored over 90, compared to the survey average of 46.2. The Profile of a High Detail Dreamer (below) shows what else these dreamers have in common.

Profile of a High Detail Dreamer ✔
(Meet the top five for dream detail recall)

*This illustration summarises the similarities between the five survey
dreamers who scored over 90 for dream detail as described in this chapter.
Each of the following points is true for at least four out of the five people.*

THEY:

Exercise frequently, at least four times per week

Meditate regularly

Are non-smokers

Are stressed from time to time

Read or research areas of personal interest

Are not engaged in formal study

Have attended a workshop or lecture series recently

Believe in life after death

Believe in reincarnation

Have dreamed of being out of the body

Have lucid dreams

Change the course of their lucid dreams, but not frequently

Have psychic dreams

Experience sound and touch as well as sight in their dreams

Have made decisions based on their dreams

Have nightmares, but rarely recurring

Scored over 90 for dream detail

Wake up naturally

Lie in bed before getting up

Think about their dreams before getting up

Have frequent deja vu

Influence of Diet and Lifestyle

Diet and Supplements

Although meat eaters remembered a higher number of dreams,
vegetarians scored higher than average on dream detail. Dreamers

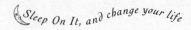

who specifically mentioned 'Chinese herbs' as a regular dietary supplement had better quality dreams too.

Stress and Meditative Exercise

Stress, either high or low, did not show an effect on dream detail score.

People who take part in some kind of meditative exercise, no matter which discipline, tend to be blessed with better dream detail recall than those who do not. Dreamers who meditate or practise yoga regularly experience enhanced memory of dream detail. These disciplines tend to be focused activities. Perhaps this trained focus during the fully conscious state aids conscious recall or observation of detail in their dreams.

> When I am doing a lot of yoga, if I wake up, meditate, then go back to sleep, I have many vivid dreams, short ones, long ones, a whole assortment of clearly remembered dreams.
>
> (Claire, child care provider)

> When I go to bed I can open my chakras and allow white light to flow through. This way I fall asleep immediately and I dream my most vivid moments.
>
> (Andrew, construction manager)

Physical Exercise

While the general survey results showed no effect of regular exercise on dream detail, all five dreamers from the top dream detail profile exercised at least four times per week. It is tempting to suggest that frequent exercise boosts your chances of becoming a master of high quality dream recall.

Alcohol and Cigarettes

No effect of either of these drugs was noted. As mentioned in the previous chapter on dream frequency, this survey looked at possible long-term effects, not binges! Heavy drinkers represented too small a group to evaluate also.

Television Viewing

People who don't watch television, according to this survey, remember more detail from their dreams.

Religion and Spiritual Beliefs

The most detailed dreams were experienced by those people who described their religion with words such as New Age, love, universe, oneness or open. The spiritualists came next, with the Catholics scoring third highest.

Below average dream detail was shown by Anglicans and those who claimed 'no religion'. The other numerous religions represented on the survey had too few members to look for meaningful statistics.

So, what gives the New Agers, the spiritualists and the Catholics such detailed experiences in their dreams, or, at least, great recall of detail? Does the diversity of their dream experience reflect the importance their spirituality places on dreaming? Do Catholics dream more because their religion is steeped in symbolism, or because their religion is strict and has caused stress in their lives? Or have these people taken on these particular religious or spiritual outlooks simply because their more intensely detailed dream experiences have provided them with a glimpse of an alternate spiritual reality?

Do the dreamer's waking life religious beliefs determine the religious nature of their dreams, or do their dreams inspire their waking ideas?

Sources of Dreams

Question 6 in Section J of the questionnaire asked 'Where do you believe your dreams come from?' Don't knows or blank spaces answered for a frustrated 17.5%. While 21.3% of people wrote the single word 'subconscious', most offered a short list of possible sources. In most cases this did not appear to be a random 'chances are' selection, but rather a more carefully weighed conclusion that dreams result from a number of sources, which perhaps should not be considered in isolation from each other.

The most detailed dreams were recalled by those who included 'shared thoughts and events' as one of the sources of their dreams. The next biggest dream source belief associated with a high dream detail score was 'the collective unconscious', followed by 'a glimpse of the future', then 'spirit or deceased people' and finally, but still high on the list, 'higher consciousness'.

As a group, these beliefs generally summarise as a higher state of awareness or consciousness during sleep, which allows us to access the collective unconscious (a pool made up of everyone's thoughts, knowledge and all events, past, present but also, in this picture, future), through which we can overlap or interact with others living, dead or yet to be, and bring back knowledge from any dimension of time. Since these beliefs are associated with high dream detail scores, study of these philosophies combined with an open minded approach may increase your own dream experience.

At the other end of the scale, below the average dream detail score, are those who quote 'daytime experiences' as the source of their dreams, followed by 'the subconscious' and also 'the astral plane'. Apart from the astral plane category, these beliefs appear more grounded and conventional. Is this because the dreams, upon which the beliefs are based, are less detailed, perhaps even less persuasive, than the dream experiences which motivated the first group to seek a wider, more spiritual basis for their understanding of dreaming? Or, once again, should we peer in from another angle, and wonder how much dream detail is related to our philosophical or spiritual expectations?

Deja Vu and Psychic Dreams

People on the survey who scored high in dream detail also reported more frequent deja vu sensations as well as more frequent psychic dreams.

Sleeping and Waking Patterns

Dreamers who lie in, drop off to sleep again and then plan the day ahead (are these people accustomed to paying attention to detail in their waking lives too?) before getting up win when it comes to a high dream detail recall. There was also a tendency among those who scored high in this area to experience difficulty waking up. Time spent in limbo between the two worlds appears to be ideal for bringing the dream experiences back into waking memory.

Sense Awareness in Dreams

How many senses do you experience in your dreams? Sensory awareness in dreams is another form of dream detail. Compare your answers to Section G on the questionnaire with the survey findings:

> *Ms Survey Dreamer mostly dreams in colour (89.4%), with an intensity similar to waking life (65%). She doesn't dream in black and white (53.1%) and doesn't recall experiencing dreams without visuals (85%). She hears sound (67.5%) and feels touch (58.1%), but doesn't notice smell (68.1%) or taste (rarely mentioned).*

Of the survey dreamers who experienced the five basic senses (sight, sound, touch, taste and smell) only six also had dreams in a colour more intense and more vivid than that seen in waking life. These six became the 'strong senses group' from which I compiled the Profile of a Strong Senses Dreamer (below). The profile shows what else these people had in common.

Profile of a Strong Senses Dreamer ❀
(Meet the top six for strong sense recall)

This illustration summarises the similarities between the six survey respondents who report dream experience of at least five basic senses and dream colour that is intense and vivid. Each of the points on the list is true for at least five of these six dreamers.

THEY:
Meditate regularly
Do not drink alcohol
Are non-smokers
Eat sugar often
Take time out for relaxation
Also read for relaxation
Believe in life after death
Believe in reincarnation
Dream in intense colour
Dream sounds
Dream smells
Feel touch in their dreams
Dream tastes
Have no dreams without visuals
Also dream in black and white
Have lucid dreams
Visit educational places in their dreams
Wake up naturally
Understand less than half of their dreams
Think about their dreams before getting up
Experience deja vu

Vision: Colour and Intensity

Of the survey respondents, 35% reported dreaming in intense, vivid colour from time to time. Although many people found it hard to comment about colour until they 'slept on it' and checked through a dream first, only five people decided they only dreamed in black and white alone (7.4% remained unsure!). Results showed that 45% of survey respondents had experienced some black and white dreams in the last two years. A few reported sepia coloured dreams, and both the black and white and the sepia dreams often related to a flashback dream segment, using that well-known cinematic technique of reverting to monochrome to indicate the past. Occasionally, black and white came up in dreams which were associated with depression, as did greyish or brownish scenes.

It was interesting to discover when I prepared the Profile of a Strong Senses Dreamer that the top six strong sense dreamers also experienced dreams in black and white. It seems that for these intensely sensual dreamers, black and white shading is an additional descriptive tool rather than a default because the dreamer hadn't found the paintbox!

Blind Dreams

We generally accept that our dreams are visual, so it was interesting to note that 14.4% reported experience of non-visual dreams. They quoted dreams composed of voices, other sounds, forces, smells, emotions, feelings of speed, sensations of presences or the presentation of knowledge, with no accompanying pictures. Footsteps, laughing, feelings of expansion, music, being pushed, instructed or reassured were also experienced. Dreaming is strongly correlated with rapid movement of the eyes which can be observed by others even through our closed eyelids (REM sleep: see Chapter 23). Scientists have carried out experiments whereby they wake sleeping subjects and ask them to describe what they were watching in their dreams. It turns out that the observed eye movements did correlate with what the people were watching in their dreams. So, do our dreamers who recall some non-visual dreams show little or no eye movement during these types of dreams, or are they, in fact, a different kind of dream taking place in 'non REM' periods?

In my own experience, I often wake up with knowledge of several distinct dreams but also with a feeling that there has been a long, drawn out contemplation of an issue, or a background idea, equation, debate or feeling. I can usually summarise what I have *learned* from that background information, although the details are often beyond the grasp of words.

These concepts frequently involve formulae or visual metaphors which I fully comprehend while asleep, but which defy intellectual understanding on waking. Certainly other researchers in dreams have put forward the idea that non REM sleep is accompanied by some sort of mundane thinking process which is

Dream Detail

not easily recalled, but these personal experiences are certainly far from mundane.

Touch, Pain and Sex

Asked which touch sensations were felt in their dreams, 20.6% mentioned temperature, both hot and cold. Feeling (or being felt by!) other people was offered by 13.1%, with a further 10% specifying sexual touch. Others mentioned the texture of skin, blood, clothes, doors, walls, in fact the whole range of waking life touch feelings.

Pain was mentioned by a few, associated with having teeth pulled out, for example. Of the many dreams of deaths and accidents that have been described to me, very few are associated with pain. Often the dreamer notes the absence of pain with amazement, and this painlessness becomes the focus of the dream. This perhaps underlines the symbolic nature of many death dreams, where death is presented not as painful but as an ending: death of the old ready for birth of the new. Other dream pains can be extremely severe, as I know from dreams of having my ankles bitten, or being injected with a hypodermic syringe. Once I had to wake myself up because a pig had locked its sharp teeth into my buttocks and I couldn't shake him off. That pain was excruciating!

I dreamed I had a terrible pain in my eye, only to be woken by my daughter banging on the bedroom door in tears. She was in agony with a pain in her eye. We found out later it was due to her leaving her contact lens in too long.

(Lesley, home duties)

Did Lesley tune into her daughter's pain or was her daughter verbally complaining as she knocked on the door, so that the notion of pain was incorporated into her mother's dream? Either way, the mother *experienced* the eye *pain* as she would in waking life.

How much sensation in dream originates from the body, or from what is happening around you as you sleep, and how much is just good, realistic dream detail or symbolism?

Symbolism apart, external sensations most definitely invade our dreams:

As a teenager I dreamed I was falling under a waterfall and I woke as the water hit my face to find my father standing over me squeezing a wet face cloth in an effort to wake me!

(Geoff, priest)

When it comes to sexual sensations in dreams, how much is physical (such as hormonal levels, or unfulfilled sex drive) and how much is symbolic?

I have felt people touch me frequently sexually and have even had orgasms.

(Fiona, retired medical secretary)

The symbolism of dream sex is discussed in Part Two, but orgasm as a real physical sensation was regularly reported by both sexes on the dream survey. 'Wet dreams', it seems, are no longer exclusive male territory!

Sound and Things That Go Bump in the Night

It is taken for granted that we usually hear speech in our dreams, but other sounds commonly reported included: music, animals, water, cars, bangs and explosions, wind, guns, bells and laughter.

I sometimes wake up hearing songs, a title or melody repeating itself, or a piano playing.

(Madeline, retired office worker)

Of course, external noises creep into our dreams too:

Dream Detail

> *I dreamed I was near a football arena and I heard someone talk over a loudspeaker, then a loud buzzer sound. I woke from a deep sleep to find my alarm going off.*
>
> (Nancy, checkout operator)

Our perception of sound in a dream can be so intense that we are left wondering about its source:

> *I have heard my name called and woken up instantly. I have felt someone touch me to wake me. I have felt someone in the room. This is all very frightening because I don't know if it's real or a dream.*
>
> (Amelia, secretary)

My personal experience of this dates back some fifteen years, and there is a very definite sense of the external, but inexplicable. In one case I awoke as a 'cold finger' touched my forehead. I lay alertly awake behind tight-shut eyes, but that finger was still there. A few hours of rigid sleeplessness later, the sun came up and I bravely went about investigating the situation. There was no way I could have touched anything, not even a wall or bed head. It remained a mystery for many years (my understanding can now at least partially encompass the event), although I did note, as I woke in the morning, that it was my parents' wedding anniversary: also the anniversary of my baptism as a baby. Things that go bump in the night are discussed later in this book.

Taste and Smell

Dream tastes are usually nasty, like tomato sauce and apricot jam which turned me off both for months!

(Fiona, retired medical secretary)

Among the dream smells, survey dreamers reported perfume, the ocean, trees, petrol, food, blood, excrement, animals, people, childhood memory smells, dirt, puss, rotting meat, farms and salt. The most commonly mentioned smell was flowers, followed by perfume. Smell perception can be symbolic and, like our other dream senses, can also enter our dream consciousness from our external world.

> *I recently dreamed about an incident in my grandmother's house. The room smelt as I remembered it.*
>
> *(Dorothy, retired teacher)*

Telepathy and Other Extrasensory Perceptions

Telepathy most certainly occurs between sleepers as well as between a sleeper and someone who is awake, and this is adequately covered in other parts of this book. Kate's description of the sense of telepathy operating *within* the dream was a common experience:

> *I can communicate with animals or they 'talk' to me in English without moving their mouths. I hear it in my mind. Sometimes I can see what people are thinking: a heightened perception of their motivations.*
>
> *(Kate, unemployed)*

Many commonly experience an awareness of another presence as in Lucy's case:

> *I often have a sense of awareness in my dreams of a presence or someone being close to me, or entering a room, or breathing or watching me.*
>
> *(Lucy, home duties)*

Emotions

Emotions and feelings in dreams are covered elsewhere in this book, but I was surprised by the number of people on the survey who responded to the question 'Are you aware of any other sense coming into your dreams?' by writing 'strong emotions and feelings'. These were not the kind of 'senses' I was referring to, but I mention them here, in passing, for those readers who would have been left wondering, 'What about emotions?'

My emotions in my dreams are very intense, from sexual to crying, to ecstatic to devastation.

(Frances, actor)

I often feel very deeply in dreams and am much more perceptive and emotional than I am in everyday life.

(Kate, unemployed)

As will be seen later, with our conscious, more rational self turned down low while we sleep, our subconscious, more emotional, feeling-orientated self can really let rip. To feel our emotions so intensely in our dreams, without the need to check ourselves for fear of judgement by others, is to begin to know who we truly are. Monitoring the emotional content of our dreams is also one of the major keys to their interpretation.

CHAPTER 5

Recurring Dreams and Nightmares

How often do you have recurring dreams or nightmares? Check your answers to Section H on the questionnaire with Ms Survey Dreamer's experience:

Ms Survey Dreamer has recurring dreams (63.1%), mostly one (20.6%) or two (20%) different ones. Her recurring dream is frequent (31.9%), but although it follows a recurring theme, it is not usually the same in great detail (41.9%). Her recurring dream is most likely to be about restriction or loss of some kind, or chase and escape which commonly makes her feel anxious or afraid. She has experienced nightmares in the last two years (67.5%), but these are rare (25%) and not recurring (50.6%).

Although recurring dreams can be positive, even ecstatic, the survey dreamers highlighted the more troublesome recurring dreams or nightmares. Insufficient people emphasised the positive recurring dreams, so I was unable to prepare a Profile of Happy Recurring Dreamers! Seven people regarded their recurring nightmares as 'frequent' and these became the 'nightmare group' from which the Profile of a Frequent Nightmare Dreamer shown below was drawn. The profile shows what else these dreamers share in common.

Profile of a Frequent Nightmare Dreamer ✦
(Meet the top seven for frequent nightmares)

This illustration summarises the similarities between the seven survey respondents who suffered frequent nightmares, at least some of which were recurring. Each of the following points on this conglomerate list holds true for at least six of the seven people.

THEY:

Approach their problems by thinking or talking them through

Don't drink coffee

Drink tea often

Eat white meat often

Read or research areas of personal interest

Are not engaged in formal study

Believe in life after death

Believe in reincarnation

Sleep for eight hours a night

Sleep neither deeply nor lightly, but between the two

Have frequent nightmares some of which are recurring

Have lucid dreams

Have psychic dreams, but not frequently

Talk to their partners about their dreams

Don't keep a journal

Experience deja vu, but not frequently

Influence of Diet and Lifestyle
Junk Food

The survey did show a tendency among those who eat junk food at least every other day to report more nightmares. It is wise not to jump to any conclusions and suggest that junk food impurities or the high sugar or fat intake cause nightmares. The common psychological patterns behind eating junk are well documented, and it could plausibly be argued that the issues we try to soothe and ignore through nurturing our palate, opting for chocolate euphoria or hitting the fast food, are the same issues the nightmares are more insistently bringing up for our urgent recognition. In the meantime, cutting down or eliminating junk food in quest of more peaceful dreams can only be beneficial to our overall health.

Stress and Nightmares

The survey showed that people in the high stress groups had more frequent nightmares as well as more frequent recurring nightmares.

Problem Solving

People on the survey who described themselves as worriers, unable to relax, let go or just plain ignore their problems during the day, suffered more recurring nightmares than average.

Television and Nightmares

Television characters do crop up in our dreams, and many people commonly blame the impact of television for giving us nightmares or for fuelling the 'vivid imagination' which pervades our dreams.

Surprisingly, recurring nightmares did show up, not for those who watched heaps of television, but for those survey participants who viewed only one to ten hours of television each week. A tentative suggestion is that many people only watch an hour or so of news or current affairs on weekdays and this daily injection of gloom, doom and high anxiety, especially when it is not balanced by lighter, more entertaining programs, may trigger nightmares.

Nightmares and recurring dreams are addressed in Chapter 10, Recurring Dreams or Themes.

CHAPTER 6

Unusual Dream Experiences

Check your answers to Section I on your questionnaire. This section was left open ended so as not to limit the survey dreamers' responses. Much of the material the survey dreamers sent me has been discussed in Part Two of this book, especially in Chapter 19, Time Travel and Chapter 20, Housekeeping or Voyaging the Astral Plane? Meanwhile, compare your answers with Ms Survey Dreamer:

> *Ms Survey Dreamer has psychic dreams (71.9%), but rarely (31.9%), and experiences deja vu (88.1%) frequently (40.6%). She has lucid dreams (78.8%), can change the course of these dreams (58.8%) and frequently does (25.6%). She has neither had an out-of-the-body experience in waking life (65.6%), nor dreamed she has been out of her body (50.6%).*

'Psychic' Dreams and Deja Vu

'Have you ever had a psychic, ESP or prediction dream which came true?' I did not define the word 'psychic' in the questionnaire, and no-one asked me for clarification, yet almost three-quarters of the people surveyed answered 'yes' to this question. According to *The Concise Oxford Dictionary*, 'psychic' means 'inexplicable by *natural laws*' and a 'dream' is a 'series of pictures or events *in the mind* of a sleeping person' or 'a state of mind without *proper* perception of *reality*' (my emphasis). Perhaps it's time we changed our perception of the natural laws to fit what is being experienced by a large proportion of dreamers.

As a scientist I might have been extremely sceptical about the first few completed survey questionnaires I received. It would have been harder to hang onto my scepticism after reading thirty or forty more questionnaires. The scientist in me would have had to concede and publish the information. As a precognitive dreamer myself, I was excited to see that others had similar experiences, and to realise just how widespread these 'psychic' dream phenomena are.

People on the survey who scored high in dream detail also experienced more frequent deja vu and more frequent psychic dreams.

Sometimes my dreams are prophetic but only concerning myself—to the point where I have been able to alter deja vu situations.

(Tom, archivist)

I believe that we relive a huge proportion of our dreams although we are often oblivious to the fact. Survey dreamers who claimed no experience of psychic dreaming scored low on deja vu experience. For the rest, we shake our heads, momentarily overcome with that odd sensation of deja vu, unaware of the original dream. Once we learn to become more adept at recalling detail from our dreams, we can use this knowledge to our advantage.

When I was in my early teens, my father had a very serious drinking problem. I dreamed my mother came to me with Dad's rifle and asked me to hide it in the bottom drawer of my chest of drawers, and not to say anything if Dad should ask. That night, in the dream, as I lay in bed, Dad was even more cruel and irrational than usual. I knew he was hurting Mum badly. I took the rifle and told my father to stop it. He turned and laughed in my face and I shot him dead.

I woke from this dream with a strange, nervous feeling. It turned out to be a predictive dream. Mum came to me and asked me to hide the rifle exactly as she had in the dream. As with the dream, my father was horribly violent. I was very scared. I thought of the consequences of killing my father. I would have loved him to die, but I knew there would be court and more problems for my mother. I chose to stay on in bed. I remember holding the sides of the bed so hard it shook as I listened to my parents arguing.

(Hannah, home duties)

This kind of predictive dream was widespread throughout the dream survey, being a chance to preview a situation, exactly as it would later unfold, and to experience the consequences of possible outcomes beforehand.

Dream sharing was mentioned by several people, and this is a phenomenon I have personally experienced too. Robyn's example illustrates:

In my dream, I walked slowly along the rocky shore of North Coogee Beach, holding the hand of my five year old son. A large wave comes in and separates me from my three year old son who is tagging along behind us. I am not very worried though. I have a happy feeling that he is okay.

In the morning my younger sister told me her dream. She was walking along Coogee Beach holding her three year old nephew's hand. Her five year old nephew is running up ahead. A large wave separates her from him. She does not panic as she has the feeling that I am up ahead with him.

We frequently shared dreams during the time we lived together, when I was 25 and she was 18. We often wrote our dreams down, then exchanged them so the accounts were accurate.

(Robyn, sculptor)

Lucid Dreams

Sometimes the dream is boring me, so I liven it up a bit.

(Seeker, astrologer)

This is known as lucid dreaming. You are dreaming and you suddenly realise you are dreaming. You become fully conscious while still dreaming. At that point you may choose to create

54

anything in your dream, or go anywhere you wish. Anything, absolutely anything, is possible once you are aware of your dream state.

Lucid dreaming can be used mildly to get out of a tricky situation without waking up.

Alternatively, this realisation of dreaming may be just enough to relax and feel safe enough in the dream to stand back and watch the action without fear of danger. In many of my own lucid dreams I choose to observe myself and the dream from my conscious state. I'll often interpret a dream while its happening, with my conscious mind making comments such as 'That's a good symbol' or 'I must remember that part in the morning,' or 'This is a long dream, I wonder if I'll manage to get to the end before my alarm goes off?'

Lucid dreams can be used to role play situations you are confronting in waking life, or to bring in a specialist, Einstein, for example, and ask him a few questions about quantum physics, or to travel to the other side of the universe and back. Since the senses are always highly accentuated and potential is unlimited, lucid dreams are totally exhilarating, yet as real as any waking life experience.

Lucid dreaming is what got me started. It's absolutely out of this world. When it first happened to me I really wondered what on earth was going on inside my mind. The only way I can describe it is to say if this room was in pitch darkness, that would be your normal dream. In a lucid dream you see a door in a wall and you walk through it into brilliant sunshine and you get all five senses highly accentuated. If I could live there permanently, I would, because it's less dangerous, you're in charge, you don't interfere with anyone else's life and you can have an absolute ball.

(Alex, clerk)

So how do you get into a lucid dream? How do you take control? The first step is to program yourself to look for signs of dreaming. Stephen LaBerge and Howard Rheingold's excellent book *Exploring the World of Lucid Dreaming* suggests many methods. A popular one is based on the assumption that we tend to dream about what we have been preoccupied with during the day. The idea is to write on the back of a business card 'Am I dreaming?' and to take this card out of your pocket every half hour or so during the day to read it. You then seriously contemplate the question. You look around you to check whether anything in your environment looks unusual or bizarre. You may try to push off on your toes and fly. The chances are that this mild obsession will creep into your dream, and you will apply the tests and realise that you *are* dreaming. At this point, the dream is yours to control. Another good method is to wear a digital watch and get into the habit of checking it frequently. The assumption here is that it is difficult to dream consecutive numbers (a task too rational for the dreaming part of our brain). Look at the watch once, then look at it a few seconds later. If you see a totally different time, guess what—you're dreaming!

Alex tried this in a dream but:

The card was blank and I wasn't wearing a watch! I ran cautiously into a wall, jumped at it, hit the wall and rebounded. So then I walked up and gently pushed it, and that's how I always do it now.

(Alex, clerk)

I once dreamed that I was in a house opening a door to go into the garden. I opened the door, but it led to another door, which led to another door. On and on doors led to endless doors with no garden in sight. At this point I started to become lucid and also knew I needed to wake up soon. I tried three more doors, then decided to close my eyes in the dream and think myself into the garden. I needed that sense of achievement before waking up! Instantly I was transported into a beautiful garden and, shortly afterwards, woke up.

This may sound a bit way out, but having access to all my senses in a lucid dream, I want to come back with something material. I always want to get to bed quickly to get on with it. Daytime is boring compared to this! I don't think you can separate daytime life from dreams. Dreams are an extension of daytime life. They help you to grow.

(Andrew, construction manager)

It seems you can use lucid dreaming to learn more about yourself, to add to your personal development, to explore the frontiers of the mind, to escape from a bad dream, to maintain consciousness so you can study the natural course of your dreams with better recall, to escape into virtual reality or to push into the reality of other dimensions. The choice is yours.

But perhaps the best use of lucid dreaming is as a tool to investigate unusual dream phenomena. Why not open the alertness channels, take control and tune into what really *is* out there in your dreaming life?

CHAPTER 7

Understanding Your Dreams

What happens to our dreams and our lives when we honour our dreams and raise them to a place of importance? How does keeping a dream journal affect your dreams and your life? Does making a decision based on a dream alter the quality of advice in future dreams? Do we get more in touch with understanding our dreams through taking them seriously? How did the survey dreamers' lives or dreams change as a result of examining their dreams closely for this research?

Check your answers for Section J on the questionnaire with Ms Survey Dreamer's responses (in 'Importance Given to Dreams' in Chapter 2) and with the rest of the survey participants (Understanding Their Dreams in Appendix A).

Joining the Survey

Most people (73.8%) found that filling out the first questionnaire alone taught them something about themselves or their dreams or opened them up in some way. This learning had intensified for many by the time they received their End of Survey Questionnaire.

Keeping a Journal

Just over a quarter (28.7%) of the people on the survey had recorded some of their dreams in a dream journal during the preceding two years.

Of the people who also returned an End of Dream Survey Questionnaire (51.9%), most (66%) had kept a journal since filling out the original questionnaire up to six months previously. I looked at how people's understanding of their dreams had changed over this period, and how this related to keeping a dream journal.

The biggest increase in understanding their dreams was shown by those who started to keep a journal after filling out the original questionnaire. This suggests that keeping a record of your dreams probably helps you to understand them better. People who gave up writing down their dreams after joining the survey showed the smallest increase in levels of further understanding.

At the same time, though, people who had never kept a journal at any stage did believe their dream understanding had advanced during the survey period, indicating that while journalling may be a great tool, other methods are also effective. In the absence of focusing on a journal, these dreamers probably gave more attention to unravelling their dreams in different ways.

A journal can also help you to improve your recall of dreams. The greatest improvement in dream recall was reported by people who started to keep a journal for the first time after joining the survey.

> *Writing dreams down gives an almost instant understanding. They make more sense!*
>
> *(Yolande, activist, end of survey comment)*

The survey showed that there was a tendency among journal keepers to notice more psychic dreams. They also tended to be more aware of having lucid dreams, but were less interested in changing the course of their lucid dreams than the non-journallers. Perhaps people who like to record dreams find observation of their dreams more appealing than altering their content. The record keepers also tended to take more guidance from their dreams than the average person on the survey.

Understanding Dreams

At the start of the survey, 24.4% of respondents said they understood most of their dreams, followed by 22.8% with comprehension of only a few dreams, and a further 19.5% with understanding of 'several' dreams. There was a drop in numbers between understanding 'several' and 'most', almost as if there is a point at which we cross a barrier and leap from a muddled comprehension to a more definite clarity. The theory reflects the way we acquire fluency when learning a foreign language. We seem to spend a couple of years at school struggling through basic French or Japanese grammar, only to wake up one morning able to speak whole sentences. Something seems to suddenly click.

At the end of the survey, 40.6% (of those who returned their End of Survey Questionnaires) had experienced an increase in understanding of their dreams, 31.8% reported no change, while 27.6% estimated their understanding below the level reported on their original questionnaire. Those who experienced an increase in understanding tended to report a high degree of comprehension, akin to a sudden insight into the language of dreams. Most of the people in this group (59.4%) shot into the 'I understand most or all of my dreams' category. Those who recorded a decrease in comprehension of their dreams rated this drop more conservatively. They seemed to experience *shifts* down the scale of understanding rather than *leaps* up the ladder.

Perhaps tuning into our long-forgotten dream language is like learning a foreign tongue. Suddenly there is a breakthrough, a sudden insight or a quantum leap into dream fluency.

Dream Guidance and Decision Making

More than half (61.9%) of our dreamers have taken guidance from a dream and almost as many (50.6%) have carried out a decision based on a dream. Over a quarter (28.7%) have gone as far as to make a major lifestyle change because of a dream.

All the dream recall in the world is nothing more than entertainment if you do not consider the guidance dreams bring. It is best to act in small ways on your dreams at first, to test the water and watch the results. Once you begin to take action you will find that future dreams serve either to confirm your actions and advise on your next step, or to back track and point out the error of your judgement in interpreting the original dream. As you become more practised in interpretation (after reading Part Two of this book), you will gain confidence in taking action. Tales are told, in later chapters, of the dreams, decisions, actions and consequences that some survey people have experienced.

Honouring the Dream

Bow down to your dreams and respect them. The survey results clearly illustrate the importance of being dream conscious, so let's get practical.

Practical Steps Towards Dream Enlightenment

To keep a journal, start by investing in a good quality notebook and perhaps adding a personal touch such as a fabric cover, photo or drawing. If you buy a cheap exercise book and chuck it under the bed, you probably won't get around to writing anything down. Creating a journal worthy of the importance your dreams deserve, not to mention your investment of time into the project, will bring the rewards you seek. At first you may have little to record, so start by writing the date and the feeling you woke up with. Your waking emotion is often a hangover from your dream, so writing down 'I feel sad' or 'I feel anticipation' or whatever, is a start. Over a few weeks these emotions will trigger recall of tiny bits of dreams which will eventually pour out onto your blank pages.

You will probably find it enlightening to record, in brief form, the ups and downs of your waking life too. The best method is to write your dreams on the right hand page, each dated and given a title. (Give each dream your 'gut reaction' title, since you'll find this choice helpful in interpreting the dream later!)

Keep the left hand page for noting daily events or thoughts, also dated. In later months, look back over the journal and compare what was happening in your waking life with the events and feelings in your dreams. You will begin to see connections between the two which you didn't notice at the time. Caught in stressful situations or times of transition or change, we are usually far too close to the trees to see the woods. Hindsight gives 20/20 vision with its more detached view.

The way we write and describe our dreams, the words and turns of phrases we use also provide inroads into unravelling our dreams. You will find practical help in Chapter 13, Magical Clichés, Puns and Words, but try not to jump ahead just yet. Start a journal now, so that you will have material to work on when you reach that section of the book.

CHAPTER 8

The Guide to Good Dreaming
...and a Better Life

What Do You Want to Achieve?

Do you wish to remember more dreams (increase dream frequency), experience better quality dreams (increase dream detail) or get relief from nightmares until you know how to 'read' them and understand what they are telling you?

Key

For *quantity* direction (dream frequency), follow items marked ↗

For *quality* direction (dream detail), follow items marked ✔

To *ease nightmares*, follow items marked ✦

Note: The Guide to Good Dreaming is based on the results of the dream survey only. Details of these and further advice is given throughout Part One.

Guidelines in *italics* are based on the profiles compiled by looking at groups of the highest scoring individuals in various categories, rather than the across-the-board data upon which the main conclusions are drawn. The profile categories were: ↗ dream frequency, ✔ dream detail, ✦ nightmares, ✿ strong senses.

DIET

✔ Become vegetarian
↗ Drink more tea
↗ Eat more red and white meat
★ Eat less junk food
★ Reduce white meat
★ Reduce tea intake
✿ *Eat sugar*

SUPPLEMENTS

↗✔ Chinese herbs
↗ Minerals
↗ Vitamin B
↗ Vitamins

MEDITATIVE EXERCISE

↗ Tai Chi
↗ Reiki
✔ Yoga
✔ Meditation
✿✔ *Meditation*
✔ Do *something* meditative

PROBLEM SOLVING

↗★ Relax and let go of your worries
↗ Keep meditation general, not focused on your problems
★ Practise focused meditation
★ Reduce worry
★ Talk about your problems

OTHER LIFESTYLE GUIDELINES

★ Reduce stress
✿ *Take time out for relaxation*

✿ *Read for relaxation*

↗✔ Give up television

★ If you only watch news on television, either give it up, or balance it with light-hearted viewing before sleep

✿↗ *Do not drink alcohol*

✿✔ *Do not smoke*

↗ *Exercise occasionally*

✔ *Exercise at least four times per week*

✔↗ *Talk to close friends about your dreams*

WAKING UP ROUTINE

↗ Try to wake up after each dream by:
a) drinking lots of water before sleep
b) programming yourself to wake after a dream
c) setting your alarm randomly through the night

↗ Never get up as soon as you wake up

↗ Set the alarm earlier than usual, lie in bed, think about the dreams you *can* recall, then go back to sleep

✿ Allow time to wake up gradually: don't worry if waking is difficult

✿↗✔ *Wake up naturally: no alarm*

✿✔ *Think about your dreams before getting up*

↗✔ *Lie in bed before getting up*

STUDY

↗★ Read and study the subject of dreams

↗★ Start to make decisions based on your dreams

↗ *Take guidance from your dreams*

✔★ *Start to make decisions based on your dreams*

↗★ Keep a dream journal

↗✔ *Read or research areas of personal interest*

✔ *Attend workshops or lectures on areas of personal interest*

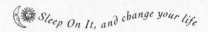

LUCID DREAMING

✔ Experiment with lucid dream induction methods
❀✔ *Notice lucid dreaming*
✔ Try changing the course in your lucid dreams
✔ *Change the course of your lucid dreams occasionally*

PHILOSOPHY

✔ Look into New Age and spiritual philosophies
✔ Open your mind to the idea of the collective unconscious
✔ Open yourself to acceptance and experience of psychic dreams
✔ *Open yourself to experiencing psychic dreams*
❀✔ *Consider life after death*
❀✔ *Consider reincarnation*

Postscript

What is the purpose of improving your dreaming if you do nothing with it other than enjoy the ride? Perhaps the fun and adventure are reason enough, time out, escape, but this survey has shown that dreams, once understood, have the power to improve your life. The key words are 'once understood'. So, come now, let's visit the Magician on the Astral Plane, where all that is bizarre begins to make sense, and where dream interpretation magic empowers you to 'Sleep on it ... and change your life'.

PART TWO

HOW TO INTERPRET YOUR DREAMS AND CHANGE YOUR LIFE

The Magician on the Astral Plane

The Magician on the Astral Plane

Make me a wish
Spin me a tale
Throw a gold coin
Deep into the well.

Throw the I Ching
Watch how they fall
Frogs, toads and lizards
The future I call.

Send me a sign
I'll open my palm
Just tell me the good things
Speak please no harm.

Win me the lotto
You know the score
Give me some numbers
I always want more.

To the north and the south
west, east, high above,
Down under, up over,
Seeking destiny, love.

Exhausted, no progress
No oracle true
I travelled the Astral
Met someone I knew.

Myself in a dream
The wisest old sage:
My Astral Magician
Freed me from my cage.

CHAPTER 9

Universal and Shared Symbols

The Thread That Binds

A baby is born, anywhere in the world, at any time past, present or future, in any culture, yet those present at the birth always see the pain that brings forth a new life, a new beginning. Whether the baby is born into peace, war, abundance or poverty, born to inherit a throne or to face death through neglect because she is the 'wrong' sex, is irrelevant. At that moment of birth, pain has given way to a new beginning. One process (pregnancy and labour) has ended and a new cycle has begun.

We share a common understanding in this experience which transcends time, language and culture. Birth can be seen as a symbol of a new beginning, often born of struggle or pain.

We spend around nine months gestating in the womb, bathing, floating, flying, weightlessly swathed in water. Our foetal senses pick up the sounds of music, arguments and laughter. We sense our mother's anxiety, happiness or anger, we relax as she relaxes, tense as she tenses. Surely this life before birth is one bathed in emotions rather than thought? Is it any surprise that we are born with a sense that water relates to emotions? After birth, water can sweep us away in a torrent, relax and soothe us, cleanse us, rain down and depress us, overwhelmingly flood us or quench us when we need it most. Water flows and changes shape, speed and temperature according to the demands imposed upon it by vessel, wind and weather, just as our emotions respond to our changing surroundings moment by moment. Throughout the world it 'sits right' with people that water symbolises our emotions.

These shared symbols which resonate deeply with all peoples of the world, giving a sense of inner recognition, and producing a similar gut reaction among us all, are known as 'universal symbols'. They are part of the common thread which binds us. Many of us, especially those raised in Western societies, have lost the ability to raise that touched chord of inner knowledge to the surface, to recognise and label it in waking life. As soon as a dream heavy in symbols is interpreted for such a dreamer, their recognition is immediate. It's as if the dream speaks to them at a very deep level, and the dream interpreter simply puts that inner understanding into everyday, practical terms. Rediscovering that link between the subconscious understanding of your situation and its practical application in everyday life is what tuning into universal dream symbols is all about.

As the world changes, and the passing centuries see roads, cars, computers and nuclear power becoming assimilated into our universal culture, we acquire new dream symbols to add to the ancient. Some, such as the flush toilet, may become shared symbols (common to many), rather than universal symbols (common to all). A subconscious recognition of a flush toilet as a symbol of somewhere to let go of waste water (waste emotions) or 'all that shit' is shared among the world's more affluent (not effluent!) peoples. Although a toilet may not be a true universal symbol, its evident symbolism is common enough to be seriously considered as a shared symbol.

Sceptics love to attack the idea of universal symbols in dreams. 'How can a tree mean the same to all people?' they ask. The answer is 'It can't, but on the whole, it does.' If you work as a water engineer, then the water in your dreams may reflect the fact that you work all day with water. Such personal associations are always more important when interpreting a dream than the universal, or shared symbols, and this is considered in the next chapter.

The common mistake in dream interpretation is to assign a universal meaning to every tangible item in the dream. This is where the old witches dictionaries (still filling many bookshop shelves) come out with entries such as the following two, selected at random from a 1980s dream dictionary (*Your Innermost Thoughts Revealed: Dreams: Hidden Meanings & Secrets*, Tophi Books, Ramboro London, 1987):

'Mint Julep: To mix or drink a mint julep in a dream foretells enjoyment through making an effort to understand the viewpoint of others.'

'Collecting: A dream of collecting stamps, bird's eggs, old furniture, etc. foretells meeting celebrities of the screen, stage or television.'

Most words in a dream account can be broken down and interpreted in some way, but only a proportion of this analysis is done using universal symbols. It is vitally important to realise that universal symbols can supply the skeleton, or comment on the general area of concern in a dream, but other methods of dream interpretation must also be used to fill in the fine details or capture the dream's true essence, without which the dream has no life or individuality of its own. These other methods are spelled out in further chapters.

Occasionally, usually at major transition points in a person's life, a short dream composed almost entirely of universal symbols will appear. Such dreams should be treated with great respect. They often reflect in symbolic form major changes that the dreamer is experiencing in life, as if in confirmation and comfort for the dreamer in times of personal transformation. Alternatively, these apparently bizarre symbol dreams may emerge as cries from the soul, tempting us to cross a barrier into a new domain, to have courage and move on to the next stage in life's journey or further along our personal path of enlightenment. The dreams may symbolise our current situation, inspiring us to reject and move forward, or they may symbolise our future situation as it could be, the dangling carrot to reach out and claim. Time almost becomes irrelevant. The focus of these heavily symbolic dreams is on the state of flux which contrasts the status quo with the potential for change.

Practicalities

If you have skipped ahead to Part Two before reading Part One, stop! This book has been designed to lead you through levels of looking at dreams and beginning to understand their nature from page 1. Start at the beginning and journey with the book. What you need to know will unfold to you page by page, calling out and resonating with your own dream memories until everything falls into place. Your deepest dream language is being rekindled, step by step, so that it may burst into full flame and continue to burn brightly, bringing clarity and insight to your dreams. While you will find this chapter useful to refer back to, it is important that you arrive at the right place at the appointed time.

   You might also find it useful to refer to the interpretations of common recurring dreams and nightmares in the next chapter, Chapter 10.

Practising Allegory: Regaining the Wisdom of a Child

The symbolic dream is an allegory, like a children's fairy tale or mystical picture book. Nothing is as it seems and nobody is who they appear to be, but to the child, all is clear. Paint a picture of a rainbow and any child will tell you it holds promise and riches. The child has never seen a witch, a locked chest or a magic seed, but when you introduce them into a bedtime story they need no explanation.

   To understand dream symbols, imagine you are the teller of tales, creatively weaving an ancient magical myth to be passed from generation to generation. Pick and choose from some of the universal and shared symbols described below, then let more fill your mind. Think back to the old legends and fairy tales, and see, in reflection, the symbols they contain and their relevance to our ancestors, ourselves and our future generations as we all experience the same cycles of life. Think of your own situation or the problems and circumstances of those close to you, and transform them into allegory and symbol, whether prose, poem or painting. With practise, you will find yourself gradually tuning into, even thinking or talking in, this 'new' language.

Your own dream experiences, whether they originated from your subconscious mind or from external physical or spiritual sources, were captured and recorded in symbol form by *your* mind. You selected the images to best fit what you experienced or learned in your dream. In all likelihood you subconsciously chose universal symbols, or those shared in common with many others. Some symbols may have more personal relevance. In the end, *you* were the dreamer of the dream, so you are the best person to break the code. Use the following, therefore, as a guide only.

Basic Universal and Shared Symbols

Note: Figures in brackets show the percentage of survey dreamers who have dreamed this symbol regularly in the last two years.

A. Journeys

Most dreams comment on our journey through life, or on our reluctance to travel further when we opt for the rut of routine in preference to the challenge of personal growth.

1 THE ROAD

Paths, streets, roads and highways symbolise the way you are travelling through this part of your life. Is it an easy road, or are there obstacles? Is it level or hilly? Do you walk alone or in company? Do you know where you are going, or are you lost? Do you walk or travel freely, or is it difficult to move? Are you looking for a turning, an alternative route or a way back? How do you feel on this journey? Is there danger? Is the path well travelled or is this a pioneer's route? Are you travelling in the same direction as others, or against the flow? Are you at a crossroads? Is there plenty of time? How much baggage do you carry? What kind of terrain are you crossing? What kind of information do these observations give you about your present journey?

(City streets 41.9%; Small town streets 29.4%; Back streets 25%; Main roads 23.1%; Highways 15.6%; Village streets 10.6%.)

I often have to turn back and find another road.

(Seeker, astrologer)

(Seeker is not getting through and needs to look for alternative paths.)

2 THE LANDSCAPE

Mountains *(36.9%)* are the challenging and difficult aspects of your journey, but can also be the most exhilarating. The way may be hard and steep, or you may fly easily to the peak. Is the view from the top rewarding and clear, or misty and cold? Do you look back to see how far you have come, or look ahead? What is ahead of you? Did you make the decision to climb freely or did you feel under pressure? Did the climb present you with danger, precipices, knife edges and avalanches? How did you handle them? What does this say about how you are handling life now? Or did you stay at the bottom, in safety, but without progress? How far have you come on this journey? How does this relate to your waking life now?

Valleys *(23.8%)* are the downs between the ups. You may rest and recuperate in a valley or you may feel low, lost, even depressed. How did you feel in your dream valley and how does this relate to your waking life?

Forests *(35 %)* are made up of many trees. Trees symbolise our individual physical or personal growth, from our beginnings in the roots to our new growth at the tips of the branches. The shape, species and condition of the tree gives more information. The tree may also symbolise the 'family tree' and our feelings about our family and our place in it, while a forest of trees may show the growth of those around us.

Bush and wilderness *(bush 30.6%)* are places where the vegetation grows natural and wild. Nothing bears the cultivated touch of civilisation. Dreams set in the bush reflect your journey into your natural self, that part of you which is untouched by society, manners and expectations.

Jungle *(8.1%)* territory is where we survive or die. Perhaps you meet the wilder parts of yourself, or get lost in the tangly vegetation.

Farms *(23.8%)* show life in the raw, natural instincts, or domestication. Compare the dream action with its farm background, and see the connection between the two.

The coast *(56.3%)* is the place where the sea *(34.8%)* (the deeper emotions, subconscious and collective subconscious) meets the land (the conscious, practical, more grounded self). Here you stand or paddle on the edge of your emotions, lingering between delving deeper into your subconscious emotions and playing it 'safe' in ignorance.

The sea *(34.8%)*. The sea can symbolise the huge emotional reservoir of our subconscious right down to the way it mingles with the oceans of the world, in the same way that we communicate with all others in the realm of the subconscious.

Water *(81.9%)*, representing the emotions, makes sense when you consider its form in the dream. Look at a river *(36.9%)*, for example. If you encounter a river on your dream journey, is it free flowing, dammed, stagnant, torrential, murky, clear, bubbling, deep, uncrossable or navigable? Does it present you with a challenge in your dream (a river to cross) or a way forward (you can travel on it, go with the flow)? A pond *(15%)* has stillness and many levels. Who knows how deep it goes? What would this say about the depth and unruffled layers of your emotions? Do you know what is at the bottom of your emotional pond? Play with the feelings the water symbols inspire, match them with the story-line of the dream, and play detective until the 'truth' hits home.

(Edge of the sea 55%; surf 31.9%; deep sea 31.3%; swimming pool 24.4%; stream 24.4%; lake 19.4%; waterfall 13.1%; bath 10%; tank 2.5%.)

I am usually involved with a body of water, running river, ocean, pond, underwater lake. I may swim, drown, float or usually observe. Sometimes I see myself watching.

(Mason, unemployed hospital orderly)

(Mason is facing his emotions and working out ways of dealing with them.)

A cliff edge or precipice *(cliff 25.6%)* gives a view from on high, but may also spell danger if it is narrow or overhangs the water. There may be a danger or fear of falling. Do you feel in control on this cliff edge, or are you subject to the winds with the prospect of falling to your death (an end to something) or of landing in deep water (emotions)?

I had a recurring dream of going down, either into a pit, down stairs, underground in the dark and being unable to get out, or falling into water and all going black, or being trapped by waves, balancing precariously high in the air on something just big enough to support me.

(Pearl, secretary)

(Pearl, at this period in her life, found herself living on the edge, barely able to support herself and fearing being trapped by her emotions. She teetered between keeping her head up and going down into her subconscious where she felt depressed and overwhelmed by what faced her there. She felt she could neither delve within nor stay where she was.)

Cities or towns *(city streets 41.9%; small town streets 29.4%)* symbolise civilisation and your relationship to other people and society.

Deserts *(9.4%)* have little water (emotions) so they are symbols of emotionally deprived areas of your life.

Foreign countries *(42.5%)* especially ones you haven't visited and have no personal association with, represent uncharted, unfamiliar territory. Here you find yourself journeying through areas in your life which you do not consciously recognise, meeting new situations which feel foreign to you.

Bridges *(20.6%)* take you from one area of life to another, usually by crossing over water or a busy road. Bridges often bring a sense of finality, a one-way crossing, or a bridging of the gap. They tend to symbolise age transitions, such as adolescence, parenthood, marriage, divorce, the menopause or older age. Take nothing for gospel though. Get a feeling for the bridge symbol, and apply it to the rest of the dream.

(Other landscapes: park 19.4%; plain 16.3%; rich areas 13.8%; poor areas 10.6%; other planets 9.4%; playgrounds 6.3%)

3 MEANS OF TRAVEL

Cars *(73.8%; car park 9.4%)* have been accessible to many of us for no more than a few decades, yet they have become a shared symbol because they have become part of our (almost) universal landscape. They represent a means of power-assisted travel and also our 'drive' or motivation, since we select, in our dream, what kind of car, how to drive it, where to go and so on. Are you driving *(58.1%)* (in control) or are you being driven by (controlled, going along with, or following) someone else *(36.8%)*? Is the car fast and showy, slow and falling apart or average and boring? Does it accelerate well? Is it going too fast for you? Do you occasionally lose control? Are the brakes in good order? Can you stop safely? Does the car move forward or slide back? Have you locked yourself out or lost the keys? Is the car burned out? Do you find yourself in the back seat and feel the need to take control from there? Is your way clear or is the traffic heavy? Are you blocked from the fast lane? Are you in the fast lane and unable to exit? Did you miss your turning? What would these details suggest about your drive, motivation and the way you are approaching your journey through life? Your ease of travel comments on your waking life journey. Contemplate the following results from the survey. What would each situation tell you?

(Ease of travel by transport: I drive 58.1%; I reach my destination 41.9%; someone else drives 36.9%; I am chased 35%; the ride is fast and easy 34.4%; I get lost 33.8%; I go uphill 30.6%; I get delayed 30%; I go downhill 26.3%; the transport crashes 21.3%; the ride is slow and difficult 18.8%; I miss the bus or transport 16.9%; the transport breaks down 15%; I am chasing someone else 8.8%)

I dreamed I was coming home from work and my car crashed. I was crushed in a rolling tossing mess of crushed metal. I heard a noise like a helicopter and a gust of wind lifted me up to safety. One or two weeks later I got sick and gave up my full time job.

(Micheálla, natural therapist)

(Micheálla's dream warns of her imminent crash and ending to that part of her life's journey, yet the helicopter (life-saving transport) shows she can survive in a different way.)

Motorbikes *(14.4%)* symbolise the new found power, energy, noise, and showy dare-devil attitude, or sexuality, of adolescence or youth.

Bicycles *(15.6%)* only work when you put in the effort to push the peddles. The faster you push, the faster you go. Riding a bike in a dream may be a measure of self-motivation, of getting there under your own steam, of self-sufficiency. Or perhaps you find yourself, in the dream, wishing you had a car. What would this mean to you?

Boats and ships *(33.8%)* are means of journeying across water, across the emotions. Is the journey rough or smooth? Is there danger of drowning, or is the boat leaky? Who is in control? Where are you going? What does your dream say about how you approach your emotional journey?

Planes *(41.3%; airport 20.6%)* symbolise high flying ideas. They may take off, not take off, crash or arrive safely (be completed successfully). They may be big or small, you may pilot or be a passenger. How do you feel about your plane journey? What does this tell you about your approach to getting ideas off the ground?

Trains *(31.3%; train or bus stops 23.1%)* travel well-worn routes and stick to the rails, so they can be seen as a rigid but safe way of journeying. You travel with others as a group, all 'in it together'. They may also symbolise 'training'.

Buses *(27.5%; bus or train stops 23.1%)* are similar to trains, although perhaps less restrictive in terms of destination but slower to arrive. They may represent travelling within the safety of numbers, but without individuality.

Horses allow you to travel with a sense of freedom, in touch with your animal passion.

4 PERSONAL MOVEMENT

How do you get around in dreams when you don't use transport? The ease with which you move gives clues about the way you move through your waking life. Consider the following results from the survey. What does each suggest?

(Ease of personal movement: normal 77.5%; fast and easy 46.9%; stuck

or held back 38.1%; slow 24.4%; fast but hard work 22.5%; very slow 8.1%)

Swimming *(31.3%)* is a way of moving through water, which is symbolic of your emotions. Are you getting right into the emotions, diving into emotional depths, going against the flow, or barely skimming the surface? Is the going easy or hard? What do these dream situations say about how you handle your emotional life?

Running *(45.6%)* may be for fun or exercise in a dream, or may be a means of escape. Do you run fast, get stuck, feel your feet glued to the ground, or keep falling down? How does running make you feel?

Flying *(55%)* may be for pleasure, escape or speed. It can afford us a bird's-eye view and a feeling of freedom, or it can inspire a sense of potential.

Falling *(33.1%)* can be a relaxing feeling of letting go, or a panic ridden feeling of falling behind and getting nowhere, or losing out. It may be a fall to death (to an ending of some sort) or falling into a depression. Be guided by how the fall makes you feel.

It is a fallacy that you never hit the bottom when falling in dreams, I certainly do.

(Robyn, sculptor)

(Robyn survives to experience the results of letting go. With this information she is better prepared to make decisions based on her dreams.)

(Other forms of personal movement: walk 83.8%; stand still 38.8%; sit still 21.3%)

5 THE WEATHER
Sunshine symbolises happiness, clarity, light and understanding.

Storms indicate inner turbulence and brewing emotions about to erupt. Expect a 'storm' in the form of an argument, emotional struggle or breakdown. A storm clears the air. Your dream warning of inner explosiveness may enable you to soften the effect of the waking life storm because you have seen it coming.

Thunder and lightning stabilise the electrical imbalances in the atmosphere. They can symbolise nervous imbalance, perhaps soothed by taking vitamin B complex or paying attention to sources of stress. Emotions have built to flashpoint, and the lightning symbolises the flashes of insight which can accompany the release of pent-up anger.

When I dream of an earthquake it usually foretells a big change in my life or [that of] another person in the dream.

(Jasmine, teacher)

(Earthquakes, rather like storms, show the very ground or foundations of our beliefs or personalities erupting explosively to allow change. Often change cannot occur effectively without this pent-up release, showing that emotions, whether we regard them as good or bad, need to surface and be released for progress to take place.)

Wind can represent the winds of change, ill winds and so on, depending on the content of your dream, but a tornado is a common universal symbol, similar to the meaning behind a storm.

Rain (water: emotions) can be refreshing, a gentle sprinkling of comforting emotional or spiritual support, particularly if you also feel the sun on your back or see the promise of a rainbow. Heavy rain indicates depression, being washed out by emotions.

Floods (water: emotions) symbolise insurmountable emotions. You may fear drowning in your emotions, or find your home (symbolising your mind or a current situation) overwhelmed by a flood of emotion.

Rainbows symbolise promise, reminding us not only of their awesome beauty, but also of the sun which shines through rain.

Tidal waves *(19.4%)* (water: emotions) are huge inescapable emotional deluges, symbolising feelings which have been repressed for too long and which can no longer be held back.

Snow and ice (frozen water) represent frozen or cold emotions.

Clouds may be fluffy, white dreamlike clouds, or big heavy rain clouds. Clouds may have silver linings or bring heavy rain (depression).

B. Cycles and Seasons

Birth *(pregnancy 31.9%; birth 26.9%; cradling an infant 36.9%)* New beginnings, often born from pain, or from death of the old. Try to see the baby as a symbol of something new, something to be nurtured, or of your inner child, rather than as a real person. Chapter 15, Who Are All Those People? will shed light here.

Death *(serene death 17.5%; accidental death 27.5%; murder 25.6%)* Death of the old, endings, often making way for birth of the new. Serene or painless deaths or killings show acceptance of the importance of letting the old or the past die to give birth to new growth. Consider the dream feelings and story-line to understand more. Again, do not focus on the person who is dying, for they are often symbols too. (See Chapter 15.)

Union, marriage, sex *(sexual encounter 56.9%; kissing, cuddling 48.1%; marriage, engagement 14.4%)* Fruition through inner integration. Look beyond the person you are marrying or making love with, and see instead what they represent. Their character (or other aspects) may symbolise what you need to integrate into yourself to progress and grow. (See Chapter 15.)

(16.3% did not dream of any of the birth, death or union symbols)

Day, sun By the light of day we see what is around us. Daylight symbolises what we have become enlightened about, what we have moved into consciousness, what we can see clearly. Daylight is our conscious self.

Darkness We cannot see clearly in the dark. We walk around, not knowing where we are or what is there. We walk the unknown, the subconscious. Dark night surroundings symbolise our subconscious self.

The full moon, if present, represents intuition, psychic sense and female (Yin) qualities. Dream moonlight opens our eyes to see what has, until now, been subconscious.

Spring New beginnings and potential for growth.

Summer Maturity and light.

Autumn Fruition, harvest, reaping the fruits of your previous labours.

Winter Endings and death of the old, or a period of hibernation, in preparation for a new beginning. Winter may also symbolise cold emotions.

Mornings are fresh beginnings with plenty of time ahead.

Afternoons see time progressing, perhaps with some achievement.

Evenings spell endings, time running out or time to draw to a close, to retire or to rest in readiness for a new day, and a new beginning.

C. Houses and Gardens

Our house or dwelling place, be it castle, igloo or cave, symbolises our state of mind.

In waking life, our house, body, clothes and possessions are all extensions of who we are and the circumstances we find ourselves in. Since we arguably create our own circumstances, all these things can be seen as symbolic of our mental state, in waking life as well as in dreams. It is the power of the mind which creates personal material wealth or poverty, subjugation or personal freedom, growth towards full potential or stagnation. Our deepest knowledge of this truth, that it is how we choose to use our mind that creates our destiny, is revealed in dreams by our depiction of dwelling places as symbols of our state of mind. We dwell, or live, within the freedom or restriction of our individual minds.

Dreaming of the house you live in now *(28.1%)*, or houses you used to live in *(55.6%)*, or other houses you know or knew, may be symbolic, but generally tends to refer to time periods (the time when you lived in that old house, you had a particular attitude, etc.), and this topic is covered in Chapter 11, Personal Symbols and Chapter 10.

Frequently my present home gets mixed up with homes I have lived in before.

(Fiona, retired medical secretary)

(Fiona is going through the same patterns of behaviour, and the dream reminds her of this by showing the interchangeable houses spanning the years.)

Common dream house *(dream house 60.6%)* scenarios include looking for a new house (considering changing your mind), or moving house (experimenting with changing your mind or thinking in a different way), finding yourself in a huge house with many extra rooms (discovering unused mental potential), or being in a small house with no easy exit (feeling mentally cramped and restricted). Houses that are dream houses but seem to belong to someone you know, may reflect that person's state of mind.

I sometimes dream of being in the house of a relative or friend, but in the dream the house does not appear as it does in waking life.

(Gillian, school student)

(Instead, Gillian glimpses the mind-set of her relative or friend.)

There have been times when I don't recognise the house but I know I've been there before.

(Valerie, teacher)

(Valerie recognises this state of mind since she's been in this position before.)

1 TYPES OF DWELLING PLACES

Castle Defensive or acquisitive mind, depending on context of dream.

Historical, old building Old (decrepit?) state of mind, or traditional viewpoint. May reflect mental tendency to refer back to the past, or to live in the past instead of going forward. The historical perspective may indicate a sense of family history and standing in the mind of the dreamer.

Mansion, palace Huge potential and richness of mind.

Derelict house Derelict state of mind. Such a mental attitude may be showing up in the dreamer's physical health, so this symbol may indicate or prelude physical disease in waking life.

Small house. Small mind, feeling mentally restricted.

Open-plan house Few walls, or a house that is open to the elements may indicate an open mind, unrestricted by partitions between one area of your mind and another, a 'unity' of mind. Alternatively, this dream house may suggest that you are easily influenced by your surroundings (open to weather), vulnerable and unprotected. The context of your dream will give the appropriate meaning for you.

Apartment block The symbolism depends on the dream, but can reflect 'identical units', uniformity, or feeling the same as everyone else. It may symbolise 'pigeon holing' or, depending on the placement of the apartment within the block (high or low?), it may refer to the higher or lower levels of the mind.

Hotel or holiday house *(hotel 16.3%; holiday house 13.1%)* Temporary state of mind, or need for time out or rest.

Shop *(shopping centre 22.5%)* A place of choice. Mental choices available.

These symbolic connections should seem obvious to you by now, but if you have difficulty working out the symbolism behind a building or type of dwelling place, go back to the children's fairy tale exercise outlined earlier in this chapter. Fit the dream house into fairy tale context and its meaning will become evident.

2 ROOMS

If houses symbolise the mind, then individual rooms represent individual areas of the mind, and the levels within the house indicate levels of the mind.

Bathroom *(16.3%)* Cleansing (especially of emotions: water). Getting rid of mental impurities and cleansing the mind, perhaps by expressing emotions.

Toilet *(15%)* Place to get rid of waste emotions (water symbolises emotion, and urine is waste emotion) and 'all that shit' that you have been carrying around. Cleansing. Mental privacy to release the emotions or the past.

Bedroom *(41.3%)* Privacy, sex, rest and sleep.

Basement, cellar *(cellar 9.4%)* Unless you have a specific horror of demons in the cellar, these lower areas represent your mental foundations: the subconscious self. You may find dead bodies (things from your past) or lost treasures (forgotten gifts and talents) in your dream cellar. Going down can also indicate depression, as you slip into the lower levels of your mind and cannot find a way up and out.

Attic *(6.9%)* The higher you climb in your dream house, the higher the level of mind you are experiencing. These higher levels, such as the attic, may symbolise your higher intellectual mind, or your higher spiritual mind (your Higher Self: the wisest part of you). Fear of ascending to the attic, unless you were raised on tales of ghosts in the attic, may reflect fear of seeing the truth of your higher mind, or fear of honestly meeting your Higher Self.

Lift *(13.8%)* Elevators move you up to the higher mind, down to the lower, more physical levels, or deeper into your subconscious. The ride may be swift, may go in the opposite direction to your expectations, may get stuck or you may not be able to get out at the right floor. Add story-line to the context of your dream to deduce the meaning of your dream. See also Basement and Attic.

Stairs *(staircase 25%; upstairs 25%)* Similar to lift. See Lift, Basement and Attic.

Kitchen *(22.5%)* Part of the mind concerned with nurturing (feeding) and nourishing. Food is what we take in to nourish ourselves and help us to grow. Food can symbolise what we need for nourishment and personal growth, and can also represent fodder for ideas (food for thought). In cooking we combine various basics to concoct different dishes, so symbolically we are mentally combining basics and coming up with new ideas or new ways of nourishing, or thinking. The cook in the kitchen is also the provider.

Dining Room *(11.3%)* Part of mind which takes in nourishment or new ideas and may share these with others if the dining is social. Who you are eating with (what they represent to you) in the dream may give you a clue as to the ideas you are 'chewing over'. See also Kitchen.

Lounge Room *(33.1%)* Everyday part of mind, or relaxation, entertainment or relationship to family area of your mind.

We sit in rooms with rivers running through them, except the actual room is like a prison cell that is orange. We sail paper boats on the river to each other.

(Jill, school student)

(Jill feels emotionally restricted in her family environment. They do not communicate directly, she feels, but across an emotional (water) gulf.)

Study/ Office *(12.5%)* Learning or studying attitudes.

Garage Since the garage houses the car, and the car represents drive and motivation, the garage may symbolise the motivational area of your mind. If you keep your junk in the garage, your dream garage may symbolise your mental garbage heap!

Hallway or passage If the hallway is long and thin, like a corridor, it can have powerful symbolism as a birth canal. To find yourself walking through a passage may represent a mental or spiritual rebirth, so note what you are looking for in the dream, and see where you end up.

Doors *(28.8%)* Doors and doorways are ways through from one mental area to another, so they symbolise opportunity and progress, or connection between one area of the mind and another. If your dream doors are closed, stuck, locked, or lead to unexpected places, what does this tell you about the way you approach opportunities? The front door symbolises how we welcome or approach the public, whereas the back door leads to the more private, or inner mind.

Windows *(29.4%)* We see out and in through windows, so these are symbols of our ability to see deeper or beyond our current position. They represent a viewpoint, so note what you are being shown through a dream window. What significance would misty or curtained windows imply?

Garden *(dream garden 33.1%; own garden 10.6%)* We cultivate our gardens with plants of our choice. A dream garden is therefore symbolic of what we have chosen to cultivate within ourselves. It represents our personal growth. Is your dream garden fresh, alive and full of colour, or dry and overgrown with weeds? Is it large and sunny, or small and overshadowed? What might these details tell you about the state of your personal growth? What jobs need to be done around your dream garden, and how do you relate this to what needs to be done in your waking life? The front garden can symbolise which parts of ourselves we show to the public, while the back garden is our more private personal development.

Verandah, balcony Close to the house, yet not quite a part of the garden, these areas may symbolise our reluctance to leave the safety of the house (mind) and really cultivate our desires (garden).

3 FURNITURE

Furniture tends to symbolise aspects of the area of the mind represented by the room, so consider the state of the furniture in any room to enhance your understanding of your mental attitudes as portrayed by your dream. Is the furniture old-fashioned, uncomfortable, falling apart or luxurious?

Tables tend to symbolise relationship with those sharing your table, or a meeting point where ideas are shared. The table, like a chair, may also be your position in life.

Chairs are symbolic of your 'seat in life'. Is it a throne or a floor cushion?

Cupboards represent areas of our mind where we have stored memories away, or where we prefer to keep aspects of ourselves hidden.

I dream of the home where I was first married. I love looking through the rooms, opening cupboards and seeing the changes made to the home and surrounding area.

(Nadine, secretary)

(Nadine compares, in her dreams, her present life to the way she thought when she first married, and observes the mental changes she has made since then.)

Bookshelves house knowledge.

Ornaments may indicate the pretences we display to others, or may reflect our personality or the depth and value of our many memories.

Carpets give an indication of the richness or poverty of our grounding, our mental base.

Television *(10.6%)* Watch out for television or videos, cinemas and theatres. When a dream is dealing with an explosive or vulnerable aspect of your life which you do not recognise, it will often set you up as a viewer or a member of the audience. As an objective observer, you are more likely to see your truth.

D. The Body

Our legs get us from one place to another, so it is not surprising that we see legs in dreams as symbols of our direction or ability to make progress. We talk of 'shouldering responsibility', so we see our shoulders as symbolic of responsibility, and we describe someone as being 'spineless' if they are weak, so we perceive the spine as being symbolic of inner strength. Our everyday language is pervaded with examples of body parts symbolising the mind. So it is in dreams too.

In common with many others, my personal philosophy is that our physical body is also a reflection of the mind; that what we believe we also create. Most Western doctors now agree that most diseases and illnesses start in the mind (usually through stress) and are capable of being cured through positive mind techniques such as meditation or a changed belief system. It is but a small step to see your body and everything around you as a physical manifestation of your own thoughts and the power of your mind.

When a dream speaks its symbolic language, we therefore see our thoughts or our minds expressing symbols of what may later become physically manifested (within the body or within our surroundings or future circumstances). It's as if, in my opinion, the dream takes a step into the future and shows you the potential your current state of mind has to become your future waking reality. In waking and comprehending the dream, you then have the choice of changing your mind-set if your potential future was not to your liking, or of making it happen fast if it looked good.

1 PARTS OF THE BODY

Head Thought. Head as opposed to heart.

Eyes Seeing or not seeing. Window of the soul.

Mouth, teeth With these we eat, or take in food for thought and nourishment, and we also communicate. When the dream emphasises the mouth or teeth, it may be drawing your attention to what you are, or are not, taking in, or to what you are, or are not, communicating. Losing your teeth may reflect your anxieties over life's changes or ageing (we lose milk teeth as we change from childhood, and lose our teeth as we get old), but may also symbolise not being able to communicate what we really want to say. As we lose our teeth, perhaps our power recedes.

Ears emphasise listening and hearing. Take heed of what is being said in the dream, it is important.

Nose The nose can represent intuition or curiosity, a 'nose' for something.

Throat, neck These are powerful symbols of communication, also known to many as the site of the fifth chakra, the communication energy centre.

Most vivid to me was a man taking me to a field from my house. I was lying down and he slit my throat as I lay there. I was not frightened.

(Jayne A., home duties)

(Jayne's communication centre was opened and freed.)

Hair Hair grows from the head, as ideas do. Hair tends to symbolise our ideas, which is why people we know often appear with different hairstyles and hair colours in our dreams. Baldness may indicate a lack of ideas, long thick hair may show the opposite. Combing your hair may symbolise straightening out, or untangling, your ideas.

Heart Feelings. Coming from the heart not the head.

Legs Direction and movement forward. To find yourself in a wheelchair without the use of your legs indicates a loss of direction or a loss of power over exercising your direction. Is someone else pushing you along or are you letting someone else control you?

Knees We bend our knees in humility or servitude, so this body part tends to represent these qualities.

Hands With these we create, give, receive and handle our world. Symbolic of our dealings with creativity or willingness to give and receive.

Stomach We get butterflies in our stomach when we're nervous, or vomit back food we cannot accept. The stomach is symbolic of nervousness, vulnerability and acceptance or rejection of what we take in about our environment.

Chest A knife in the chest is a killer. We speak of 'baring' our chest when we are being brave, or of 'getting it all off your chest' when something needs to be said. The chest can be symbolic of these qualities and is therefore representative of our vulnerability.

Back We can get stabbed in the back, turn our back on something, put our worries behind us, look back, never look back, have some backbone or be spineless. Look at the context of your dream to gain understanding.

Shoulders Symbolic of our ability to take responsibility, wide shoulders in a dream indicate the bearing of heavy responsibilities. Someone placing their hands on your shoulders may symbolise an imposition or simply be an emphasis on your responsibilities.

Buttocks The buttocks are the 'seat' of your power or ego. Look at where you place them in the dream!

Right side The right side of your body is controlled by the left hemisphere* of your brain, which also deals with what we see as the male (Yang) qualities of logic, rational thought and our relationship to the challenge of our outer world. Any emphasis on the right side of your dream body (right eye, right hand) combines the symbolism of that body part with the challenges of your outer world. The right eye, for example, may symbolise looking at your outer world, while the right hand may comment on how you deal with work or emphasise what you give to the world. See also Left side and Balance.

Left side The left side of your body is controlled by the right hemisphere* of your brain, which also deals with what we see as the female (Yin) qualities of intuition, creativity, emotional nurturing and our relationship to our inner world. Any emphasis on the left side of your dream body (left shoulder, left leg) combines the symbolism of that body part with the emotional requirements of your inner world. The left shoulder, for example, may represent your emotional responsibilities towards your inner self or the way in which you take on responsibility for the inner wellbeing of others. The left leg symbolises your emotional support (your leg supports you) or emotional, inner direction. See also Right side and Balance.

* *The left hemisphere is 'Yang' for 95% of right-handed people and for 10% or more of left-handed people. The hemispheres are reversed for the remainder.*

Balance All of us, whether man or woman, ideally need a balance between these male and female qualities of Yang and Yin. In other words, we need a balance between our involvement with the outer world and our inner world. This theme of left and right pervades other symbols apart from body parts. You may notice right or left turnings in your journey dreams, or in the placement or position of yourself, others or objects in your dream. A client once dreamed he sat at the head of a long table. To his right all the seats were occupied, the full length of the table, all taken by men. To his left, only one seat was filled, by a woman, and the rest were empty. This man's position in life, and most of his dealings, were with his outer world. He had fully developed his male qualities, and although he was aware of his inner, female side, he had suppressed her. He had not dealt with his emotions and had tried to sublimate them through his dedication to his highly successful working world, his family's financial 'needs' and charity work. This dream was one of many that signalled a turning point in his life, and a necessity to redress the balance by paying attention to his inner needs.

2 CLOTHING THE BODY

Clothes cover and protect our bodies and also signal our atti-tudes to others. We dress in business clothes to project credibility in the workplace, wear a long, thin, black evening dress or a dinner suit to give an impression of elegance, or wear slogan emblazoned T-shirts to advertise our preferences to the world. In the same way, dream clothes symbolise the attitudes we show to others, and behind which we feel protected. Look at your clothes in dreams and ask yourself what they say about your attitudes, given the context of your dream.

Naked. Without the protection of clothes we appear vulnerable. Nakedness is 'baring' the truth, being vulnerable and being honest. How we *react* to our nakedness in the dream is the more telling part!

Shoes represent our standing in life. What kind of person would these dream shoes belong to? What attitudes would they reflect? Are they appropriate to the dream scene, or are they out of place? Being barefoot in a dream may symbolise being in contact with the ground, without pretence, or may indicate poverty, obviously depending on the dream context.

I dream often about clothes and colours seem important in those dreams. Shoes also seem significant and I'm often changing them.

(Jaquelyn, librarian)

(Jaquelyn may be experimenting with how to present her attitudes to others, what position to take in certain matters, or with seeing the point of view of others by 'standing in their shoes'.)

Jewellery adorns us and symbolises our riches. Jewellery can appear in a dream to draw attention to a body part and its symbolic meaning. An earring, for example, may underline the importance of hearing, or a soft, amber necklace may ask for a honeyed approach to communication. Rings may have obvious symbolism such as marriage or engagement, but, on the whole, precious jewels symbolise precious qualities, talents or gifts. Was the jewellery given to you? Did you discover it hidden away somewhere, lost and forgotten, or did you find yourself looking for lost jewellery? What would each of these tell you about your special talents and gifts?

Baggage What do you carry with you? Do you struggle through your dreams with your own heavy luggage, or are you asked to carry everyone else's? Do you put your bags down and decide to travel light? How much old baggage from the past do you carry around with you? Do you need to lighten your load?

E. Institutions

School *(some kind of educational place 50.6%; high school 22.5%; primary school 20.6%; university 15%; college 13.8%; short course 5.6%; kindergarten 5%; weekend learning retreat 4.4%)* Learning or teaching. What is the lesson in this dream?

I seem to be undergoing tuition a lot in my dreams, but never in an earthly place.

(Amanda, astrologer)

(Is Amanda learning about concepts and ideas which are alien or esoteric to her, or is she learning about alternative realities through dream travel?)

Hospital Healing (hopefully!). Your dream may perceive a hospital as a place of sickness and death, or it may hold the joy and promise of a maternity hospital. Either way, a hospital is a place dedicated to healing and renewal. Which aspects of your life are highlighted in your hospital dream? How can these be healed? Does the dream give you clues about what you need to do, or about attitudes you need to take, to heal yourself or your relationships in waking life?

Library *(9.4%)* A place where all knowledge is stored, and where you search for something you need to know. What are you trying to discover in your dream?

Prison Restriction, subjugation or perhaps feelings of self-inflicted punishment based on guilt. What are you feeling guilty about? Is this valid? What can you do to release yourself from guilt, or to release yourself from someone's overbearing manipulation or restrictive control? How does the dream advise you? In which other respects might you be feeling a severe lack of freedom?

Monastery The spiritual or religious aspects of your mind, according to the context of the dream. A monastery may also symbolise a place of solitude, a need for peace, meditation or prayer, or a need for a temporary escape from the world.

F. Animals

Animals symbolise our instinctive drives, or animal passions, our inner wildness or drive to live life and respond according to our in-built, pre-domesticated nature. As always, if you have a pet, or a personal feeling or association about a particular animal, this becomes more important than any universal symbolism. Note the species or breed of animal, its behaviour in your dream, and the surrounding circumstances to get an accurate picture.

Sometimes people become animals and vice versa. I'm often caring for young animals, and the animals change into other animals or human babies.

(Annie, home duties)

(Annie sees the animal instincts behind her dream characters and how one instinct can give rise to another according to the influences around her and the actions she takes in her dreams. Her nurturing suggests she needs to nurture these qualities in herself.)

Cat Usually seen as feminine, the cat symbolises intuition and psychic power, although may also represent independence, 'cattiness', or 'prowl and pounce' behaviour. The type of cat should shed light. A wild cat may indicate wild passion, while a domestic pedigree suggests expectations of pampering, or eccentric misplaced affections.

Dog Our natural instincts are often portrayed by a dog in dreams, and the breed of dog enhances this. A wolf (untamed) or German shepherd (protector or aggressor) conjures a different picture from a greyhound (eager, competitive?), a Saint Bernard (loyal rescuer) or poodle (fussy, pampered).

Horse More than any other animal, the horse inspires us, worldwide, with a feeling of physical passion, particularly the strength and fluidity of sexual passion.

Insects Little annoyances or irritations in your life can 'bug' you and often crescendo to a point where they can drive you mad! A swarm of mosquitoes, or biting ants have the same effect. While insects may symbolise unnoticed irritation which is building up to something big, different species may have specific meanings. Termites or bees may represent altruism and labour. Consider the overall effect of hundreds of workers each performing their small task to contribute towards a massive structured society which protects its own. Do you feel society treats you as just another worker, or that you are contributing to a greater whole? Or are the termites symbolic of being undermined?

Spiders Spiders weave unseen webs that can trap the unwary, and the female spider of some species is widely known to eat the male after mating. Spiders are also seen to have tenacity, spinning new webs every time the old is destroyed. To be covered in dream spiders may symbolise a feeling of becoming entangled and trapped. To stamp on spiders indicates an attempt to stamp out this feeling of being manipulated or engulfed by an insidious power. Above all, the notion of the female eating the male leaves the spider universally symbolic of the overbearing power of a woman, usually the mother, mother-in-law, wife or girlfriend of the dreamer.

Birds Throughout myth and legend birds are seen as symbols of the soul (as are butterflies, although these can also be seen as ephemeral, flighty, fancies, here one day, gone the next). The bird, like the soul, flies free and high and, seeing far, can assess a situation with the benefit of distance. Consider the species in your dream. An eagle, with its high circling and incredible eyesight symbolises ultimate wisdom, whereas a sparrow might inspire a feeling of everyday ordinariness. Magpies may be possessive, ducks impervious to criticism ('water off a duck's back'), and swans may symbolise the beauty that grows from the poor 'ugly duckling'. Is your dream bird free or trapped in a cage?

Fish Living in water, fish symbolise instincts closer to our emotions, closer to our heart, unable to survive in the 'air' of our thought-filled heads. The spirit or soul is also closely related to our emotional self. The biblical image of Christ and his disciples fishing for souls, and the parable of the loaves and fishes, adds emphasis to the soul or spirit symbolism of the fish.

Sharks Bigger, more dangerous fish have a different and obvious meaning! It is common to dream of watching the sea and slowly becoming aware of sharks below the surface. Since the sea is our emotional and subconscious self, the sharks represent the fears which lie below the surface. Consider what particular fears your sharks represent, given the context of your dream, and work on facing them and making them disappear.

Whales and dolphins Not fish, of course, but mammals, these creatures are symbolic not only of the New Age, but also of the huge, gentle, intelligent, soft wonder that lies within our subconscious. These creatures, but particularly the whale, are glimpses of our true magnitude and 'goodness'. Personal symbolism of the cruelty associated with whaling, or the feeling of encountering something too big to handle, may also be important in whale dreams.

Elephants may represent something too big to cope with, something too slow, or plodding, or a memory from the past since 'elephants never forget'. Personal associations with persecution through hunting for ivory may also be indicated by elephant dreams.

Lion What nature does your dream lion exhibit? Universally the lion tends to represent strength, but a strength, as in the legends of Hercules, that is better handled with gentleness and respect than with force. The lion symbolises your inner strength to overcome adversity.

Snakes Freud's much discussed symbolism of the snake as the penis (more so than his long list of other phallic symbols!) has left us, in modern days, with a remnant of belief in the snake as representative of male sexuality. This belief alone, because we have taken it on board, does mean that the dream snake will sometimes carry this meaning.

The snake has enjoyed several millennia of symbolism. For around a thousand years before the birth of Christ, the ancient Greeks took their physical, emotional or spiritual concerns to one of some 300 healing temples. Here they would generally go through various cleansing rituals and meditations, then be sent to sleep in a room alongside harmless snakes. The snakes were representative of Asclepius, the Greek god of healing. In the morning, the people would recount their dreams to their healers, who were dream interpreters. The interpreters would suggest the cure, based on the dreams. Hippocrates, now known as the 'father of medicine', was a student of dream interpretation at one of these temples around the 4th century BC. He realised that many dreams reflected the physical state of the body, whether it was already diseased, or whether conditions were building which, left unchecked, would result in illness. When Western doctors were required, in the past, to swear the Hippocratic oath in his memory, they did so under the symbol of the snake entwined on the caduceus.

Many ancient initiation rites involved spending time in a snake pit, where the bite of a poisonous snake was believed to be overcome through self-healing. The biblical snake in the Garden of Eden is believed to represent our instinctive urges, presumably our sexual urges, while in Indian Tantric philosophy the snake, known as Kundalini, is a source of spiritual energy which lies coiled at the base of the human spine. Through a number of procedures, including meditation and ritual sexual intercourse, the Kundalini snake is raised towards the head, travelling through and igniting the seven chakras (energy centres) along the spine, raising consciousness towards enlightenment as it goes.

Putting all these powerful snake symbols together gives an overall feeling of the power of the life force to draw healing and transformation through the bite of poison. The bite bestows healing through the pain of facing up to fear or adversity.

Pigs Some cultures revere the pig, but in Western cultures we see the pig perhaps as symbolic of greed, selfishness or male chauvinism.

Rats and mice These rodents gnaw and bite, overrun our space and may bring disease. They may symbolise the gnawing annoyances that chew away at our lives, undermining us, or bringing destruction and disease.

G. People

This is a complex subject that has been given the whole chapter it deserves. See Chapter 15.

Further Information

If you are interested in a deeper study of universal and shared symbols, consult Carl Jung's work. One of the few genuine modern dream dictionaries is Tony Crisp's *Dream Dictionary*, which was first published by Optima Macdonald in 1990.

Please beware of getting too attached to interpreting dreams through universal or shared symbols because this can become a rigid, unbalanced approach which may generate false advice. Whether you are interpreting for yourself or for others, it is vital to remember that the dream always belongs to the dreamer, and that only the dreamer can confirm a feeling of resonance, a 'Yes! That's it!' socked in the guts, maybe even tear-jerking response. It may take several days for a dreamer to reach this stage, especially when they are dealing with deep-seated blocks, but if the interpretation is correct, it will come.

A professional dream interpreter walks a thin and careful line between showing a dreamer the blocks they may not acknowledge, and ultimately bowing down to the dreamer's personal reaction to the interpretation. The interpreter should beware of imposing his or her personal or learned symbolism, and should avoid declaring a sense of finality or diagnosis. The role of the dream interpreter is rather to walk a step ahead of the dreamer, using a more experienced eye, a practised inner knowledge and, if lucky enough to be so blessed, a dose of psychic insight, to clear the mist from the path so that the dreamer can make his or her own discovery.

With only one set of tools in your dream interpretation bag, it is now time to travel further into Part Two to gain more.

CHAPTER 10

Recurring Dreams or Themes

Why do dreams recur? If our dreams give us information about our deeper selves, shouldn't they disappear once the message has been delivered?

According to the Talmud, 'A dream that is not understood, is like a letter not opened.'

In our present world, where we have lost touch with the language of our dreams, the postman always knocks twice, thrice ... or more, until we finally understand!

A dream message may slowly trickle through at a deep sub-conscious level, but until recognition of the dream's meaning percolates through into our waking consciousness, we make minimal progress. If an important issue repeatedly comes up for us in waking life, but remains unresolved, it will continue to be addressed in our dreams.

Often, the dream seems to grow in impatience as time passes, becoming more insistently graphic or exaggerated. What we once regarded as a recurring dream may grow to become a recurring nightmare, causing us to wake in a sweat of fear and panic. For others, the dream trudges itself out in regular cycles, as they go round and round in never-ending circles, having the dream, doing nothing about it, facing the same issues in the same old (obviously unsuccessful) way, having the dream, doing nothing about it, facing the ... How do we break the pattern and learn?

Many people find their recurring dreams are more recurring *themes* than exact word for word, scene by scene repetitions. These dreams can be easier to crack, to begin to understand,

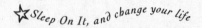

once you focus on what the recurring dreams have in common. Often this will either be a precise symbol (a tidal wave, for example), or a feeling (such as loss).

The examples in this chapter illustrate some of the most common recurring themes and explain what they mean. Check these categories against your own recurring dreams.

Chase and Escape Themes

Run and Hide from a Pursuer

I'm being chased, but I don't know who by. I feel frightened and know I'll be okay if I hide. Over the last 15 years, I've hidden in roofs, cupboards, libraries and rainwater tanks. I always realise it's 'only a dream' towards the end and experience a great sense of relief.

(Isabelle, legal secretary)

We often run away from the things in life that we fear, and can spend much of our lives in avoidance and escape rather than confronting our fears and resolving them. Isabelle has been running for 15 years, and it is her sense of relief on waking to find the experience was 'only a dream' that prevents her from taking the dream message seriously. She wakes as if hearing her mother's voice from the past, stroking her forehead and assuring her, 'Don't be silly, it's only a dream.' So, if it's 'only a dream', why has it returned for 15 years to haunt and frighten her?

> **Meaning:** *Chase and escape dreams indicate that you need to confront something in your life and put an end to it through resolution.*

Run from a Tidal Wave

I am on a beach with a wall behind me. There are many people. I see a giant wave coming and run for the wall. I never make it and wake up as the wave is upon me.

(Annie, home duties)

Tidal waves found their way into 19.4% of the survey dreamers' dreams over the last two years, while 5.6% of these people dreamed of tidal waves more than any other kind of water situation.

Water represents our emotions, and the ocean itself can symbolise our subconscious self, which, of course, largely speaks in terms of emotions. A tidal wave therefore conjures up an enormous, overwhelming, inevitable wave of emotions which are going to knock you flat. Whether these emotions are good or bad, this type of recurring dream tends to suggest the dreamer is subconsciously aware of the emotions which he is ignoring in his waking life. He keeps these emotions dammed up deep inside, refusing to express these feelings by allowing them to surface and flow out. There comes a point where the pressure of these emotions becomes too great, regardless of the dreamer's attempt to hold them back.

> *Meaning*: You are repressing your emotions and not facing up to your feelings, but you can't run away from them forever. This dream begs you to let your emotions flow freely and find expression.

Finding yourself ecstatically floating on a tidal wave, however, is bringing awareness of the freedom which is released on expressing your more positive emotions or in letting go and flowing with them.

Lost and Found

We spend much of our lives looking for what we feel we have lost or left behind or cannot find.

Can't Find My Way

I dream of a street scene, where I am walking to a known destination, then losing my way. I can see where I want to be, but I cannot get there.

(Lesley, home duties)

In dreams we often travel endlessly, through streets, roads, highways, towns, cities even foreign countries, sometimes with ease, but sometimes losing our sense of direction altogether. These dreams reflect our individual journeys through life. There are times when we know exactly where we want to be, but get lost or can't find the way, like Lesley. As she says herself, 'I can see where I want to be, but I cannot get there.' Lesley's dream reflects her frustration at, perhaps, being so near, but so far.

Meaning: *You, or your situation, is preventing you from getting to where you want to be.*

Losing or Forgetting the Baby

I would be given a baby to mind and was supposed to breastfeed it. I would put it away and remember some days later. I felt absolutely dreadful, sure it would be dead. I'd get to it just in time with very real relief. At the time of having these dreams, I didn't have much time for myself. The dream stopped after I realised, after ten years, that the baby was my child within that needed attention.

(Wendy, home duties)

To dream of a baby or child generally either refers to some new (baby) project or idea you are trying to 'foster', or is symbolic of your 'inner child', that tender, growing part of you which still needs attention, love, care and nurturing.

Meaning: *Dreams of losing your inner child, or seeing your inner child in danger, are clear pleas from your dreaming self to give yourself more loving attention.*

Buried Body Resurfaces

Sometimes the prospect of finding or discovering a lost part of yourself, or a memory, is scary and threatening. We may dream-picture lost skills, opportunities, emotions or past times as 'dead and gone'. We may even have been guilty of the murder. It is common to go through a dream with that haunting suspicion that you have killed something which has remained dead and buried for years, but which is now threatening to be discovered:

I am located near a creek that runs under a road crossing. Although I cannot remember harming anybody, my brain tells me I have killed a woman and buried the body under the pebbly crossing. A rainstorm is coming and I am worried that the body will be uncovered by the storm water. I have no idea who the woman is or what she looks like.

(Joseph, communications tradesman)

A woman in a dream can symbolise the female side of ourselves (Yin); that creative, nurturing, intuitional, expressive aspect which understands our inner world. Joseph has possibly killed this aspect of himself at some time in the past, and although he has not consciously noticed the lack and has felt unharmed so far, it seems he is approaching a time when he will be confronted with the loss of these qualities from his life. The emphasis on water in this dream, particularly storm water, suggests stormy emotional times are ahead, and these circumstances are likely to confront him with this loss.

Meaning: *You are becoming aware of something you have buried in your past, or a part of yourself you have 'killed off'. It is about to resurface, or needs to. Try not to get bogged down with the feeling of guilt in a recurring dream like this. Guilt, in a dream, is more to do with how we have cheated* ourselves *than how we have treated others.*

Restrictions and Hesitations

I'm Late!

The main theme of my recurring dream is time. I'm late for appointments, dates, or catching a plane or train. All manner of incidents keep delaying me. No matter what I do to overcome one thing delaying me, something else will crop up causing more loss of time.

(Joe, catering attendant)

Would you believe that a recurring dream involving being late for everything is usually the province of very successful people, or, at least, people who are always on time for their waking life appointments? These dreams can hinge on anxiety born of being overworked and under pressure to perform and run to deadlines. The greatest fear of such people is often failure, and it can be that very fear of failure which urges them ever onward to achieve success in the eyes of the world.

This type of dream also belongs to those who feel constantly under pressure of time, perhaps not so much in work, but in terms of feeling that life is running away from them and that time is running out. They would like to achieve more, but something always holds them up.

> **Meaning:** *Your possible fear of failure sees you living out one of two choices: to hesitate and not put yourself in the vulnerable position of being seen to fail, or to go for it to the exclusion of all else to ensure that you are perceived in the most successful light. Which are you, and why might you fear 'failure'? In what way have you restricted yourself?*

Going Up and Getting Stuck

I see myself walking upstairs and when I reach the door on the landing dividing the rooms, an overwhelming feeling takes over and I cannot move. I wake up. This dream gives me the feeling that I must overcome my fear and open the door, and all will be well.

(Lainey, home duties)

Recurring dreams of going upstairs often symbolise ascending to the higher mind, intellect or higher consciousness. Lainey, like others who share this common recurring dream, wants to understand more from a higher point of view, but hesitates. The door is the gateway from one place to another: an opportunity.

> **Meaning:** *You fear what is on the other side, or fear taking the*

next step. It is only your own hesitation which is paralysing further progress.

Swimming on Dirty Water

I'm swimming in a pool and the water is dirty, not clear. I can't get down into the water properly. It's as if I'm swimming on top of the water.

(Stella, home duties)

Since water represents emotions, dirty, unclear water symbolises unclear emotions. Stella wants to get into the emotions around her in her waking life, but feels they are too murky to see her way through.

Meaning: *Swimming on top of the water can show your hesitation to really get into difficult emotional areas.*

Can't Find a Suitable Toilet!

I am desperate to go to the toilet and everywhere I go there are people looking at me, or the toilets are visible with no privacy, or they are all taken.

(Cassie, recruitment consultant)

Urine, being waste water, can be seen as waste emotions. We all need time and privacy to let go of our emotions, and Cassie obviously feels she doesn't have this. A full bladder can cause a dream like this, with the hesitation about relieving yourself stemming from the fact that you know you are in bed and would end up with a wet mattress! However, people frequently wake themselves up from such a dream, get out of bed, go to the toilet ... only to find that there was no need.

Meaning: *You need to find more time for peace and privacy to deal with your private emotions and let go.*

Overburdened and Stressed

Can't Feed Everyone

My recurring dream is one where I have lots of guests for a dinner party and suddenly I am unorganised and can't find any food in the fridge. People are hungry, and when I start cooking, everything goes wrong. I am so panicky and nervous.

(Michealla, natural therapist)

This can be a variation on the 'late for everything' dream described earlier in this chapter, but it usually belongs more to those who become overburdened by the demands of others. Michealla is a natural therapist who is much in demand both by her clients for her healing skills, and also by her young family. People are dependent on Michealla to provide and the dream shows her feelings of inadequacy when she occasionally finds she cannot nurture and feed everyone.

Meaning: *You may have taken too much responsibility for the welfare of others, and need to re-evaluate issues of dependency and responsibility at these times. You may also be feeling insecure about performance.*

Crashing or Out of Control Car

During the time my business was going down (I became bankrupt), I had a recurring skidding car dream. It was always a Mercedes Benz or a big Ford. I would start out by myself, going to a business meeting, but out in the bush mostly. Often there would be storm clouds and I would think, 'I hope I can get through and don't get bogged.' Then came the uncontrollable skid and crash. The car would be wrecked, but I would be okay.

(Seeker, astrologer)

Cars are the modern day symbol for the way we go about our life journeys. Seeker travelled his working journey in expensive style indicating the extravagant approach he continued to take in his business even though he was aware, in his dreams, of the threatening storm clouds ahead. His dream showed that hope alone would not be sufficient to get him through the storm, and that his expensive all-risks attitude would cause him to skid and crash, which he did, all the slippery slope way to bankruptcy. If Seeker had fully comprehended the message in this recurring dream, he could have perhaps pulled back on his expenditure and got out of his business without the crash.

Meaning: Recurring car dreams ask you to look at what is happening to the dream car, and therefore to you, and to compare this with how you are going about your daily life.

Back to the Past
The Old Days
I am often living back in Ireland in my dreams, even after ten years of being in Australia.

(Brigid, personal assistant)

Recurring dreams set in places or houses we have lived in before (in *this* life: past lives will be discussed later in the book!) generally compare how we were then to how we are now. They give a time scale or may even pinpoint a past event or the birth of a particular attitude or behavioural response.

Meaning: When you find yourself constantly revisiting an old home or country, look at the rest of the dream and try to see what it is telling you about the experiences you had during those times, the way you thought and the way you felt compared to now. Why do you need to see this now?

The Past Looks Different: Big and Small Rooms
I go back to houses I have lived in. Sometimes the rooms are really huge, much bigger than the size of the house, yet this seems normal. Sometimes I am in a room and the walls close in leaving a very small exit.

(Lesley, home duties)

Lesley's experience of room sizes possibly reflects her feelings at the time. Walls that seem to close in leaving only a small exit indicate the feeling of oppression that she must have felt in those days, and her perception of being trapped, with only a small chance of escape to the outside. When her rooms are large, this may either indicate the room for potential growth or enlargement that was there at the time (whether she took advantage of it or not), or it may be the dream's way of emphasising and drawing attention to the room, in the same way that dreams will produce huge birds or oversized spiders and so on just to make sure we don't forget them!

Meaning: Ask yourself how those past years, rooms and feelings seem relevant to whatever you were experiencing around the time of the dream.

Past Traumas

Specific events and traumas such as incest or violence may be the cause of recurring dreams or nightmares, but it is easy to translate a dream too literally and jump to conclusions about terrible things which happened in your past, when, all along, the dream was symbolic of something else. Nevertheless, this aspect of dreaming of the past is important, and if you feel a dream is trying to focus your attention on a blocked trauma, you would be wise to seek professional counselling to guide you through your interpretations and discoveries.

I am a child or I am small compared to a huge, dark, long staircase. I never know who or what is at the top. Once or twice I have been up the stairs and see a door. I can only remember empty rooms but feel someone or something is there.

(Philippa, media assistant)

Meaning: Is this type of dream a blocked childhood memory, or is it symbolic of feeling overwhelmed about the unknown?

Attackers and Presences

An Evil Presence

Someone is standing over me, looking down at me while I sleep. It is only a dark figure but it is absolutely evil and I am very vulnerable. Sometimes I think it is Death.

(Polly, rose grower)

This terrifying recurring dream experience is very common, right down to the dreamer's feeling that the presence is Death. While presences and twilight experiences are addressed later in this book, we do also dream of presences in a symbolic way. Our emotions and feelings are accentuated in dreams, and since most dreams are also visual, we seek pictures or symbols to represent those powerful feelings. The very word 'presence' conjures up a feeling that is so close it sticks to the bones, a feeling that we cannot escape, that pervades the air. Presences in dreams may be good or bad, angelic or evil, god-like or demon. They may be inescapable because they are indeed a part of ourselves, our own feelings which we disown, preferring to see them as separate from ourselves and belonging to some other entity or presence. Polly may have an overwhelming sense of mortality and fear of death, which lingers and will not dissipate and leave her in peace.

> **Meaning:** *What might you be rejecting and disowning about yourself? Psychologically, this is known as your 'shadow self' which needs to be accepted and recognised as being a part of your own feelings, so that you can then set about coming to terms with your more negative emotions, memories or fears. After facing them you can let them go.*

Under Attack

I had to close all the doors and windows in our house as extremists were coming very near. Every time I thought everything was closed I had to run to and fro to close a door or window I had forgotten.

(Evelyn, home duties)

Another common recurring theme is that of being under attack, either in a house, like Evelyn, or in a war or siege of some kind. This usually indicates the dreamer is feeling unsafe and vulnerable to attack from others, mentally, spiritually or physically. Evelyn describes her attackers as 'extremists', suggesting, simply from her choice of words, that she fears extremist points of view. She may be dealing with extremists in her waking life, or she may be fearful of her own growing extreme attitudes.

Meaning: *You are feeling under attack, either from yourself or from others.*

Snake Attack

A snake attacks me or my children. The dream used to be worse, but in the last one, about three months ago, I held the snake as it struck me and I finally felt no fear. I won. I left the nightmare knowing I had beaten it.

(Alison, nurse)

Alison's description of finally facing up to her fears and coming to terms with them is classic. The sense of absolutely knowing that in confronting an issue, even in a dream, she had robbed it of its power to harm her was totally freeing, not only in her dream state but also in her life. She had finally 'come to grips' with both the snake, and the fear. She is healed.

Meaning: *You feel under attack, or in a state of conflict. If you face up to the fear and let it bite you, you come to terms with the fact and overcome it: you heal yourself.*

Physical Warnings
Personally Symbolic Recurring Dreams

I have had this dream when I have been sick with high temperatures. I start in an attic where there are lots of interlocking wheels similar to that of a large watch. They turn and turn and get bigger and bigger.

There is an indescribable vulgar smell and I find it hard to breathe. Then I am falling or riding a bike madly, out of control, down a steep, sandy hill. The smell gets worse, I can't stop and I can't get away from the wheels or the worm. Don't let me fall! I used to be an epileptic and would take fits at high temperatures. This dream occurred whenever I had a fit. Mum would wake me by shaking me and I would find myself out of bed, huddled in a ball, crying in the corner of my bedroom.

(Peta, architect)

The other night my son wet his bed and as my wife and I were talking about it I suddenly recalled a series of dreams I had as a youngster of seven or eight years, which were preludes to my bed-wetting. The dreams were always about harvesting wheat and I seem to recall the harvesters were horse drawn. There were still some horse drawn harvesters around in those days, but one of the last dreams had a red tractor instead of the horse team. As I got to recognise those dreams for what they led onto, I was able to wake up in time and so avoid the embarrassment of a wet bed.

(John, town planner)

There is great practical potential in learning to recognise the onset of recurring physical symptoms through their preceding recurring dreams. Further examples are given throughout the book.

Potential and Progress

Not all recurring dreams are bad, let alone nightmares. The survey dreamers were asked what feelings their recurring dreams gave them. These ranged from fear, worry, confusion, loss, panic, frustration, claustrophobia, dissatisfaction and anguish to tranquillity, great love, happiness, pleasure, mystery, magic, relief, serenity, warmth, achievement, exploration and resolution.

My Amazing House
I am showing people my dream house which I have worked hard to decorate. As I lead the people through the doors, corridors and

archways, I am amazed at how beautiful and perfect it is. Usually the colours are brilliant and it is like a rainbow, one room or one colour graduating into another. I am amazed I could create something so perfect.

(Hannah, home duties)

A dream house is often symbolic of the mind. In Hannah's own words, she has worked hard to create her present mental attitude and to develop her creative skills.

Meaning: Such a dream can be an inspiration to you, like a progress report sent at a time of achievement to underline the sense of satisfaction and wonder that your progress has instilled. It urges you forward, for, as the dream shows, you are capable of creating perfection.

Breaking Through the Recurring Dream!

As a university student I had endless dreams of going to the station and buying a ticket, only to see the train departing without me. (I didn't travel by train in those days.) On the night before I sat my Finals, I dreamed I caught the train. I sat back on the luxuriously padded carriage seat, looked at the man sitting opposite me, and laughed myself awake!

This marked both the end of that recurring dream and the end of my 'training', as I perceived it at the time, combined with the freedom to begin a new journey meeting the outer world (man) face to face.

Meaning: Like Alison's snake-bite dream earlier in this chapter, this is a progress dream, of the type which commonly signals transcendence of a problem.

Practicalities

The most obvious way to get rid of undesirable recurring dreams or nightmares is to understand their meaning through interpretation, which is the focus of Part Two, although if you share one of the common dreams described here, you may be well on the way to seeing yourself and your attitudes in a different light. Realise that these were given as general guidelines only, and that each dreamer's situation is individual. Remember also that interpretation alone is not enough, and that you need to act on your new understanding to make the changes in your life which bring personal growth and relief from the old recurring dreams.

Keep a record of the dates of your recurring dreams, and write down any events, arguments, feelings or issues that came up in the day or so before the dream. Then note the same for the day or two after the dream. Once you have recorded this information over several repeats of your dream, you will begin to see a pattern in your waking life which is associated with the dreams. It may be that the preceding days show tension or the recurrence of an issue which the dream then addresses. It is then easier to relate the interpretation of the dream to the problem itself.

It is possible to program yourself so that next time you have that recurring dream you will turn around and face your enemy, grab that snake, take that other road, or whatever dream action you feel might conquer a fear, or explore a new facet of your inner self. Simply spend time during the day visualising the normal course of your dream and then seeing yourself take this new action. Soon this habitual vision will happen in the actual dream too, often putting an end to the recurring series. This visualisation process will also change your waking life attitudes in a beneficial way.

Children's Nightmares

It is better to let children sleep through a bad dream so that they can get closer to the end of the 'story', to experience what the dream is telling them. They will always awaken if it gets too much to bear. Take steps not to dismiss the dream. Hold the child close to give comfort and security, and encourage her to tell you as much about the dream as she can. Alternatively ask her to draw, paint or model something from the dream. A tiny child may pick a colour that seems to be 'like the dream', or may even dress up or act out a character from her nightmare. Children are more tuned to an innate understanding of their dreams which becomes clearer to them as they relive their dreams through these methods. In a safe, loving environment she can come to terms with the emotions and feelings brought up by her dream, and act to 'kill the demon' by acknowledging it. She can play act beyond the story-line of the dream and slay her dragon, throw magic potion on the witch or whatever it takes to regain control.

Adults can do the same! What we can role-play and experience in drama, visualisation, paint or clay, we can take forward and apply in 'real' life.

CHAPTER 11

Personal Symbols

Mention 'pear tree' to me and my mind immediately flits back to my final year at university when I lived in the basement of a beautiful, stately, Victorian stone house in Scotland. Peering through the barred cellar windows, amidst the smell of damp and mildew, I watched the pear tree and the collared doves which sang there. My professor, who owned the house, told me the pear tree featured in a well-known, but not well-written, Victorian novel. Strangely, it was while browsing through a second-hand bookshop in Bangalow, New South Wales, that I saw that book for the first time, one of a limited edition published in Glasgow. I bought it, but I must have lost it since. Which reminds me of that old edition of *Treasure Island* I had as a child. Now, what happened to that? And the four-leaf clovers (yes, genuine!) that I found by the school library and pressed between its pages. Just like the rose petals from Granny's garden ... oh, I've just remembered her dog, running between the roses, almost bigger than me as a child of four. 'Gipsy', that's right. We used to have gipsies (tinkers) knocking at our door in those days, and tramps who chalked crosses on the walls of the houses which gave food ...

What's all this got to do with dreams? Just about everything!

We've all played word association games at some stage. The popular idea of a psychiatrist used to be someone who sat beside your reclined body, bouncing words to and fro, hurriedly scribbling down your responses for deeper analysis. I might have wandered along my own track, starting with 'pear' and ending with 'gipsy'. I wonder how many other people would link pears to gipsies?

We tend to do this in dreams too. A dream interpreter might look at my dream of, for example, my grandmother looking for four-leaf clovers on Treasure Island, and not know where to begin. It would be very helpful if I explained how these very personal symbols were related to each other inside my head. Stretching back over all those years though, it's just as likely that I might have completely forgotten all of that, and the symbols might have popped up out of my misty subconscious, shaking their heads and rubbing their eyes after their long hibernation.

'Ah,' you might think, 'that just goes to show that dreams can be mish-mashed jumbles of old memories randomly surfacing and mixed into a dream cocktail!'

My experience as a dream researcher and dream therapist has convinced me that this is rarely, if ever, the case. If I had dreamed of my grandmother on Treasure Island, I may have been able to put these symbols together and relate them to the days previous to my dream. Perhaps I had been contemplating how unfortunate it is that my children's grandparents live on the other side of the world, and this had triggered *treasured* memories of my *grandmother*. Perhaps I needed to be reminded of how *lucky* I am to have known her. Or maybe there are *personal treasures* or *hereditary talents* that have become *buried in the past* that I need to uncover, and which will bring me the luck I need. Who can tell? In fact this particular 'dream' was totally fabricated to entertain you and illustrate a point, although the pear tree and gipsy story was real!

The point is, associations stemming from the dreamer's life, history, thoughts and philosophies will appear in dreams, and these personal symbols will always be more important than universal or shared symbols.

Difficulties in interpretation arise when the dreamer is not consciously aware of his subconscious associations or 'lost' memories. The fact that the dream has recently surfaced does imply that these forgotten details are no longer beyond retrieval. It may be simply a matter of the dreamer re-entering a 'subconscious' frame of mind to get back in touch with the meanings behind his personal symbols.

Apart from clinical hypnosis or regression, there are several tried and trusted practical techniques to achieve this.

Word Association Game

Just sit back, relax and play the old game. You know how it goes. Or write it all down. Start with one word from your dream and let word associations pour out. The secret to success is to do this quickly. Try not to think or to produce a calculated response. Let your associations flow because that's how you do it in your dreams. Once you have produced a long list, look back and highlight the words which seem to jump off the page at you. Many of these will have some bearing on your dream. Sit back and treat these words like pieces of a jigsaw puzzle. You don't have all the pieces, but try to fit together the ones you do have and see what you get.

Time and Place Association

Take the personal symbols from your dream and try to get a time or place frame. If you keep dreaming of hearing collared doves sing, try to recall when you first heard this song or where you were. Rebuild a picture of what was happening in your life at that time, or what your associations with that place were. Try to fit some of the other dream symbols into the picture. Ask yourself what is happening in your life now that might be causing you to refer back to those times. What was happening for you then?

Seeker spent some time contemplating the 'gramophone needle' symbol which appeared in a worrying dream. In this dream he had found himself in a clinic where:

Inside it was pretty dark and I told the men to leave me alone, but they wouldn't. The older one held me down while the fat one stuck 'acupuncture' needles in me: mainly in my face and top lip. The needles hurt and it turned out they weren't acupuncture needles at all, but old-fashioned gramophone needles made from steel. They shoved a lot in my lip.

(Seeker, astrologer)

He associated the gramophone to a time, place and event as he relates:

Old gramophones to me represent cheating. I used to have an old gram my dad gave me for a birthday present when I was little. Years later he sold it to an Aboriginal stockman on the place and trousered the money. I felt very cheated.

(Seeker, astrologer)

This dream occurred when Seeker was concerned about a friend who, he feared, was being influenced by a man who was leading her in a dangerous direction, 'cheating' her.

The pins in my lip, I felt, were designed to shut me up, to stop me speaking my truth to her about this man.

(Seeker, astrologer)

Seeker felt he couldn't say anything to stop this 'cheating' process.

Painting, Drawing, Sand Play, Art

Select your best loved art medium and play. Start with a symbol or two from your dream and watch what you create. A feeling, an emotion, a memory, thought or an idea is likely to hit you as you relax and create.

Meditation

Meditate on a symbol from your dream. Focus on the symbol for a while before you let it change and show you what you need to know.

Talking to Your Symbols

Get yourself out of earshot and relaxed and have a conversation with one of your dream symbols. At first you will feel absolutely crazy and may also think 'This is silly, I'm just making all this up', but bear with it because this is often the most successful way of finding out why a certain symbol is in your dream.

One way is to ask your questions out loud and 'imagine' you hear the answers. For example:

You: Four-leaf clover, why are you in my dream?

Clover: I'm a symbol of luck, you know that!

You: There's more to it than that, I know. I had one once.

Clover: I remember when you picked me, it was a sunny day.

You: So why have you come into my dream?

Clover: Don't you remember that boy (what's his name?), he pushed you over and tried to steal me?

You: Vaguely. What happened next? Did I keep you?

Clover: I wish you did. He gave you a black eye and soon forgot about me. Why didn't you stand up for yourself?

You: Is that why you're in my dream, to tell me I should stand up for myself?

Clover: That's it. I brought you a piece of good luck in the end, didn't I? Even if it took me 20 years and I had to do it in a dream!

Or, you may decide to take the part of the symbol and tell your own story. For example:

Clover: I always wanted to bring someone good luck, but I felt like a needle in a haystack until the day this beautiful little girl came and plucked me up. She smiled at me, but her sunshine was overshadowed by the bully ... (etc.)

I urge you to try this out, because it really works well. A less bizarre alternative is to type the 'conversation' straight onto paper, as I have just done in my imaginary scene! At least you feel a little more academic about the exercise! Again, the important thing is to do it fast, maintaining a flow, letting the heart speak, not the head.

Looking at Previous Dreams

Your dreaming self may make associations to previous dreams, as in this quaint example:

> *The other night I dreamed of a bread man, like you sometimes see specially baked in a hot bread shop. The figure was already sliced ready for eating. Was this a continuation of my other dreams about fields of wheat, now ripened, baked and ready for eating?*
>
> *(John, town planner)*

Keeping a Personal Symbol Dictionary

Buy a notebook or alphabet-indexed journal to use as a personal symbol dictionary. Note the major recurring personal symbols that appear in your dreams, whether or not you understand them. You might, for example, frequently dream of using an old-fashioned silver hairbrush, or of eating jelly beans. Enter 'hairbrush' under 'h', and 'jellybean' under 'j', and write the dates of your dreams by their entries.

After a few months, look back through your dictionary and see how many times you dreamed of a 'hairbrush' and when. Look over your waking life diary and try to see a connection between your life or your thoughts in the day or two preceding your 'hairbrush' dream. Over a period of time, some of your personal symbols will start to mean something to you. In some cases, you may never work out *why* you have a connection about a silver hairbrush, because the original association may be too far forgotten, but the symbol still emerges. For example:

> *Eating raw meat, for me, foretells deceit and trickery from others, whereas eating cooked meat foretells good times and happy company.*
>
> *(John, town planner)*

> *Occasionally I dream of a small room which is bright and clean. A single bed stands to one side of the room and above it is a closed*

window. The room itself is very peaceful. I have a strong feeling that someone has passed away, and some days later will hear about a relative or someone I know that has taken ill, or passed away.

(Lainey, home duties)

If I dream about being near a fire, the next day, I usually have a fight or an argument, generally with my husband.

(Stella, home duties)

In this last case, fire can be a shared symbol of anger and burning feelings as well as enthusiasm or fiery energy. Stella's dreams may reflect mounting anger which she expresses shortly afterwards. Whether the symbol is more personal or universal is not as important here as the fact that she has worked out what she regards as a personal symbol, by herself, through personal observation.

Dreaming in personal symbols can be very effective and concise as recently experienced by Eloise:

My precognitive dreams have become more refined since joining the survey. They are now effectively reduced to several symbols or images which I can interpret easily. A recent example of this is my Eryl Mai dream.

Eryl Mai Jones was a nine year old girl who died in the Aberfan disaster in 1966. She had what must have been one of the most tragic precognitive dreams ever recorded. On the morning of her death she told her mother that she dreamed a black cloud covered her school, and she wasn't afraid to die as she would be with her friends.

I read this story about five years ago, and thought nothing more of it, until a dream I had a few months ago. I dreamed of Eryl Mai's face appearing twice, quite clearly, then fading away. When I woke up I immediately made the connection between Eryl Mai and her death: 'avalanche'. There were two avalanches that next day, one in Turkey and one in Norway, and both were newsworthy.

Personal Symbols ☆

I felt that this dream was clear and to the point, and effectively got the message across, whereas another person would have made no sense of Aberfan at all.

(Eloise, unemployed receptionist)

Like Eloise, you may find that getting to understand your personal symbols may provide you with some great dream interpretation short-cut tools. Please remember, as with universal symbols or any other method of dream interpretation, that the best results are achieved through combining several different techniques. As you continue to discover the Magician's secrets you will see that understanding how to interpret a dream by looking at the emotions, or by considering how you act in a dream, for example, will supply many of your missing jigsaw puzzle pieces and help to build the overall picture of the meaning behind your dreams.

CHAPTER 12

Feelings and Emotions

I act out a lot of verbal and physical confrontations in my dreams, stuff I shy away from in my conscious life. I guess this type of thing is the brain doing a little midnight therapy.

(Mell, writer)

In dream life we are free to express ourselves and explore our emotions and feelings without fear of judgement from others or concern for the waking life consequences. Our subconscious has full rein to vent and express itself, and its currency is the language of emotion and feeling. Have you ever tried to calculate numbers or think through a rational process in a dream? It rarely works, unless you are a lucid dreamer. I have woken many times remembering dates, times, phone numbers or equations I thought I had forgotten, but these were found buried in my subconscious, as if I had rifled through a filing system. Their recall was not the result of calculation or any rational thinking process.

No, our dreams are not the stuff of rational calculated thought, but the unfettered, unrepressed expression of our emotional selves. We may come to conclusions in dreams, but these are based on feelings. I believe feelings and emotions form the core of our nature, and that facing our feelings and then making (perhaps rational) decisions based on our understanding of those emotions is the best way to live.

Emotional Hangovers

The dreams I write down are not always understood by me, but for some reason they affect me.

(Brigid, personal assistant)

Our emotions, especially when expressed freely in dreams, speak to us powerfully, even though we may not be able to explain their impact in rational language.

I am curious about the feeling, after certain dreams, where the dream is okay, but I wake up with a feeling of sadness or depression.

(Stuart, postal worker)

Dreams can uncover feelings we do not acknowledge in waking life. Without interpretation of the dream, it may be difficult to see a connection between the story-line of the dream and the emotions it evokes. People who say they never dream, or find it difficult to recall dreams, often have emotional blocks they do not wish to bring to waking life. It is safer to forget the dream. Writing down the feeling you wake up with each morning is a way of getting back in touch with your dreams since that feeling is residual from the night's dreams. That old 'I got out of bed on the wrong side this morning' feeling suggests a night spent reviewing issues which were neither resolved by the dream nor brought into waking consciousness. The irritable feeling signals 'unfinished business'.

One excellent dream interpretation tool is to look at the feelings expressed in dreams. If you write down your dreams in a journal, take time to express how different parts of the dream made you feel. Then go back with a highlighter pen and mark all the feeling words. The meaning of the dream is likely to be much clearer. If you don't recall how you felt in the dream, close your eyes and watch the dream again in your mind's eye. Note how you react, and record those feelings instead.

Bryan asked me to ride on an apple-green ferris wheel, saying, 'Trust me, it is safe,' convincingly. The plastic wheel arms attached to my chair broke, and I was left hanging on to the outside wheel. Later I got off and walked away. 'Now I am safe,' I thought.

(Rosemary, secretary)

Much later, Rosemary left Bryan, and that was when she recalled the dream. The dream underlined her lack of trust in Bryan, and the knowledge that she would feel much safer without him. In retrospect she saw the accuracy of her dream.

I was with some girls and I had won a jumping race, although I'm always last in life. We walked home under an underpass that was light (it had always been dark as a child). At home, I opened a door without a key. I didn't feel safe.

(Serena, administration officer)

Why didn't Serena feel safe? Her dream had shown her to be successful twice. Firstly she won a race, and secondly she found it easy to open the door. In her waking life she is always last in races, and the dream also implies that she expects doors (opportunities) to be locked. It is interesting to note that the tunnel was light, as if light were being thrown onto her situation by the dream. Serena didn't feel safe with success. Recognising this attitude could be a turning point for her.

That Sinking Feeling

Look at the number of feelings expressed in Erika's dream, and try to get a 'feeling' of its meaning as you read:

Dream Title: 'Here Comes That Sinking Feeling'. I was a passenger on board a cruise ship that had anchored itself offshore of some beautiful, tropical Mediterranean islands. There were many people swimming from the ladders off the ship and the waters were warm. Everyone was wearing old-fashioned swimming togs from the fifties or sixties. I swam round and round and began to look below the surface, then swam under the water. There were people under the water trying to save others by making them swim up. One woman just didn't want to go and offered no assistance to the man who was trying to help her. I realised that I had been swimming around down there for some time. I tried to swim up but it was no use. The harder I swam, the further I was going down. Some strange music filled my mind and the voice of Annie Lennox and the Eurythmics sang in with 'Here Comes That Sinking Feeling', strange and melodious. I was being calmed. I had no control over where I was going, but I knew it was okay. Deeper and deeper I went, almost feeling enlightened. I woke up with that music playing in my head and it has often returned.

(Erika, administration officer)

The overall feeling from the dream is that Erika's road to enlightenment is to be found by letting go, sinking deeper, rather than by fighting her feelings.

The rest of the dream can be interpreted symbolically to underscore this conclusion. She is at a point in her life where she feels safe (anchored and warm) enough to delve into her emotions or subconscious (sea). She is either relating to years past, represented by the old-fashioned togs, or looking at 'old-fashioned' feelings. She is prepared to look below the surface and dives deep. She sees two options: to bring 'things' to the surface and 'save' herself, or to let go and sink deeper. At first she tries to come to the surface for survival but finds that trying hard and fighting the feeling are not enough. She is later calmed to see that going deeper into her sinking feeling is the way towards enlightenment.

Erika reported that the song has often returned. She would be wise to note her emotional circumstances at these times, and heed her inner advice to 'let go for enlightenment'. Any day-time memory, or return of part of a dream, tells you that *this* is the type of situation the dream was advising you on.

That Flying Feeling

One of the most powerful, emotionally charged dream sensations is flying: without the plane, of course! The following examples reveal the 'meanings' behind flying dreams for different people, showing how important it is to focus on the feeling to fully understand the dream. The sensation of flying in a 'dream' can also accompany an out-of-the-body or astral travel experience, but this is described in a future chapter. On now with the symbolic:

> *I fly around and sometimes I don't know where I am. I breaststroke as I fly, but if I stop, I start to go down. This dream gives me a sense of* freedom, *a sense of* power *and more* psychic, intuitive *abilities.*
>
> *(Isabelle, legal secretary)*

> *I'm flying and I am the only one who can. People ask me how I do it. I always tell them it's easy and that they can do it if they choose to. It's simply a* state of mind. *One* meditates and simply lets go. *However, I'm the only one who does fly.*
>
> *(Alex, clerk)*

Alex feels he has simple answers that others do not trust. The dreams see him enjoying this knowledge and also urge him to fulfil his highest potential by following his own advice.

> *I am a flier. Flying has always occurred in situations of* escape. *However the* terror *of the situation never completely overrode the* exhilaration *of the flying experience, consequently there was a degree of* pleasure in the fear *which gave me* balance.
>
> *(Dorothy, retired teacher)*

Dorothy's flying dreams perhaps reflected her love of living on adrenalin, of thriving on danger, which gave her a sense of balance in her life. Dorothy's love of dream flying prompted her to carry out her own research:

In the last couple of years I have been inquiring of family and friends if they are fliers, and my research has shown:

1~ *Only the women are fliers, and we are all reasonably alike physically and mentally.*

2~ *Each flier has flown since their earliest childhood memories and have all flown less as they have grown older.*

3~ *My family fliers all fly in situations of escape.*

4~ *My friend flies for pleasure.*

5~ *My mother, nieces and I all land because our feet get caught up, in my case always on tree tops, my mother and one niece on fence tops.*

6~ *I take off by running and springing up. This would not have been influenced by things like Superman as I was a bush kid and did much flying before seeing such movies. I remember my initial reaction to Superman being 'He does it like me, sort of!'*

(Dorothy, retired teacher)

Although my survey and counselling experience suggest that just as many men, if not more men, as women fly, Dorothy's observations probably show an emotional family trait, particularly because she noted their similar mental characteristics.

Flying less as you grow older is generally acknowledged among fliers, although an increase in flying, or a whole new aeronautic interest, is often sparked in older age.

A few years ago I had another spell of flying. This time I was not being chased, but exploring the road ahead. I usually started at a real life road or place, and then would discover new paths and ways. A most beautiful experience and peaceful waking up.

(Amleh, receptionist)

Amleh's flying has become a way of seeing ahead and looking at possible new directions in her life. A bird's-eye view gives a sense of peace. Her waking feeling of peacefulness underlines the message of the dream, which is to explore new avenues and ways of being.

Acting on a Feeling

The waking feeling is often sufficient to inspire action with no need for further interpretation, as shown by Jaquelyn's dream. Note the feelings described in her report.

I was on a busy highway, although no other cars were in sight. I was searching for a car but needed to get off the highway. I knew of an entry on my left but I couldn't make an exit turn there. The road surface became very bumpy and soft. Then I was in a car park with my husband but we were sitting against a wall between the cars. He said he was going away for a week. I said I wanted to come too, but he didn't want that. I tried to argue with him, but he will never argue. He remained adamant. I became upset. I heard my mother two cars away and hoped she wouldn't see us, but she did. I then left the car park and headed back with a small child. We crossed an unfamiliar road which seemed difficult to cross due to traffic and people. Once in a small room, which presumably was home, the child hid and I tried to tempt him out with marbles. I felt lonely as if no-one wanted me, and I resolved to book my own holiday.

After this dream I did arrange to have a week's break with my sister. My husband and I are on good terms and he is always happy for me to go everywhere with him, but I was beginning at that time to feel the need for a break away from the regular routine. Of course I did feel revitalised on my return from the holiday and changed some aspects of my life which had become a bore.

(Jaquelyn, librarian)

Jaquelyn's dream is full of symbolism too, with details of her need to get off the busy highway of life and change direction, the difficulties she foresees in doing this, crossing unfamiliar

Feelings and Emotions ☆

territory, tempting her inner child to come out into the open and play and so on. All of this gives detail, but Jaquelyn innately understood the meaning of her dream and took the appropriate action, not only by taking a holiday, but also by instigating changes on her return.

A simple feeling, gleaned from a dream, can give a whole new direction to life, as shown by Erika:

> *I was driving in a snow-filled car park in America where the snow was about a metre deep. There were paths everywhere and a lot of* plastic people *(yuppies who look the same, confused, scurrying about), but there was also a tall Negro man wearing a long coat. He was very distinguished and I knew he was a judge, kind and just. He stood still and used his open hand to wave me in the right direction. It was a great feeling to be helped like that.*
>
> *(Erika, administration officer)*

Erika needed to accept more help from 'real', non-plastic people in her life, as indicated by the positive feeling she had in her dream when she accepted the Negro man's direction. She would have been wise to check that she herself was also coming from a 'real' perspective, being true to her native (Negro) instincts, responding to and supporting what was kind and just, and not being plastic to suit others' expectations. Stillness, openness and distinguished (wise?) poise were all that was required. The snows (frozen emotions) of a more 'yuppie' approach were, no doubt, melted by the more genuine, warmer (tropical Africa?) approach.

Contacting the Dream Feeling

Another way to get in contact with your feelings in dreams is to paint, draw or use some form of creative art to express your dream.

> *I'm an artist and I draw a lot of my dreams immediately I wake up. I'll find I'll be drawing and then I'll say, 'Oh, what's that?'*

As I look at my drawing all these emotions will come up. The actual process of drawing seems to bring out more for me than writing the dream down.

(Robyn, sculptor)

Try poetry, story writing, acting, miming, dancing, playing music, or any creative medium which may work for you, which may draw out your feeling connection with your dream and lay it bare for you to experience and acknowledge. When dealing with children, always ask them 'How did the dream make you feel?', or get them to paint, draw or simply choose a colour to represent the dream.

Whichever method of dream interpretation you choose, none is complete without checking the emotional content. Feelings and emotions are our cornerstone and without their expression, our dreams, like our waking lives, would be meaningless. Use the emotions in your dreams not only as an interpretation key, but also to colour your waking life perspective and to help you to become a full expression of your true self.

CHAPTER 13

Magical Clichés, Puns and Words

I'm with my ex-husband and the water is lapping around my home and feet. There is a flood. I call my parents and family and they experience this too. The world is in a flood situation; the 'end of the world'.

(Frances, actor)

Was this a precognitive dream about the end of the world, or did Frances feel that this was the end of her (personal) world? At the time of her dream, she was still flooded with emotional issues (water) which were affecting both her position (feet) in life, and her mental attitudes (house). Her family and friends shared her feelings. The use of this old cliché 'the end of the world' summarised exactly how Frances felt.

I'm in a pitch black room unable to find my way out. I wake up screaming or trying to find my way through a wall. I feel like I'm still dreaming until the light is put on. I don't have these dreams often now, but a few years ago I had them nearly every night for months. This was during a marriage break-up.

(Annie, home duties)

In cliché-land we 'try to find my way through a brick wall', 'bang my head against a brick wall', 'climb the walls', get 'driven up the wall' and so on. I suppose clichés exist because, as a human race, we all tend to experience similar situations at some stage in our lives. It becomes easier to describe your state as 'being driven up the wall' than to go into a long explanation of the frustration of an unyielding daily life. Those few words deliver the feeling as it is.

Acting Out a Cliché

Many people have found themselves, in dreams, in the passenger seat of a car, being 'driven up a wall' by someone, or perhaps being 'driven round the bend'.

Have a closer look at the actions in your dreams. Have you ever found yourself in dreamland 'bending over backwards' to fit in with someone, or 'letting your hair down', or 'going round in circles', 'keeping your head above water', 'walking on ice' or even 'slipping up'? What would these literal clichéd dramas in your dreams say about your waking life?

You may act out a host of clichés in your dreams, making their meaning quite clear as Paula discovered:

Mainly in my dreams I am unable to find my way out of strange buildings. Corridors and stairways always bring me back to the same starting place, but in a recent dream every corner I turned led to a dead end and every door I opened had a brick wall behind it. I am confused and frustrated.

On another occasion I dreamed I lost half of the index and second finger of my left hand with no idea how it happened. I just looked at my hand and saw two clean, neatly healed stumps. I remarked to someone that I could feel the tips of my fingers even though they were no longer there. (Dead ends?)

These dreams started after Paula's retirement three years ago.

Never in my life have I experienced any doubts about where I was going, how I was to get there or what to do when I arrived. I always knew and just simply got on with it. Now it seems all I find are closed doors, corridors leading me round in circles and brick walls.

(Paula, retired graphic artist)

Alternatively, you may find that when you describe your dream to someone else, or, better still, when you write it down, you choose clichés to describe the action or feelings, or you choose words that speak loud and clear.

Millions of things like ants were marching towards me, coming right up to my face, right in front of my nose, almost pushing me into the pillow. It's like they create a barrier right in front of my face, closing me in. I can't get past this barrier.

(Claire, child care provider)

Whatever was clearly annoying (insects) Claire at this time, and forming a barrier to hinder her progress, was, in her own words, 'right under her nose'. She needed to look close to home to identify the source of her frustration.

Revealing Words and Puns

Our choice of words when talking about our dreams in general, or when summing up their basic content can be revealing too.

I have often commented to my wife that if I could remember my dreams they would make great movies. They usually started at a reasonable pace with reasonable actions, but as the dream progressed I would get more and more into situations that I could not get out of.

(David, surveyor)

David's business life and the decisions he made in waking life always seemed reasonable at the time, but as he took on more and more responsibilities, he got himself into situations that he

138

couldn't get out of. When David joined the survey, he felt he was on a treadmill with no way out.

To get the most out of this angle on dream interpretation, write your dreams down then take a highlighter pen and mark any clichés, puns or turns of phrase that seem suggestive. Then stand back and string them all together. If you do not have time to write, try telling your dream to someone, or recording it, and listen to the words you use.

The dream we receive, from whatever source, is translated into 'hard copy' by our brain, so that we have some kind of record in everyday language or picture form that we can refer back to. If you are a word-orientated person, you may find a predilection for using telling words or acting out clichés in your dreams. I love puns, and tend to notice these in my dreams.

My husband is with his nephew, Jay, *who throws something onto the railway line, then jumps down to pick it up. We both gasp at the* danger *involved, because the train* tracks *carry live electricity in this dream. Jay gets back onto the platform safely.*

(Jane Anderson)

At this time my husband was taking risks with his career (*'training'*) and experimenting with new ideas. He would wander down this or that *track* to see what it had to offer. This was *risky* to our financial situation, but necessary to find alternatives. The dream showed this *'Jay walking'*, while apparently dangerous, would probably give us a few scares but would ultimately result in our safety.

Look for the *spoken* words in a dream. Often simply highlighting the conversation in a dream brings instant understanding, as in Brigid's account:

I was in the waiting room of a hospital with Craig, my four year old son. There were other people with children there and someone was organising individual baby-sitters for them, so that they could go and be with their relatives. I went through to the labour ward

Magical Clichés ☆

where Carl, my husband, was in labour. My thoughts were 'I must be with him as he was with me.' He was on a bed and a middle-aged lady was helping him deliver. The baby's head was visible, very blonde, and although Carl was in labour, he didn't seem in that much pain, although he was perspiring. I remembered wondering about a womb and birth canal and his tummy was very flat. I was wondering if it was a boy or a girl and then I thought, 'He will get what he wants.' It was a girl.

(Brigid, personal assistant)

Brigid's husband was working (labour) at something new in his life and needed her help and support. She reflected on the fact that he has stood by her in the past, but also notes her feeling that he always gets what he wants (perhaps implying that she feels that she doesn't). What this dream does is to set out the situation as it is, so that Brigid can make a decision based on a better understanding of all the factors involved.

Time for a pun:

I saw Dad suspended over a spit roast thing but there was no fire. I realised that he was dead. I told Mum she had killed Dad with all the stress she puts on him.

(Isabelle, legal secretary)

Dad got a real 'roasting' from all Mum's 'spit' (spite?) and the stress she ladled onto him. Isabelle sensed this had killed something in her father.

And another:

My husband, Glenn, put in a quote to design an unusual Christmas display for a centre which included the word 'mirage' in its name. A few weeks later, I had a dream which included:

Kirstie is pregnant and is worried about the labour. I put my arm around her to comfort her. Just as we are on the threshold of a coffee shop where Glenn is giving a quote for a Christmas display I look up into the sky and see a very realistic Santa's sleigh disappearing into the distance. The reindeer look like dappled pink horses and I can see the detail on their thigh muscles as they weave through the sky. It's stunning to watch, but I turn to Kirstie and say, 'It's a pity it's an illusion', at which point it disappeared in a puff of mist.

(Jane Anderson)

Kirstie sounds like 'Christmas', which was obviously the theme of the dream, and the pregnancy and worry about the *labour* reflected Glenn's concerns over who would win the *job*. *Illusion* for me was a dream pun on *mirage*, and because it was a *pity*, and it *disappeared*, I knew the contract would go to someone else. It did.

Try this one. Look at Joe's dream and, remembering that a car tends to symbolise motivation or direction in life, focus on his use of words to deduce the meaning of his dream:

I am being driven in my four-wheel drive. I am in the back of the car. Later we stop and all get out and I go looking for the driver. I see the interior of the car glowing as if it is on fire. Someone has lit a kerosene pressure lamp on the back seat and the heat from this is causing the leather upholstery to blister and sag. I shout for help but everyone is too busy. I am angry, thinking that this is going to be a big repair job, then ask myself, 'When did my car have leather upholstery? It has cloth upholstery.' I wake up, still very angry.

(Joe, catering attendant)

Joe was not in control of his direction in life, and not able to follow his own basic drives and motivations since he perceived someone else as being in control, in the driver's seat. As a result, he was feeling under pressure (in the back seat) and the heat of his anger and frustration was burning him (car) up. In the dream he is beginning to acknowledge the source of his frustration and even begins to look for the driver (to find the part of himself who needs to be in control). He also realises that rebuilding his motivation and taking back control of his drive and direction in life is going to be a long process: 'a big repair job'.

Magical Clichés ☆

I once had a long dream, full of key words for interpretation, during which:

> *Glenn (my husband) and I are in a plane and we see a huge tidal wave below. Although we are safe, I suddenly see and feel the panic through the eyes of Glenn's son, who is on the beach. I start to speak in his voice, crying for his mother and suffocating. Then Glenn and I are suddenly in a long, dark corridor, where Glenn is sitting cross-legged, halfway along the passage and I am standing. There is a knock at the door and I can see a peaked cap through the frosted glass panel. I think it is a policeman and I close the backroom door to keep our daughters safe. I open the front door to see a Salvation Army lady who points at Glenn. He goes outside.*

> *(Jane Anderson)*

I saw the symbolism in this dream as a birth, and it was only on closer reflection that I realised how accurate this dream account of Glenn's actual birth had been. The key word here was *Salvation*. Glenn was born by *caesarean section* ('saved') after a protracted attempt at a *breech birth*. The breech birth is symbolised by his cross-legged sitting position (not moving) in the birth *passage*. The tidal wave symbolised the overwhelming emotions he must have felt, and which I experienced in the dream through his son, who must have represented Glenn's inner child. The suffocating and the cries for his mother added to the stuck birth feeling. Closing the backroom door to protect the girls may have been symbolic of putting his mother under anaesthetic, because once this was done, the *Salvation Army lady led Glenn outside*. (He was *saved* and born.)

So, place another tool now in your magic box of dream interpretation methods, and journey on to discover further secrets of the astral plane, locked in the action of your dreams.

CHAPTER 14

All in the Action

How do you act in your dreams? Are you the hero of the story or do you run away and hide? Do you fly higher than any person has ever gone, or do you dig a hole in the sand and hibernate? Do you say what you really feel, express yourself, perhaps even violently, or do you bow to the wishes of others? Are you right there in the midst of all the action, or do you watch at a safer distance?

How you act and react in your dreams gives an insight into how you handle your waking life. One lady told me how she repeatedly dreamed of kicking her first husband, so much so that she often found herself physically kicking him as she awoke. She did not express her frustration directly to him during her waking hours, but her dreaming self was releasing her true emotions. In the end she had to acknowledge the way she felt and do something about it. Our dreams, then, may play our waking behaviour back to us, like a private movie for our consideration, or they may show us how we truly feel, giving us an insight into how much we mask our real emotions during waking life.

It is sometimes helpful to regard all the characters in your dreams as aspects of yourself, but let's just consider the one who looks like you: your 'dream ego'. Look back at your question-naire and check your responses to Section U. Are you generally active or passive in your dreams? What conclusions can you draw before reading any further?

Active or Passive?

Most of the survey dreamers take a fairly active role in their night-time encounters, although 67.5% have found themselves watching or observing the action at some point.

More than half (63.8%) commonly take decisive actions in their dreams, while 15.6% have found themselves regularly acting against their will.

I Take Part in the Action

Most people (91.9%) commonly take part in the action of their dreams.

I Take Control

Just under half (48.8%) have found themselves taking control of the action.

> *I caught someone working undercover and made him pull off his mask/face. He would have killed me otherwise. I feel this dream shows the self-destructive aspect of myself.*
>
> *(Serena, administration officer)*

Serena interpreted her unmasked undercover agent to be an aspect of herself she had not recognised until the dream.

By taking control in her dream and facing the unknown, she learned something about her tendency to sabotage herself in waking life.

Fiona's dream shows a change of attitude, a turning point where she takes control at the vital moment:

> *I was in the water at the mouth of a river, with some other people, clinging onto a huge brass buoy. As we grabbed at one side, we dragged it over, so that the rim we were holding onto was submerged. I lost my grip and a current swept me out to sea. In that moment of panic I decided I didn't have to drown and could try*

and save myself. *I started to swim with* strong, *swift strokes and almost immediately was back in the river. Incidentally, I'm a very poor swimmer!*

(Fiona, retired medical secretary)

Being in the water, Fiona's dream was looking at her emotional or subconscious self, and shows she felt as if she were losing control. In her own words, her dream report reveals she felt she had '*lost her grip*' on life and was being swept along by her emotions or perhaps by the emotional needs of others. Her dream showed Fiona that she had two choices: to continue to act passively (and drown, or 'go under') or to take control and save herself. The moment she decided on action she was back in the river (flow of life?). Fiona's very positive dream experience gave her a sense of elation at taking control and perhaps gave her courage to apply the same sense of control in her waking life.

Another person (let's call him Marc) in a different phase of life, may have found himself drifting *peacefully* out to sea, without Fiona's sense of panic. Marc's dream suggests he should relax and go with the flow of his emotions for a while, and that such passive action might bring a much needed sense of peace. It is important to realise that there are times for being active and times for being passive, and that 'active' is not always better than 'passive'!

Why have I interpreted Fiona's dream as showing a need to be more active and take control, whereas I have taken Marc's dream to indicate a need for passive relaxation? Their dreams were similar. It is important to look not only at how their dream egos *act,* but at how this action makes them *feel*. Fiona felt panic when she was being passive, but felt strong when she was active. Marc felt peaceful when he was passive.

When you look at how you act in dreams, take care to consider the attached feelings and use these to guide your interpretation.

All in the Action ☆

I Make Decisions

Results showed that 63.8% of the survey dreamers commonly make decisions in their dreams. How many of these dream decisions can be carried forward into waking life?

I was going to some sort of meeting place and met a girl heading for the same place. She walked in some kind of brace and said she was going to this place for a cure. We became very close over the next few days. I helped her out of her harness and fondled her breasts, giving us both much pleasure. We seemed inseparable and comfortable with each other.

Then some members of my family turned up and this seemed to split us. I felt lost, alone and unhappy without this girl who had become a 'part' of me. I saw her passing here and there and she was not happy either. She told me she was leaving to go back home, without her brace. I wanted to come too but she wouldn't let me and seemed angry at me.

I seemed to be busy but not getting anywhere. About every five minutes one of my family members would want something of me. It was all very messy and the house started falling apart: a board missing, something broken, steps gone, a fence or gate in need of repair. The girl said, 'I'm going away now. I'll always be there for you, but you must clean up your own mess before you can come.'

The old man and woman who seemed to own this 'health farm' were all in favour of us being together, and the old man said, 'You go. I'll fix all this. You must go.' I made up my mind I would go and be with her and then woke up.

(Seeker, astrologer)

Full of universal symbol language, this dream shows Seeker's need to *meet* and integrate with his inner female self to recover his health and wellbeing. He is looking for a *cure* when the girl, in his own words, becomes *'a part of me'*. This integration is underlined by the sexual fondling which brings pleasure, as well as by the other emotional expressions in this dream. Seeker's family split this relationship by imposing too many demands and this is indeed reflective of Seeker's life where his dedication to supporting his birth family has denied him of the time and space to find union with his inner self.

The dream goes further to illustrate the devastating mental and physical effects which Seeker has suffered because of this imbalance in his life. The dream house (mental and physical self) fell apart as soon as the family made its constant demands on him. Seeker wishes to go with the girl, but she stops him. She tells him what he needs to do to find her again: he has to clear up the mess he has got himself into before he can truly be whole.

The old man is symbolic of Seeker's wiser self (his Higher Self, his inner words of wisdom). This man takes an opposing view from the girl. He urges Seeker to drop everything and *go now*. He implies that the mess will sort itself out simply because he makes the decision to *act* now. Seeker agrees with the wise old man in his dream, and *makes the decision to take action* and go with her.

On waking, Seeker had experienced the positivity of his dream decisiveness and was left to contemplate translating his dream decision into waking life.

Eleanor has recurring dreams:

Sometimes I'm exploring the interior of an empty house to see if it suits me to live in it, and sometimes I'm exploring a street of house exteriors.

(Eleanor, homeopath)

Looking for an alternative state of mind (house), both on the inside and on the outside, Eleanor spends her dreams searching, in the process of decision making. A helpful exercise for Eleanor would be to relive her dreams in a relaxed state, while awake, and alter the course of events. She could experiment with deciding to buy this house, or that, allowing herself to daydream about taking decisions and about living here or there. She could feel her emotional responses to making this or that decision, and perhaps move closer to making a decision in her waking life.

All in the Action ☆

I Lead Others

Leadership qualities were commonly displayed by 40.6% of the survey dreamers.

> *I had a very technical dream in which I was explaining town planning and land-related matters to some people. When I had finished, I woke up, glad that it was over and that the inquirers had gone away satisfied. I went off to sleep again and had a lovely refreshing dream that made the rest of my day go off with a zing.*
>
> *(John, town planner)*

In competent leadership fashion, John took control of unfinished business in his first dream. The second dream reflected the peace of completion.

I Watch and Observe the Action

We may watch from a vantage point within the dream, be an onlooker to the main scene, watch from a cinema seat or through the lens of a camera, or we may feel disembodied, viewing the action from some overhead or distant point. Watching and observing the action commonly occurs for 67.5% of the survey dreamers.

Observing can be a very positive experience, as Amanda illustrates in this learning dream:

> *I dreamed that a man was showing me how thoughts create our reality. I watched while he held a thought in his cupped palms, and out of a misty sort of substance the thought became a solid object. Naturally I was completely mystified. I asked him if he were a magician, and he said, 'No, this is what really happens to your thoughts, but you don't have the power to see the process. You just see the consequences, but now you know because you have seen with your own two eyes.'*
>
> *(Amanda, astrologer)*

It may be wise to remove ourselves from the dream action periodically, taking the time to stand back and learn from others.

If a dream is concerned with something that may be painful for us to experience, or difficult for us to acknowledge, we may find ourselves viewing the dream from the distance or watching it as if it is a film or a play. An unusual camera angle may indeed give us a view of our life from a different 'angle'. These tricks give us a more objective viewpoint.

Note the point at which Davina removes herself to third person status in her recurring dream:

In this recurring dream, my mother and I drive along a road by the sea among dull brown colours. Our car breaks down and a man comes from the opposite direction, sees us broken down, and parks, like us, very close to the edge. He gets out of the car and by this time I am no longer there. Instead I am in the third person, like a camera. The man and my mother talk, he goes away and she falls off the cliff in her car.

(Davina, shop assistant)

I have noticed that people who dream of watching a murder often find themselves sitting next to a dream-friend (stranger in waking life) or talking to someone who feels very familiar to them shortly after the gruesome event has occurred. The dreamer will often listen to what this familiar soul has to say, and will frequently conclude that this friend is very wise. After the dream has been interpreted, the dreamer will often see the relevance of the drama they witnessed (perhaps, in this example, symbolising an ending to something in their life). Listening to the point of view of the 'third party', the dream-friend, helps the dreamer to see his situation from a different angle. It is but a short step from there to realise that this dream-friend may be an aspect of oneself, slightly removed for objectivity and comfort.

I Don't Take Part in the Dream

Not taking part in their dreams was a common experience for 13.1% of survey dreamers. This was, in hindsight, a badly worded question, so I don't know how many of these people meant they were observing, and how many meant they weren't *even* observing.

When the dreamer is not there at all, either as actor or observer, she may be practising the ultimate form of disassociation from the content of her dream. In these cases, the dream scenario may be so potent that the dreamer needs total objectivity to make any kind of assessment of her situation. Such a dream may also belong to a dreamer who is feeling distant and removed from her own life. She may perceive her waking ego as totally alien to her inner self, and not invite it into her dreams.

Many people experience dreams as someone else. I once dreamed I was a man:

> *I was part of a labouring team and I had missed the work truck because I was talking to another man in the locker room. He was hiding and I didn't want to be associated with him, so I left and walked fast to catch up with the truck. My punishment for being late was to be shot at close range by a catapult which would drive a silver screw into my forehead: my third eye. I was scared, but the man who was appointed to do this to me checked that the boss wasn't looking then rubbed the screw over my forehead to make it bleed and pushed my face into the ground to get gravel into the wound. This was supposed to be lenient, saving me from the catapult, but it still hurt! It was a 'cover up' job.*
>
> *(Jane Anderson)*

Dreaming that you are someone else and experiencing life through their eyes is stunning, and dreamers are often convinced that they have relived a past life or jumped into another body. I believe all these things are possible and also that they do happen. However, I also believe that we sometimes have dreams that are symbolic of our present life, in which we experience the dream through the eyes of other aspects of ourselves, not through our dream ego. In my dream I was that man just as much as I am Jane Anderson.

Perhaps such dreams are simply our way of being able to 'stand in someone else's shoes' and see things from the point of view of other personality types in our lives.

I Follow Others

Familiar to 18.1% of dreamers is the experience of being a follower rather than a leader.

There are times in our lives for leading, and times for following, although sometimes we may be in the habit of leading when we should follow, or vice versa. When you interpret a leading or following dream, look at the feelings leading or following gives you, and use these to guide your interpretation. (Refer to 'I Take Control' earlier in the chapter for illustration.)

I Act Against My Will

Some 15.6% of survey dreamers have succumbed to the power of another in a dream.

I used to dream I was blown off a cliff or was driven off by fire. I hit the bottom and died the last time five years ago.

(Annie, home duties)

There was a very steep mountain with cable cars and I recall standing at the bottom of the slope where the cable car terminated. I looked up and saw the cable car tracks, one up, one down, vividly, including all the contours. The cars operated on tracks rather than being suspended. Then I was in the car and I was absolutely terrified. I was belted in but there was no cage surround. Therefore, you sat with your back to the mountain and you looked straight into space and down into ...

(David, surveyor)

When I act against my will it is like being a puppet.

(May, day care provider)

Does May feel like a puppet sometimes in waking life? If so, who pulls her strings? Who controls her? If May examines her dreams she will be able to pinpoint the circumstances which cause her to passively respond in puppet fashion instead of cutting the cords and acting for herself.

What do the other examples (above) suggest to you about the dreamers? Could they make changes in their lives to regain control?

Scotty's recurring dreams revealed that he felt he was being driven around (controlled) by others, acting against his will:

Usually (in dreams) I drive. However, when someone else does, I start feeling upset and try to get out, or I'll say, 'I'll drive.' A month ago we nearly made a major investment in real estate as a partnership. It was rushed and we got to the point of signing bank and vendor contracts. I realised at the last minute it was too risky and sought legal advice, managing to get out of the deal at some expense. I was emotionally and physically sick with worry and my dreams reflected this. Going back over the last six months of my dreams I had over half-a-dozen dreams warning me of this situation.

(Scotty, petrol tanker driver)

Had Scotty been as adept at interpreting his dreams then as he is now, he would have been able to see his sliding loss of control and take action at an earlier stage, perhaps preventing the emotional and physical sickness that he endured as a result.

Heather had a number of dreams which prompted her to take more control of a certain situation in her waking life. She did this, and her new attitude was confirmed in a subsequent dream:

I was a member of a committee that had to make decisions re the five living presidents of the USA! I was controlling the meeting and as several of the people present were looking towards me, I said, 'Well, we are agreed that we will establish their privileges according to priority.' The environment was plush and the lights were bright in that bright room.

How's that for taking power? *I've been laughing all morning!*
(*Heather, retired psychiatric nurse*)

Apart from observing your actions in dreams, it can be helpful to rewrite a dream in the morning, changing all the actions. Take Serena's dream:

I was walking in the countryside with my daughter. We were dehydrated after three weeks with no water. A man gave my child a crystalline substance but I didn't ask for anything. We kept walking and I collapsed at a friend's house.
(*Serena, administration officer*)

How might you rewrite this to give Serena back a sense of control? Here's my effort:

'I was walking in the countryside with my daughter. We were dehydrated after three weeks with no water. A man gave my child a crystalline substance. I thanked him and explained that we both desperately needed water. I hadn't noticed his campsite behind the old ruins. In a moment he was pouring fresh water from his billy can and we drank to our hearts' content. Refreshed, I asked him to explain how the crystalline substance could help us further. We left his camp and reached my friend's house well before dark.'

Symbolically, Serena's dream reflected her huge thirst for emotional (water) nurturing and caring from others, or even from herself. It also showed how she neglected herself by not asking for what she needed.

Practical Summary

Write down your dream and use a highlighter pen to underline the action in the dream. If you were observing, do the same for

All in the Action ☆

the actions shown by the main characters, since this will bear some relevance to you.

Note how many actions were active and how many were passive. Look at the feelings or emotions that accompanied your actions. Decide which actions felt good and which felt inappropriate or unsatisfactory. What did each action lead to? Does your dream suggest 'If you do *this*, then *that* will happen'?

Rewrite your dream (maybe several different ways) and change some of the actions. Make up what happens after each changed action. Play around with possible outcomes from different actions. See how these alternative ways of approaching life, of acting, not acting or reacting might be worth trying in your waking life.

What was happening in your waking life in the day or so leading up to your dream? Why might this have triggered your dream? Does the dream suggest a better way of dealing with your waking life?

Ah yes, it's all in the action!

CHAPTER 15

Who Are All Those People?

There they are, nightly, throughout almost all your dreams: people. People from your distant past, people from your daily life, the lady who cuts sandwiches at the deli and the man who smiled at you on the bus. An old boyfriend kisses you, a deceased friend has a lengthy philosophical discussion and the man who used to read the six o'clock television news ten years ago offers you a cuppa and a chat. Then there are all those strangers, some of whom feel so familiar, the tiny baby you nestled in the crook of your arm all night, the angel who parted the seas for you and the destitute old man who asked you for a dollar.

We often cry with laughter in the morning as we recall how our staid and sensible neighbour climbed out onto her roof and sang with the alley cats in our dreams, or about how normal it seemed in dreamland to see the boss conducting a business meeting wearing his pyjamas and cuddling a pink teddy bear.

Why, out of all the people you have come into contact with throughout your life, out of all the people you have noticed from the corner of your eye, did you dream about those particular people last night? Why did you need to bring in a whole bunch of strangers? Were they just 'extras' needed for your dream drama, or did they have a specific purpose which could help you to unravel the meaning behind your dream?

Who do people dream of most?

Check your questionnaire answers for Section S.

Asked who they dream about most of all, the survey dreamers picked:

First:
Themselves 79.4%

Second:
Close relatives 30%
Other people in their life now 21.3%
People from the past 10%
People known, now dead 3.8%
Middle-aged strangers 3.8%

The overall responses in the survey showed:
1. Self 95%
2. Close relatives 83.8%
3. Other people in their lives 79.4%
4. People from the past 70%
5. People known, now dead 58.1%
6. Young strangers 49.4%
7. Middle-aged strangers 48.1%
8. Child strangers 38.8%
9. Other relatives 38.1%
10. Baby strangers 31.3%
11. Adolescent strangers 26.9%
12. Elderly strangers 24.4%
13. Mostly men 23.1%
14. Spirits 20.6%
15. Mostly women 18.1%
16. Dead strangers 10.6%
17. Extraterrestrials 6.9%

Ah, But Who Are All These People Really?

It can be helpful to regard all the people in your dreams as representing different aspects of yourself. Some of the dreams related earlier in this book have been interpreted according to this idea, so if you are reading this book chapter by chapter, the way it has been designed for maximum understanding, you will already have an idea of how this concept works.

Sometimes, though, the people in your dreams are simply being themselves, and are there to illustrate how you relate to them, or to give you an insight into who they really are. They may be there symbolically to give you a time or place reference, or they may be there in 'thought' through a telepathic link-up, a connection with a deceased person, alien or other entity, or perhaps you are tuned in to someone you are yet to meet in your future, as in a precognitive dream. If that's all too much to take in at once, let's move on swiftly to look at these possibilities individually and to discover practical approaches to sorting the sheep from the goats.

Dreaming of People Known To You

Yourself

It is not surprising to discover that most people dream of themselves. If you have any confusion here, refer back to Chapter 14, All in the Action.

Dreaming of yourself when you were younger is a way of comparing how you were then to how you are now. Events in your present life have probably brought up old issues which will make more sense to you if you consider how you behaved and what was going on around you at the age you were in your dream. Often we go back in time but stay our present age, as commonly experienced in the 'back to school' dreams, where you attend, as a 35 year old, your old school where everyone else is still 11. This also serves the purpose of questioning how you act and think now compared to then. Note your dream observations about school, the other kids and the teachers, and ask yourself how much you've changed and how much you've stayed the same.

Dreaming of yourself as older than your present age is the dream's way of projecting your present lifestyle or anxieties about the future forward. This is a great opportunity, albeit in a dream, to experience older age, with the bonus of being able to come back and make appropriate changes to your diet, health, relationships and so on! This type of dream is also helpful for being able to see things from an older person's perspective, which may have a bearing on your present-day relationship with older folk.

Dreaming of yourself acting out a role, like a queen, bishop, world leader or road sweeper is the dream's way of showing the roles you tend to play in life, or in relationship with whoever else is in your dream, or in given circumstances such as those the dream portrays.

So much of this book concerns the experiences of the dreamer in his or her own dreams that I feel this section needs no further explanation.

I have met myself in dreams. There are two of us, an identity crisis or something.

(Kate, unemployed)

Close Relatives

My recurring nightmare during 1980–86 was of my ex-husband killing my children. We left him and the state in 1985, so it took a year for the nightmare to stop. I was living with constant emotional and physical abuse and great fear.

(Stacey, unemployed technical assistant)

This is probably one of the most debatable areas of dream interpretation. When is your husband in your dream representing himself, and when is he representing the 'male half' of yourself?

In Stacey's case, she understood that the dreams were a reflection of the domestic violence that was occurring in her waking life and she took the best action in moving interstate. On a deeper level, it could be argued that all was not well with Stacey's inner male, the part of herself that relates to her outer world. How did she get herself into a relationship with this man in the first place? If his violence grew after her marriage, why did she allow it to continue to such a terrifying stage?

158

Looking at Stacey's male side and how she deals with the challenge of the outer world might have helped her to understand why all of this was happening and what her real options were. Did she run away as an escape or did she also make changes in her life to strengthen her male side and prevent herself from falling into a similar relationship later? As well as physically saving her children in waking life, did Stacey save her own 'inner child'? Was she able to understand why she had allowed her inner child to be neglected and abused rather than be nurtured towards growth? I know Stacey has spent several years looking at all these issues to her great advantage.

The important thing here is to note that the dream may be applicable on two levels. We can see Stacey's ex-husband both as representing himself, and as representing the self-torturing aspects of her inner male.

Consider Micheella's comment:

> I dream of friends and family and they confide in me and tell me when they will need help and when they will prepare to die and what is troubling them. I also do spiritual hands-on healing on others in my sleep state.
>
> (Micheella, natural therapist)

Micheella is well respected as a spiritual healer. Like most of us, she dreams about her work, but she is also perceptive enough both on a day-to-day basis and also on a telepathic and spiritual level, to continue her work while she sleeps. While she accepts this and is happy to work this way, she is wise to also consider whether the people she meets both in her dreams and in her waking life are also teaching her something about herself. I know she does look at life this way. Again, dream people can be themselves and yet they can also represent parts of ourselves.

As a general rule, consider close relatives in your dreams to be themselves first, and take what you can from the dream by looking at it from this angle. If it makes sense, go with it. If the sense is confused, try looking at your close relative as an aspect

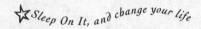

of yourself. If you are brave, try both: sometimes it takes courage to view life that way.

Other People in Your Life Now

The further away from close relationship the people in your dream are, the less likely it is that they represent themselves. This is only a rule of thumb, but it is probably safe to interpret these characters as representing aspects of yourself first. If the dream does not make sense that way, try again, allowing the people to be themselves.

OTHER PEOPLE AS ASPECTS OF YOU:
Get a piece of paper and write down the names of all the people in your dream. Next to their names, write down three words which describe each individual's personality. Then add a sentence to summarise their approach to life. Your notes might read:

~ *Peter: Happy-go-lucky, generous, faithful. He is an opportunist, and tries most openings that come his way.*

~ *Andrew: Careful, serious, emotionally cold. He prefers not to take risks and puts self-protection high on the list.*

Now, if your dream showed you kissing Peter after murdering Andrew, what conclusions would you draw? The dream perhaps suggests that you should kill (put an end to) the more serious, distrusting side of yourself, and take on more of the Peter-type characteristics of being more openly trusting. Have a look at the background situation in your dream to make your interpretation more precise. If the backdrop was work, try being more open at work, but if you found yourself by the sea in your dreams (water: emotions), try being more trusting in your emotional relationships or with yourself.

Most times in my dreams, people I know look different but I know who they are.

(Chiron, astrologer)

160

Chiron's observation holds true for many dreamers. Interpret according to who you know the dream character to be. Consider their physical differences in the dream as symbolic to add to your interpretation. For example, since hair tends to represent ideas, you might expect people's hair to be a different colour or style to their 'real' hair. They may be bigger than usual if they are overbearing, a tower of strength, a father figure or simply trying to make an impact on you, the dreamer. They may be tiny in your dream to symbolise their lesser significance or to underline their meek attitudes.

OTHER PEOPLE AS THEMSELVES:
Look at how you act towards them and how you react to them, since their role will be to shine a light on your own behaviour when confronted by such personality types. You may experiment, in your dream, with different ways of relating to these people, and you may, on waking, decide to try out some of these new approaches in waking life.

Perhaps you are a psychic dreamer, very much tuned in to these other people's lives or their dreams, so that you can wake and decide whether to enlighten them as to what you've learned about them in your dream, or whether to keep it to yourself. It is best to be extremely cautious if you feel you have messages for others from your dreams, and wisest of all to say nothing unless the occasion arises that the person comes to you seeking advice. This area of dreaming is addressed in Chapters 19 and 20.

Other People You Knew in the Past

It puzzles me that people I haven't seen or heard of for 20 years can appear in a dream.

(Jayne S., home duties)

Well, Jayne, you shouldn't be puzzled any longer after reading the last section! Apply the same principles to these people as you would to those from your present life who make dream appearances. Get out the piece of paper, make the lists as described above, and take it from there.

Sometimes we go back into the past to search for the person who best describes the personality or approach to life that fits the needs of our dream. On other occasions, though, the person is more symbolic of a place or a time in our past. The appearance of your ex-wife in your dream may be symbolic of who you were and how you acted in those days. The dream may also highlight how much you've changed in the intervening years, making this a 'progress report' dream. Look in the dream for anything that might connect your present relationships and challenges to the past, to the years when your ex-wife was more prominent in your life.

Old Mrs Smythe-Jones who used to shout abuse at you over the garden wall when your childhood games interrupted her afternoon sleep might reappear in your dreams to remind you of those days for some particular reason. Interpret the dream according to her personality, and if that is not revealing, spend time imagining being a child again during those years and try to connect those feelings and the events around that time to what is happening in your life now.

We can find people from our past rearing their heads in our dreams when we need to make peace with them, or when we need to 'go back' to sort things out and make peace with ourselves.

I had three consecutive dreams over three nights. In each dream, people who have troubled me in the past appeared at my door: different people in each dream. I invited them in and made the decision to be 'pleasant even though I don't trust them'. They stood over me in an aggressive manner, but I remained pleasant but firm in my stand with them. They faded off into the distance and disappeared! I interpreted this to mean I could now 'stand my ground' with different people.

(Heather, retired psychiatric nurse)

I feel people in my dreams play a significant part. People who have led me spiritually and who are not in my life now, keep returning to give me correction and guidance.

(Brendan, pensioner)

Does Brendan bring these people into his dream symbolically, so that each is there to represent a particular way of thinking which he can apply to his present life? Or are these spiritually advanced people making contact with him (or is he making contact with them) through his dream state? Again, Brendan can investigate this through applying the same practical guidelines outlined above, and can then draw his own conclusions.

Most of the time other people in my dreams are clearly reflections of myself, yet at times they are teaching me and seem separate.

(Jade, teacher)

Psychic dreamers are often faced with the dilemma of whether to treat a dream on a symbolic level or on a psychic level. In the end, the intuitional approach is probably best, although the dreamer will frequently find meaning by considering the dream from both angles. As this book clearly illustrates, people can and do make contact with others through the dream state, and we should not lose sight of this possibility by being dogmatic or rigid in applying dream interpretation 'rules'.

My series of dreams about my friend from the past are still happening and the answers are starting to manifest. I was at the library one day and looked on a shelf and saw the Births, Marriages and Deaths records in a big folder in the computer department. My mind immediately clicked to my dream of meeting him in a Registry Office. I made inquiries and found a name through the genealogical researcher at the library that could possibly lead me to him. If there had been no dream, seeing that journal would have meant nothing to me. I am still working on it and I believe I will make contact with him.

(Yvonne, charity worker)

People You Know to be Dead

By now you will have a clear understanding of the alternatives. Look at each of the following dreams, and think about the possibilities. Are the deceased people in the dreams symbolic of a personality type? Are they symbolic of an approach to life? Are they representative of a time or place in the dreamer's past? Can we be comforted by and seek advice from our deceased friends and relatives by consulting them symbolically in our dreams, so that we speak with the memory of who they were and what they might say to us? Or are they truly contacting us in spirit?

Across all of these possibilities is the very real opportunity of making peace with our past.

Within one week of my late husband's demise, I dreamed he and I were in bed together and he pulled the sheet over him and wanted me to come underneath the sheet too. But I didn't want to. I felt if I did, I would soon be with him and I still wanted to live.

(Stella, home duties)

My deceased sister appears frequently in my dreams. She used to appear to be emaciated at first, but now appears well and healthy with flowers growing everywhere, and we seem to enjoy each other's company. She died of cancer in 1986.

(Lainey, home duties)

When I am going through difficult times I find I dream of my parents and grandmother who are deceased.

(Morag, research student)

Sometimes I get my husband confused with my dead parents and am unsure who I have been dreaming about.

(Fiona, retired medical secretary)

In this last dream, Fiona's experience more clearly points to the symbolic where she sees similarities between her husband

164

and her late parents. When her waking life relationship with her husband (who is a fair bit older than her) has shades of her previous relationship with her parents, her dream confusion may draw her awareness to her tendency to sometimes 'act the child' in the relationship.

Dreaming of People Unknown To You

A lot of the people in my dreams won't have a face. It's as though they're not relevant.

(Jayne S., home duties)

I have created a new 'character'. I have never seen this person before but I can recall the dream specifically and his looks. I often find remembering a person's looks difficult. He is what I would call my ideal partner and in the dream he was my rescuer.

(Karyn, receptionist)

Are our dream strangers just extras or fantasy characters? How many times have you had the experience of waking up to recall the exact details of a person's face, even though you have only met them in a dream? Our dream strangers can *feel* so real:

They are not all strangers in my dreams, but when I awake, I don't know who they are, so I'll call them strangers.

(Tara, medical typist)

Sometimes people's faces are blurred and I can't work out their identity but I feel as though I know them.

(Kerry, student)

Do we feel as though we know these dream strangers because we have indeed met them and forgotten, because we know them on the spirit plane, or because we have known them intimately in past lives? Any of these cases may be so, but these dream strangers are often more symbolic. They may be walking, talking symbols of other aspects of ourselves, or they may represent different personality types for us to bounce off and react to as we try out various dream roles and relationships.

Usually when I dream of unknown places I am someone else in the dream (a stranger to me). When I dream of places I know, I'm either myself or my husband.

(Annie, home duties)

Annie gives a clue when she reveals that she is a stranger in strange places, but is someone familiar in known places. To find ourselves in strange or foreign places in a dream is often symbolic of looking at unknown aspects of our lives: emotions, events or attitudes that seem 'foreign' or 'strange' to us. When Annie's dreams deal with unknown quantities, she appears as an unknown quantity too. She doesn't recognise herself in relationship to this 'foreign' theme.

Perhaps we use strangers instead of known people in our dreams when we are dealing with aspects of ourselves that seem quite foreign to us.

Obviously we cannot apply the same practical methods of listing personality and approach to life as we can for people known to us in our dreams. Instead, give your dream strangers names and write these down on paper. You may find it helpful to give them 'role' names (like nurse, healer, baddie, etc.) rather than real names. Think about how they appeared in your dream, and write three words to describe their dream personality. Project ahead from your dream experiences with these characters and imagine what their approach to life might be. Write this down too. Then stand back, exactly as described earlier in this chapter, and see if these dream strangers seem to be aspects of yourself, or whether they have anything they can teach you about your life.

My wife is in bed and I am standing naked by the bed. A very tall man with blonde hair who is naked rushes in to our bedroom and stands beside me. I am petrified and unable to move. Another man runs into the room. He is dark and stocky. He climbs onto the bed and starts to rape my wife. I am trying to move. I want to get the big Masai machete that is in another room, but the fear will not let me move. I wake up covered in perspiration and very tense.

(Joe, catering attendant)

~ **Blondie:** *Powerful, strong, 'good'. He hesitates and holds himself back from action.*

~ **Rapist:** *'Evil', physically passionate, instinctual. He acts according to his passions.*

The descriptions are mine, not Joe's, but I have discussed this dream with Joe who was able to recognise the two strangers as different aspects of his sexuality. Joe and his wife differed in their perception of 'normal' sex, and the dream showed Joe's fear of his strong instinctual sexuality, which he had come to perceive as 'evil'. In the dream, the blonde man stands close to him, showing that Joe identifies more closely with 'hesitant sexuality' in his relationship with his wife, feeling that it is right to be 'good and to hold back'. After a series of dreams focusing on instinctual sexuality, Joe moved towards acknowledging his 'dark' side as 'normal' and started a more open communication with his wife about this area of their marriage.

Stuart met an 'ugly' female (witch) aspect of himself which he had been disowning, and his dream clearly advised him to acknowledge this disowned, feminine side of himself to give more balance to his life:

I was at some kind of fair or amusement park and was wandering around when I went into a large room. Inside there was a very ugly witch. I was really scared but then she seemed to be attracted to me and transformed into a beautiful woman and we made love.

(Stuart, postal worker)

Several of Stuart's other dreams reflected this need to express, rather than repress, parts of his make-up which he considered 'ugly'. Once his dreams had been interpreted, Stuart wrote:

I took your dream interpretations to a lady who does sand-play work and she facilitated me on a sand-play on the witch dream. I became the different symbols within the dream. It was quite wonderful to embrace the different energies involved with the symbols, to own them instead of pushing them down—especially the beautiful woman.

(Stuart, postal worker)

I have experienced a physical reaction and the feeling of someone's face breathing on me, or reaching out to touch me, or staring at me, a feeling that a dream person is following me throughout my life. I feel that I will or do have a bad side that remains in my dreams until I have fixed something in my life and am at peace.

(Lucy, home duties)

Lucy was able to see the 'bad presence' in her dreams as a part of herself: 'a bad side'. She realises that she will be 'haunted' by this dream character until she fixes up the 'bad' parts of herself and her life and finds peace. Presence dreams are often, although not always, disowned aspects of ourselves: the parts we feel are too negative to belong to us.

Lucy, Joe and Stuart all had aspects of themselves they needed to own. Some aspects, once known, were worth hanging on to and developing. The only way to get rid of the more negative aspects of ourselves that we try to ignore (such as jealousy, for example) is to own it first, feel it, then, in understanding it, let it go. This process is like getting rid of an abcess by lancing it, letting all the poison come to the surface, and then letting it go.

This dream took place in what seemed to be a tent made of chamois. The lighting was candlelight, a large number of candles which lit the place softly but clearly. There were quite a few people present and at first I was aware of them but not participating in any talk or action.

A female started talking with me and she took hold of my hands and looked directly into my eyes. Her eyes were a lovely green, not emerald or dark, but clear, bright and compelling. I was drawn to these eyes and felt an incredibly strong emotion which took all of my being and drew it out and into her eyes. She stood very close to me and just looked tenderly but intently into my eyes (which are also green). This time I was not only drawn into her but was drawing from myself every emotion and feeling that I have ever experienced. I wanted to stay locked into those eyes forever.

(Carolyn, home duties)

Carolyn noted that the stranger's eyes were the same colour as her own. Was she a spiritual guide or did Carolyn come face to face with herself in this dream? Was this an aspect of her Higher Self compelling her to draw out and acknowledge every emotion and feeling that she had ever experienced? Perhaps Carolyn needed to ask why it was important, at this time in her life, to let her deepest feelings flow, to connect with her heart.

I am in a crowded place with dream people, that is, people who I recognise from past dreams but who do not resemble anyone in real life. I know that I have dreamed about them before and even though I cannot remember the dreams, they are familiar. Not everyone in the crowd is known to me, just the ones standing close to me. We are very close, moving around with our arms above our heads because we are so close together. I feel we are in a school or part school, part cafeteria. [This was part of a very long afternoon dream: Joe had been asleep for 45 minutes.]

(Joe, catering attendant)

This dream is a beautiful example of a progress report dream. Joe meets familiar strangers (aspects of himself) from previous dreams, but experiences a closeness that binds them tight. Over the years he has gradually come to know these once un-recognised aspects of himself, and the dream shows him about to integrate them into one person. They move as one, about to become one. The school setting suggests the learning that Joe has undergone while the cafeteria represents the 'food for thought' inspired by the dream.

Men, Women, the Elderly, Children and Babies

We have many complex aspects to our personalities, but it is helpful to recognise the following ones:

INNER MALE

Whether man or woman, we all have an inner male. He represents the male qualities of rational thought, intellect, work and the challenge of our outer world. According to Chinese philosophy, he is our Yang. In the Western world, Carl Jung refers to him as our animus. Any male in our dreams may symbolise our inner male.

Men in your dreams may represent your outer world.

INNER FEMALE

Whether man or woman, we all have an inner female. She represents the female qualities of nurturing, creativity, emotions and our inner world. In Chinese philosophy she is our Yin, and according to Jung she is our anima. Any female in our dreams may symbolise our inner female.

Women in your dreams may represent your inner world.

THE ELDERLY

We all have an inner wisdom that exceeds our waking grip on life! This Higher Self may appear in our dreams as a wise old man or a wise old woman. Of course, elderly people may also symbolise other qualities such as frailty or heritage, but if your elderly dream character exudes a steady wisdom, or gives you advice, then he or she may represent your wiser Higher Self.

INNER CHILD OR BABY

We all carry a part of ourselves that is still learning, growing and needing loving care. This is our inner child or baby.

A baby or child boy in our dreams may represent the part of ourself that needs further growth in our outer world, or world of work. A baby or child girl may represent the part of ourself that needs further growth in creativity or our inner world.

We commonly put our children's faces on our dream inner child which can make interpretation confusing. Always consider your children as representative of your inner child first, before looking at any possible meaning for your children. See 'Close Relatives', earlier in this chapter, for further advice.

Spirits

Dream spirits may be deceased strangers or other entities and this subject is well covered elsewhere in this book. In dream interpretation terms, spirits may represent 'disembodied' and therefore disowned parts of ourselves. Lucy's earlier example illustrated this phenomenon. Scotty describes the same phenomenon after consulting a psychiatrist about his own dream spirit experiences:

> The experience with bad spirits has been diagnosed as a type of stress-related sensory deprivation. In knowing there was practical application I haven't had any more.
>
> (Scotty, petrol tanker driver)

Robyn describes the very simple, if courageous, process of reabsorbing her disowned aspects:

> In a dream an aggressive male person/energy was abusing me with sexual intentions. I woke myself up, but as soon as I slept again he was there. This happened three times and I decided this was not a dream but an interaction with something that can contact me when I sleep. Later my aunt suggested that maybe this presence was a part of myself that I was disowning. So, before bed I said, 'I own the aggressive, demanding, male side of me', and totally relaxed while saying it. That night my partner and I had the most wild and abandoned love making we've ever had ... and the unwelcome presence has not returned.
>
> (Robyn, sculptor)

Dreaming of spirits or entities on a symbolic level may also be reflective of your philosophy of life and your needs or fears concerning your relationship with the 'other side'. Practical advice for dealing with distressing spirit experiences is given in Chapter 20.

Changing Faces

Often people in my dreams are combinations of people I know. I often get confused as to whom it is. They also change in the blink of an eye.

(Karl, student)

Our dreams may show how one aspect of ourselves can be changed into another, or how attitudes may change. Perhaps we see the similarities between people we know, and see this represented in the dream by their interchangeable faces.

> *The thing I find quite weird in dreams is that in many cases I partake in some event and then all of a sudden I become somebody else, as if I'm in somebody else's body. I feel like I am that person and at the same time I know I'm not. This occurs with both men and women.*
>
> (Kerry, student)

Like Kerry, we may 'try out' standing in other people's shoes, or see things from other points of view.

Role Characters

Look at the role characters you meet in your dreams, examine whether you know them in waking life or whether they are dream strangers. You may meet kings, teachers, politicians, doctors, priests, fathers, arsonists ... the list is endless! Sometimes these roles are symbolic of aspects of yourself: holding up a mirror to reflect the teacher in you, or the politician in you and so on. Easy! Here are a few examples to illustrate the point. Apply the same sense of translation to all other role characters who appear in your dreams.

~ **Jailer:** *Aspect of yourself which imprisons or restricts you or others.*

~ **King:** *Aspect of yourself which rules over the rest of you (this is the presumed psychology behind the mythological version of King Arthur, whose knights [parts of self] fought their various battles to become one [whole self] at the round table), or over other people. Consider what kind of king you are in the dream. Wise, caring, cruel, greedy?*

~ **Teacher:** *Aspect of yourself which has learned and is now teaching you something in the dream, or the aspect of yourself which teaches others.*

~ **Mother:** *Aspect of yourself which mothers you or others. We often take on our own mother's mothering beliefs and mothering behaviour, both towards ourselves and towards others. Look for evidence of this in your dreams. The same goes for* **Father**.

~ **Doctor, nurse, practitioner:** *Aspects of self capable of self-healing, or which can give sound healing advice in your dreams. (The advice may be symbolic: don't follow it literally!)*

~ **Politician:** *Part of yourself which has definite views, something to say or may be the idealistic aspect of yourself. This depends on your view of politicians and what the dream politician is trying to achieve and how!*

And so on.

Puns in People's Names

Take a second look at the names of all the people in your dreams, whether you know them or not. (The same goes for place names.) A stranger named Dawn, for example, may tell you something which 'dawns' on you. Tom Cruise may simply be there to symbolise a need to 'cruise' along for a while. Mrs Waters may signal something very emotional (water as emotions) and Dr Feelgood may not represent the musician or radio personality of the same name, but may be advising you to cure yourself through doing something that makes you 'feel good' for a change. These examples may sound silly, but that's the way our

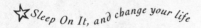

minds work when they search for symbols to capture a concept, to illustrate a point, or to paint a word picture.

Practical Summary

Never be rigid in your use of dream interpretation. Select the right tools to do the right job. Follow the checklist below to look at the people in your dreams, and then use clues derived from using your other dream interpretation tools, such as looking at the actions, emotions, universal symbols, personal symbols, clichés and so on. Settle on an interpretation only when it *feels* right to you, and be open to the idea that one dream may be interpreted in several different ways which, occasionally, can all be relevant to your situation. They simply reflect different levels of meaning.

Checklist

People you know

★ *List three of their personality traits.*

★ *What is their approach to life?*

★ *When did you last meet this person and what was happening to you then?*

★ *Do you associate this person with a particular time, place or event?*

★ *Does their name contain a pun or play on words?*

★ *What role do/did they play in life in general?*

★ *What role do/did they play in your life?*

★ *Could they represent any of your 'inner selves': child, male, mother, etc.?*

★ *Do you have any unresolved business or feelings with this person?*

★ *Do you need to make peace with this person?*

★ Were you trying out a new way of relating to this person in the dream (role-playing)?

★ Do you think this person could represent an aspect of yourself?

★ What can this person teach you about yourself?

★ Do you think this person was just being him/herself in your dream?

★ What did you learn about yourself or about this person in your dream?

★ Do you feel you were in psychic connection with this person through your dream?

★ What does the background to the dream highlight about your relationship to this person?

★ Did the person change into someone else, or remind you of someone else?

★ Was his or her appearance changed?

★ Do you feel different about your relationship with this person now you are awake?

★ Do you feel this person relates to a past life or to someone you have yet to meet?

★ If you were to meet this person today, how would you react?

People you don't know

Follow the above list wherever you can, imagining the stranger's personality, approach to life and so on from what they did or said in your dream.

Realise strangers may be parts of yourself which feel foreign to you.

Above all, never throw away the characters in your dreams, for, as Krishnamurti observes in waking life:

> *Only in relationship can you know yourself, not in abstraction and certainly not in isolation. The movement of behaviour is the sure guide to yourself, it's the mirror of your consciousness; this mirror will reveal its content, the images, the attachments, the fears, the loneliness, the joy and the sorrow. Poverty lies in running away from this, either in its sublimations or its identities.*
>
> *(J. Krishnamurti)**

In waking or in dreaming we learn about ourselves through looking into the eyes of others, for they are the mirrors which reflect our own souls.

*Quoted in A Guide for the Advanced Soul, *Susan Hayward, In-Tune Books, quoted from 'Krishnamurti's Journal', copyright 1982, Krishnamurti Foundation Trust Ltd, Kent, UK.*

CHAPTER 16

Tell Me a Story

Fairy Tales, Myths and Modern Parables

How many of us take straight facts about ourselves or about life easily? The best communicators are often well versed in diplomacy, able to spin a story, tell a tale, or somehow produce that magical mental picture: the one that illustrates far more than a thousand direct and tactless words. We get our difficult messages across to a child or work colleague by pointing to an outside situation that bears a resemblance to the more personal one at hand. Tactfully we are able to discuss this more objective situation without ever acknowledging its similarity to our own circumstances. Through such an objective eye we can more clearly judge our own behaviour or relationships.

Watch any American family situation comedy on television to see the happy family tie-ups at the conclusion of each weekly episode. Regardless of whether you endorse the morals presented, our children sit and absorb these modern-day parables. Who knows how many take personal note and become more caring towards their peers or parents as a result.

Westerners raised on centuries-old fairy tales absorb from early childhood the lessons of, for example, the Three Little Pigs (build your life from solid foundations: if a job's worth doing, it's worth doing well), or Cinderella (humility and honesty wins in the end). We see how our genuine embrace of the unfortunate can be endlessly rewarding, as when the little princess kissed the ugly frog and transformed not only the unfortunate animal but also her whole life when he became the handsome prince.

Whether our fairy tales contain great ageless wisdom, or whether they were fabricated to keep the peasants in order (a kind of
'opium of the masses') is beside the point. The point is that
stories, role characters, myths and legends capture and enrapture
us with their magical objectivity, imprinting deeply on our
subconscious selves to instill some kind of ancestral moral code.

Every culture has its myths and legends and yet, although the
names, languages and stories may change, the messages tend to
follow similar lines. We can look across the world and marry
the legend of King Arthur with the myth of the Fisher King.
Handed down to each new generation, a story may change to
suit the particular times, religions or cultures, to suit war or
famine, to suit a mountain village or a coastal town, but over
centuries the individual differences tend to get ironed out in
favour of the main story-line which always survives.

Jesus spoke in parables because, presumably, they had a more
lasting impact on the listeners. Our dreams often speak in
parables, or use fairy tale or movie characters, and, in so doing,
deliver the personal message with greater tact but far more
impact.

*When I was a child I used to dream of walking up a hill to my
grandmother's house. There would be signs everywhere saying
'Gran's House', but it was a trick. It was really a witch's house
and she would have my Gran in gaol.*

(Krystal, mother)

This recurring dream suggests that Krystal, as a child, feared
deception or felt insecure about the relationships around her.

*I read the questionnaire through before sleeping last night and had
a hugely apocryphal dream featuring Jesus, miracles, destruction of
world power figures and cataclysmic destruction, all of which my
mother, father, myself and one unknown other survived by believing
in our own reality.*

(Natalie, student)

178

When I received Natalie's completed questionnaire, she told me she had found the exercise to be great therapy, and recommended several friends to join the survey simply to reap this benefit: which they did. It seems that contemplating the questionnaire alone was enough to unleash a 'state of play' dream in readiness for her to work on the next day.

Erika's dreams bring old fairy tale characters as well as modern fictional space characters to life, allowing her to role-play and experience situations that are relevant to her waking life. As she expressed: 'A bit far-fetched perhaps? Well, how successful was *Star Trek*: to boldly go where no-one has gone before!'

I had a series of dreams between May 1988 and December 1991, which were like fairy tales, nursery rhymes or bible stories. In all of these, I was either a part of the dream or the characters talked to me. I was Grandmother Time, Gulliver, Cinderella and a mouse. I watched the man who went to mow a meadow. I sowed, reaped, worked hard and enjoyed the sun.

All of these dreams seemed to be sending a specific message to me, for example, 'do good and you shall be rewarded' or 'seek and ye shall find' and so on. I once had a dream called 'Space Fantasy' that was most impressive. I saw in it the key to life, my truth. This is that I must pass tests and rise to higher levels of achievement in my own fashion, with harmony and dignity, without abusing anyone or anything. The dream went like this:

I was on board an enormous space station where there was a ceremony taking place. I was wearing a futuristic uniform and was being decorated for some commendable act or achievement. As the decoration was pinned on my uniform I was saluted in the most honourable way by the entire crew. The many different ranks and officers were differentiated by different coloured uniforms, and the higher the office or rank, the higher they stood on a wide platform of many levels, floors and balconies.

The officer who decorated me was my brother, although he was much older than in present-day waking life. He was the most decorated and distinguished officer. Everyone else in the dream was another family member, or a person of special significance in my life. Friends, teachers, mentors, in fact anyone who had left an immoveable impression on my mind or life. The different ranks and ages of people saw the face of a person repeated over and over many times, like a large family.

This scene and the looks of hope, congratulation and expectation on the faces of all led me to an amazing revelation that this was the pattern of my life: all tests and results, achievement and triumph. I am not even alone. The dream showed the people in my conscious life were placed there to help me get through my next test. Each step in life was deliberately planned by this giant inter-galactic crew: protectors and guides for my journey home. I think of this dream every time I win or lose. I take a deep breath and experience that feeling of accomplishment and self-worth.

(Erika, administration officer)

From Dream to Fairy Tale to Enlightenment

Changing your everyday dreams into myths, fairy tales or television sitcoms can throw light on their true meanings and relevance to your life. All you need is a pen, a piece of paper or word processor and a wild imagination.

First choose your preferred medium. What do you relate to? Ancient Grecian legends, medieval folktales, Shakespearian humour or tragedy, Hans Christian Andersen, Rudyard Kipling, Woody Allen, Eastern mysticism, national politics, 'Full House', Superman, Walt Disney or *Star Wars*? Choose your weapon.

Next take each person who appeared in your dream and write down their names at the head of your page. Without too much thought, assign each person a story character. This should be a quick gut reaction response, since you are appealing to your subconscious to select the most appropriate role for each character. If you feel your final list is a bit restrictive, you can invent a few more characters to balance the baddies or whatever.

Then look at the background to your original dream and choose a parallel setting which is more appropriate to your theme. If you were driving along in a sports car, for example, and you have chosen a medieval folk tale theme, put yourself on a fast pedigree stallion. If you were trapped in a cellar in your dream, and prefer a space age script, relocate yourself to a sealed section of a space rocket which is running out of oxygen.

If your dream had an ending, translate the *feel* of the ending into an idea for the ending of your new theme. If, for example, your dream ended when you picked up a ringing phone, and your theme is fairy tale, change the ending to a messenger handing you a wax-sealed letter. If you dreamed of being saved from an awkward situation by a neighbour, and your theme is Superman, rev up the excitement and adventure and have the great hero himself rescue you from a blazing 20 storey apartment block.

If there was no ending in your dream, make one up in your story.

Rewrite the dream and don't worry if it goes off the track or if you feel you are losing touch with the dream. As long as you keep the main characters in play, and maintain the outlooks and attitudes they had in your dream, as well as sticking with the start and finish in your dream, you can be as creative as you wish. Put yourself in the dream, either as yourself or as a character which suits the original feel of the dream, and try to keep the same level of active or passive behaviour that you had in the dream. This will help you to see how you interact with the dream characters, and enlighten you about how you tend to interact with similar personalities or in similar situations in working life.

If you are not satisfied with the way you are treated or the way you behave in your story, rewrite it to satisfy you. Then translate this rewrite into a formula for rewriting your day-to-day behaviour to achieve more rewards in your waking life.

Example

Dream: I dreamed I went to see my bank manager to ask for a loan. I didn't know whether I'd get the loan I wanted, but I expected an overdraft at least, something to help me through the bad times. He refused and for the first time in my life I felt humiliated. I was also anxious about losing my home.

Rewrite: I went to see the King to ask for protection from his knights. My castle was attacked earlier in the year, and I feared for our safety. The King, usually a kindly and understanding man, had helped me on numerous occasions before. Today he seemed distant and refused my offer. I asked him why he wouldn't help me this time when he had done so before. 'Ah,' said the King. 'Last year you asked for precious gems to trade for materials to build fortifications. I gave you the gems. Where are the fortifications?' I felt humiliated and realised that I had squandered resources that were given to me in good faith. I had not honoured the hand that fed me. I wondered what would become of my home.

This fictitious example was simple and obvious, but was chosen to show how we can see ourselves and our actions more honestly if we place them in another setting, let the characters speak more for themselves and let our imagination run wild. The dreamer might have chosen to create an ending for his story:

Ending: I realised the King was right. We cannot take without giving back. I offered to repay his previous kindness by making him a gift of my finest horse.

Perhaps in waking life, this fictitious dreamer might have decided to use his car as security against a new loan while he worked to pay the debts he had accrued through overspending on his credit cards.

So much for a bit of fun, but you should have the idea by now!

We recall some dreams only as single scenes, or lasting impressions, yet can be just as puzzled by these short dreams as by the movie-length variety. Use these scenes as starting points for creative writing. Subconsciously you do understand the implications of your dream picture, or dream feeling, and this meaning will often emerge in your waking creative treatment.

You can extend the dream through story writing, poetry, or whatever medium appeals to you.

If Frances applied this method to the dream she describes here, she would gain insight into its meaning:

My dream house is always unknown, by the sea. The waves are pounding on the rocks close by. The house is so beautiful, all marble with antique but uncluttered furniture. It has huge windows and doors overlooking the water. The colours are beige to mauve, so classy and very serene regardless of the waves pounding.

(Frances, actor)

Using her dream as an introduction only, she should consider how she feels standing in this house, whether people are close by, what time of day it is, what she can see through the windows and so on.

Who knows, apart from interpreting your dream, you may come up with a prize-winning novel or script!

CHAPTER 17

But I Missed the End of the Dream!

Fragments and Frustration

How often does the alarm ring at the crucial moment? You were just about to kiss the woman of your dreams, reach the top of the mountain or open the door into a new dimension. How many more years worth of dreaming will it take before you have that opportunity again?!

Or maybe you have become very adept at waking yourself up out of frightening dreams, escaping from the clutches of a monstrous killer into the familiar darkness of your bedroom in the opening of an eye. Ah, you may have eluded that particular scene, but will you ever escape the whole recurring nightmare unless you face the end of the dream? What can an unfinished dream tell you? You need to grapple with the monster, or see what comes next to know how to resolve the waking dilemmas that the dream symbolically portrays.

Do you get frustrated by being able to recall only fragments of your dreams? You write down a snatch here, a bit there, suddenly remember the bathroom scene and then wonder how the cuckoo fitted into it all. You sit back and regard the page in your journal. Were these parts of one dream, or snippets of four different dreams? Should you be trying to piece them together somehow? Did this action cause that event, or were they unrelated? It may be helpful to realise that a night's dreaming often seems to investigate one issue in your life, as if the dreams are looking at a problem from a variety of angles, or working out several different ways of dealing with the same situation to see which is best. This approach leaves you with a number of scenes, rather like glimpses of the action seen through a keyhole at random time intervals throughout a day.

How many dream reports start along the lines 'I found myself on a boat' or 'I was swimming in the middle of an ocean.' How did you get there? Did the dream start abruptly, or has the beginning of the story been lost? Are you perhaps remembering the end of the dream, or the middle, seeing the 'effect' without recall of the 'cause'? How can you make sense of the dream's message if you can't sort out the cause from the effect?

Recognising the Unfinished Dream

The examples given in the introduction are obvious, but often we believe we have recalled a whole dream until we try to interpret it or to take action based on the dream's message. You may interpret a dream to see it is a statement of how you feel about a certain issue, for instance. Now, this can be useful information, especially if the dream reveals subconscious feelings which you hadn't previously acknowledged. This recognition alone may be enough to allow you to see what is holding you back in life, or to decide what action to take. In many cases, though, far more information was lost than was remembered.

Look at the dream you have recalled. Was each action carried through to a conclusion? When you walked down the road, did you get somewhere, or did you learn something along the way? When you asked someone a question, did you hear the answer? When you made a decision in your dream, did you stay around long enough to see the effect? Look at the beginning of the dream. Are you satisfied that this was the opening scene, or do you feel that something is missing? Would it help your dream interpretation to know how you got there, or why you were there?

A satisfying dream will frequently contain words such as

The End of the Dream ☆

'suddenly' or 'I realised', or there is a feeling that something has been resolved. Look for turning points or moments of enlightenment, then compare the action before these moments, and the events which follow them. At such points your dreams may be saying 'If you do that, then this will happen' and so on. To be complete, a dream needs a sense of *resolution*. If this is missing in your dream, try one of the following techniques.

Filling in the Gaps

There are several ways you can retrace possible gaps in your dreams, and these are explained in this short practical chapter. Each method works on the assumption that you do have a subconscious memory of your dream, or of its true meaning, and that this is best tapped into through entering a state where you are more closely in tune with your subconscious mind.

Professional hypnosis may help you to relive or recall a dream, especially if you are plagued by a recurring nightmare yet continually block recall of parts of the dream. Self-hypnosis, or a semi-trance state, can work well too, but a simple procedure of putting yourself in a state of deep relaxation or meditation is usually all that is required to get the most out of these dream re-entry techniques.

Relaxation Procedure

Allow yourself 20 minutes to lay or sit in a comfortable position, with the phone off the hook, in a place where you will not be disturbed. Let all your muscles release their tension until you feel heavy as if your body is sinking down. Just 'let go'. Check every muscle from your toes to your head, focusing on relaxing deeper and deeper with each outward breath. Finally become so aware of the heaviness of your body that it suddenly becomes as light as air and you feel yourself 'float away'. Keep your eyes closed and lay back to enjoy the ride, seeing whatever floats before your mind's eye.

You may wish to use deeper meditation or cleansing procedures, or to add rituals similar to those described in Chapter 18. This can be extremely effective, but the simple relaxation procedure outlined above is sufficient for the task.

Method 1: Re-entering the Dream

A. FINDING THE ENDING

Follow the relaxation procedure and allow the dream to replay in your mind's eye. Take time and feel free to 'stop the film' from time to time, or to replay sections in slow motion. When you reach the end of your remembered dream, don't stop. Allow yourself to daydream on, imagining the ending. The secret is to stay relaxed and to bypass your head or its thinking processes! Let your heart tell the story, allowing your intuition to be your sole guide. Don't concern yourself with the question of whether you are 'right' or not. Just let the new version unfold itself. The chances are that your subconscious will direct the new 'dream' along similar lines, if you let it flow.

You may prefer, at the end of the session, to record your feelings in poetry or as a painting rather than as a strict record of each detail of the relived dream. Follow your intuition to get the best results.

B. FINDING THE BEGINNING

Follow the same procedure as for *Finding the Ending,* but put yourself at the start of the dream and picture yourself physically turning around 180 degrees to face the other direction. Daydream yourself backwards through time, retracing your steps. Follow the same advice given above to allow your intuition and your heart to lead you. If you give yourself the freedom to enjoy this daydream, you will find enormous benefit from the exercise.

C. FINDING THE MIDDLE BITS

Follow the above procedure again, but allow your intuition to daydream the links which get you from the end of one remembered dream fragment to the beginning of the next. Explore possibilities by changing the order in which you place

The End of the Dream ☆

the fragments until the story flows and you feel a sense of satisfaction and resolution with your daytime creation.

Method 2: The Folded Paper

This method of finding an ending for your dream relies on a quick gut reaction response on your behalf, so allow yourself three or four minutes only for this exercise. Again the advice is to let the heart speak and try to bypass the brain altogether.

Take a blank sheet of paper and fold it into four quarters, then spread it open. You now have four sections marked by creases. Take your dream memory and reduce it to three main parts. Draw part one in stick person action (maybe with bubbles showing what they are saying) in the first box. Draw part two in the second and part three in the third. Very quickly, and without thinking, draw part four in the last section. This is your subconscious effort at getting the dream message across by providing a similar ending to the original dream. If you feel unsatisfied, repeat the procedure several times, and then sit back, switch on the brain again, and compare all the possible scenarios.

Method 3: Dream Incubation

Use one of the dream incubation techniques described in Chapter 18 to request either a replay of the lost dream or a substitute the next night. Relax and remember that, in the end, if the message is important enough, it will come through again.

Method 4: Fairy Tales and Television Scripts

Take your dream fragment or unfinished dream as a starting point for a creative fairy tale, television script or other story-telling medium as shown in Chapter 16, Tell Me a Story. Let your intuition pick up the theme and direct the action by letting the story flow without worrying about grammar or originality. Allow it to become as personal as you wish. You can always burn it afterwards.

Method 5: Meditation

Meditate on a symbol, or a feeling from your dream memory and let it grow and take on a life of its own. Let a story emerge and allow it to find a life of its own. Conclude the meditation by focusing on the image which inspired you most, and take this symbol and feeling into your day.

Postscript

These methods are successful if you allow the subconscious free reign. In cultivating this art of letting go, you stand to reap further benefit as you begin to allow your dream recall blocks to fade. If you find yourself 'trying hard' in any of these techniques, stop. Trying is a way of blocking success. It never succeeds. If you *try* to write a letter, for example, your paper will remain blank. The only way the letter will get written is if you *write* it. Don't *try*, *write*! *Trying* to do your best, is an excuse for failure. It means 'I won't do my best, but I'll fool myself and everyone else into thinking that I am working on it.' The only way to do your best, is to *do* your best. Don't *try*, *do*! The same applies to these 'let go' methods of dream re-entry or daydream explorations. If you find yourself thinking it's hard and 'trying', nothing will happen. *The only way to let go, is to let go.*

Always remember, too, that if the dream message is really important, it will come back. It might reappear in a different drama, with different characters, but the meaning will be the same. So, just let go!

Don't try to force anything. Let life be a deep let-go. See God opening millions of flowers every day without forcing the buds.
     (Bhagwan Shree Rajneesh, in Dying for Enlightenment)★

★*Quoted in* A Guide for the Advanced Soul, *by Susan Hayward, In-Tune Books. (Quoted by Susan as copyright to the Rajneesh Foundation International.)*

CHAPTER 18

Sleep On It—Solving Problems

Have you ever dropped thankfully into bed after a long night's drive along major highways, only to close your eyes and see more traffic signs, tail lights and headlamps, and to feel the steering wheel still vibrating beneath your hands? Or have you spent too many hours closely weeding a garden without looking up, only to see weeds sprawled before you again as soon as your head touches the pillow? Or have you fallen to sleep while reading a book, but through your closed eyes dream you are still reading, perhaps only realising you are dreaming because the book's narrative begins to take uncharacteristic bizarre twists? I have been unfortunate enough to take all of these, not to mention computer screens and dozens of handwritten dream questionnaires, into my sleep! We take our relatives, friends, work, television programs, plans, ideas, hopes, wishes and, of course, our problems to bed with us and meet them again in our dreams.

As we drift into dreaming, our conscious brain largely switches off and hands the whole bag of the day's thoughts, experiences and problems over to the subconscious and other accessible means of guidance to work on. Our dreams may try to deal with our current situation by taking us back into the past, or by projecting us forward to show how things might be if we take this or that action. Our dreams might concentrate on the relationship aspects of our natures, or on our ingrained behaviours, attempting to illustrate why we continually end up in the same kind of situations that we found ourselves in yester-day. Or we might find ourselves, in our dream state, taking a clearly focused view of one particular problem and coming up with a real eureka of an answer!

That moment of clear focus, whether it arises naturally or whether we need to program it, is the purpose of this chapter. Can we really sleep on a problem and come up with an answer, and, if so, are there techniques we can use to ask for, and get, an answer to a chosen question?

Of Science, Art and Dreams

A German chemist, Friedrich Kekulé, (1829–96), had been struggling in his effort to determine the molecular structure of benzene. Something about the structure, whenever he drew it, didn't balance. He dreamed he saw a snake swallowing its tail and found his answer. He had expected the molecule to be a string, or a string with branches, whereas, in fact, it joined onto itself and formed a circle! The dream was correct. Kekulé was apparently so moved by this dream revelation that he addressed a scientific audience with the advice: 'Let us learn to dream, Gentlemen, and then we may perhaps learn the truth.'

Early the next century, another German-born scientist, Otto Leowi, dreamed of the crucial experimental method which would test whether nerves passed their impulses around the brain and body electrically or chemically. After the dream he conducted the experiment and later collected the 1936 Nobel Prize for Medicine or Physiology for his discovery of chemical neurotransmitters.

A Nobel Prize based on a dream! Let's take a different example: Singer sewing machines. Elias Howe, an American, had tried just about everything to create a more efficient sewing machine, and was finally saved by a dream. He had been captured by cannibals, who stood in a circle around him, holding their spears. Fearing his death, he looked at the sharp point on each spear and noticed a hole just below each point. And that's exactly where the hole in the sewing machine needle is today.

Einstein, often quoted as the most creative scientific genius of modern times, traced the roots of his Theory of Relativity to a boyhood dream. In the dream he rode a sledge, faster and faster until he was travelling as fast as light itself. At this point, the stars fused into patterns and colours, and relativity was glimpsed in picture form.

Poets and authors have many times awoken with a new creative flow derived from the benefit of sleeping on it. The British poet Samuel Taylor Coleridge (1772–1834) dreamed most of the story of the Kubla Khan, awoke with a reported 200–300 lines of the poem in his head, but was interrupted and had to add the rest himself. There may have been more to Coleridge's dream than shifting writer's block, though, as the Kubla Khan palace in Xanadu was accurately described in his poem, but the manuscript containing a description of the palace from a Persian painting was not translated into English until after Coleridge's death.

Problem Solving in the 1990s

Closer to home, consider these dream solutions from the dream survey:

My brother was trying to buy a grazing station and everything was going along fine to begin with until someone began to make it difficult for him. My brother had signed an unconditional contract and had his all on the line, so he was about to lose the whole lot. He asked me what he should do, and I said, 'I don't know, but I'll tell you tomorrow!' I was too busy to think about it then. I went to bed and woke up an hour later knowing exactly what to say to him. In the morning I made the right phone calls and in 24 hours we had it fixed. We had completely aborted this other guy's efforts to abort the show.

(Seeker, astrologer)

About nine years ago I began a new job as a clerk typist. The position dealt exclusively with one of Australia's largest companies *and I was responsible for balancing the accounts to somewhere between $1.5–$2.5 million every month. This figure comprised sales to and purchases from the other company over eight different departments, so there were many areas where mistakes could be made. I was approaching my deadline by still being $7.20 out of balance on my first attempt alone. I had no idea where else I could look. I tried not to worry about it, but the problem would not leave my mind, whatever I did. When I finally got to sleep I just kept seeing figures in front of me. I was really exasperated.*

As I awoke the next morning I realised I was coming out of a consciousness where I'd been searching through documents, and had held, in my hand, a commission docket to an agency which had deducted $7.20 commission from their sales return rather than wait for us to apply the $7.20 credit to their account. Could it possibly be? At work, when I physically held it in my hand, I believed it. In fact, I was totally blown away!

(Louisa, accounts co-ordinator)

There was an occasion when I got a car bogged and there was little or no help available. After I had lunch I had a short rest, and in a dream I was able to see how I would get the car out of the bog myself. And I did.

(John, town planner)

The dream can be so literal and precise, that it is also a pre-cognitive dream. Pearl was preoccupied with her anxiety about driving a ute, as she describes:

To give some background first, I was brought up on a farm near a small country town and I was taught to drive a tractor when I was very young. Even though it was illegal at this age, I was encouraged to drive to town when it was necessary. Though I found driving the tractor fun, I was apprehensive about the ute, because its brakes weren't working. The seat was also stuck back so I couldn't reach the pedals effectively.

Solving Problems ☆

At first sight, Pearl's dream appeared to be a good example of a problem solving dream, suggesting a way of coping should an emergency arise:

In the dream, I was driving to town with Grandfather as passenger. I noticed a vehicle travelling up the hill in front of us, and as I approached it I realised it was travelling slower than we were and that I would have to change down gears. As we neared the vehicle I fumbled the gear change and stalled the engine which then cut out! The handbrake wasn't working so I applied the footbrake as hard as I could. As I began to slide further back against the seat the pressure on the brake was diminishing and the vehicle began to roll back, picking up speed.

I was frightened that I would lose control and that we would both end up in the river and drown. Then a thought came to me that I could steer the ute into the embankment on our left.

This solution was perhaps comforting. It restored a sense of control should an emergency arise. Consider what happened next:

I cannot remember how long after this dream the exact experience occurred, but as it unfolded (exactly as I had dreamt it), I thought of my dream at the most crucial time and I steered the car into the embankment.

This really scared me, both because the dream had predicted it and because I would have been responsible for Grandfather's death had the worst happened.

The dream solution probably saved both lives, and was also seen to have been a precognitive dream all along. Pearl learned two things from this experience. Firstly:

I had learned my lesson. I decided that in future I would stop prior to the climb, change down, and travel up the hill slowly, thereby alleviating the gear change further up.

And secondly:

I believe my Higher Self gave me other precognitive dreams over the years so that I would eventually begin to take notice of them and accept them as a means to give me insight into the future and eventually save my life once again.

(Pearl, secretary)

Pre-empting the Future?

Do we see here another function of precognitive dreaming? Precognitive dreaming can warn us of future dangers and save our lives. It can help us feel good when an enjoyable or peaceful prediction becomes reality and we feel a sense of confirmation about the direction we are taking in life. It can push us to look at life in a different way, to readjust our philosophy of life to fit what we have experienced in finding ourselves reliving our dreams. It can cause us to think more deeply about time, psychic senses, spirituality, our place and individual purpose in the world and so on, but Pearl's dream is more than all those things.

Pearl's dream solved a potential problem in her life by suggesting a way out of danger should her anxieties occur. It also made her aware of the risks she was taking with other people's lives. If she had acted on this awareness, she might have refused to drive that particular vehicle again, or changed her driving habits. Either of these actions would have prevented the dream from coming true. Although the dream probably saved lives, it begs the question of the necessity of a precognitive dream manifesting into waking reality. Should we be more sensitive to our dreams and take their advice more seriously? Do waking life calamities occur because we have not understood or ignored previous advice, perhaps through our dreams? After the accident, as Pearl reported above: 'I had learned my lesson. I decided that in future I would stop prior to the climb, change down, and travel up the hill slowly, thereby alleviating the gear change further up.' Was the original dream trying to teach this lesson, backing the teaching up with a safe way out (the embankment idea) in case she continued to take risks?

More precisely, do the events in our waking life take place, or

Solving Problems ☆

not take place, according to how much we have learned, misunderstood or ignored when first presented with our situation in our dreams? Do we run through our learning in our dream state, but, when this is not effective, have to be exposed to a waking life version instead? If this is true, can we change our future by paying closer heed to the teachings and advice in our dreams?

Dream Incubation: the Power of Focus

If the purpose of our dreams is to give us feedback on how we go about our lives, and to help us make wiser decisions based on this knowledge, then surely all we need to know is how to interpret our dreams. In the long term this is true, but sometimes we have a need to hurry the process along, or we feel, in waking life, a need to focus on one specific problem. While our dreams may prefer to address a difficulty in our lives in (what appears to us) a roundabout way, there are times when we have less patience. Perhaps also, especially when we are still learning how to interpret our dreams, we need our dreams to be more finely tuned, more obviously directed towards a precisely worded question. This is the process of dream incubation.

Dream incubation is an ancient technique which existed in many cultures including those in Central America, China, Africa and Aboriginal Australia, but it was the Ancient Greeks who used dream incubation as their primary healing tool for over 1000 years before the birth of Christ. Some 300 healing temples were distributed throughout Ancient Greece, dedicated to Asclepius, the Greek god of healing. Asclepius lived (and was later deified) around 1100 BC, before the Trojan Wars, and was believed to have been instructed in the art of healing by Cheiron. His symbol was the snake.

Whenever people needed a physical or emotional cure, they would go to a healing temple and be taken through various ritual cleansing processes. They would sleep overnight, often in an underground room containing harmless snakes, in deference to Asclepius. In the morning, they would recount their dreams to their healers, who were, effectively, dream interpreters. The healers would then interpret the dreams to show the cause of the person's suffering and to offer a method of cure.

This system was in place for a thousand years! Hippocrates, the father of medicine, studied at a healing temple on the Island of Kos around the 4th century BC, learning dream interpretation and its application to physical disease. I wonder how many modern-day Western doctors are aware of the origins of the snake which entwines the caduceus, the symbol of the Hippocratic oath?

Robyn has used dream incubation techniques to discover the basis of her medical problems:

Before sleeping, I asked for an answer to this question: 'Why am I consistently so incredibly tired, catching every virus and infection? I eat healthily, take supplements, don't drink or smoke and have a positive attitude.' The dream was very short and clear, one image, one sentence. I saw an enlarged cell. The nucleus was fine but the energy stores were depleted. The 'voice' came on, 'Your T cells are down.'

In the morning I decided to find out whether we have T cells, which of course I now know we do.

(Robyn, sculptor)

Scotty was anxious to know the sex of his first baby and programmed a dream to find his answer:

I went to bed wanting a sign of whether our new baby would be a boy or a girl. I dreamed I went on a fishing trip with my wife and we were on a boat. She baits up with a big round lemon-like ball. I just shrug my head and laugh. As I start doubting she gets a strike: a big healthy silver fish, a real fighter. I'm amazed. She looks up in the sky and she says, 'Look, there's the sign you wanted.' I look up, and there in the clouds, lit up by the moon, are the white letters 'boy'.

(Scotty, petrol tanker driver)

Scotty's baby boy was born on 5 August 1993.

Lainey used dream incubation to gain first-hand experience of death for her book:

I was trying to write my first book and one chapter is on death. I wondered what it would be like to experience death in a car accident. I then had this unusual dream:

I was a passenger in a friend's car which was travelling up a mountain. When we reached the top we decided to get out to stretch our legs. While resting my arm on a railing I had strong feelings that I was going to fall off the mountain, or something dreadful was about to occur, so I told my friends we should go.

We drove away and the last thing I remembered was a blackness overtaking me which was followed by a falling sensation. It was then that I realised that the car I was in, and the other cars, were falling down the mountain as trees and bushes flashed by. My thoughts were 'I am going to die!' I felt the car hit the ground with a sickening thud and pieces lay everywhere. Friends' cars lay in pieces as well. Bodies were strewn everywhere. My thoughts were 'I'm still alive', but this was not so.

I became aware that I was travelling into the air at a very high speed towards a white circle. As I drew nearer, the circle changed into a white woman with white flowing hair which broke into pieces. I then began a rapid descent to the ground. I awoke gasping for breath for a moment and it took a while to regain my senses.

(Lainey, home duties)

Dream Incubation: The Practicalities

1 *Formulate your question precisely, so that you are clear about what, exactly, you want to know.*

For example, 'How can I free myself from my financial debts?' might be too broad, whereas 'Would it be wise to consolidate my debts?' is more focused. The dream you receive may seem inappropriate at first and interpretation is always easier if you know the precise question the dream is addressing.

Once you have your answer, you can incubate dreams to look at other aspects of your financial life.

2 *Write the question down.* Doing this ensures you have indeed been precise, and also serves as a reminder of the exact question in the morning. It is easy to sleepily lay in bed and think up a dream question, have a dream, then wake up with only a blurred memory of your request.

3 *Choose a ritual that feels good to you.* You may wish to pick one (or all) of the following, or you may wish to create your own procedure. The important thing is not so much what you do, as the fact that the ritual underlines the solemnity of the occasion and your dedication to solving your problem. As you become proficient at dream incubation, you will find that maintaining the same ritual brings even greater rewards, as your dream state becomes programmed to recognise your ritual. In other words, practice makes perfect!

Suggested rituals include:

★ *Write your dream request on scented paper and place it under your pillow to 'sleep on it'.*

★ *Sleep in a different place which you reserve specially for dream incubation nights. Try a spiritually inspiring place, such as out in the open air, or camped at the top of a mountain.*

★ *Wear a ritual garment or choose a bedcover, sheet or pillow which you keep for this purpose only.*

★ *Light a candle, or several, by your bed, and watch them for a while as you contemplate your question. Then state your dream request aloud and blow out the candles before sleep. As the flames disappear, mentally dispatch your dream request to the night.*

★ *As above, but write your dream request on a piece of paper, and burn it in the candle flame, thereby sending it on its way into the night.*

★ *Pray and ask for your prayer to be answered in your dream in a way that you will understand clearly.*

* If your dream request concerns other people, place photos or letters from them around your bed to add to your ritual.

* Write a poem, stating your problem, and finishing with the precise request, then burn it or place it under your pillow.

* Take a bath in scented oils, or have someone give you a massage perhaps incorporating aromatherapy oils chosen to enhance your dream ritual.

* Choose all full moon (or new moon) nights as special dream incubation nights.

* Address your request to your Higher Self, the universe, God … whichever is appropriate for you.

* Picture a wise old woman or a wise old man, especially focusing on the infinite wisdom and kindness in their eyes, and put your dream request to this guardian of your dreams.

* Choose a ritual of your own.

4 *Place paper and pen, or a tape recorder by your bed to record your dream.* It is common to wake in the middle of the night with an illuminating dream which you are certain you will never forget, but which remains only fleetingly in the morning. Program yourself to wake up and write your dream down, or record it onto tape, as soon as you have experienced it.

5 *Don't discount a dream* because it does not bear any literal resemblance to your request. The dream may be highly symbolic, so spend time applying all the dream interpretation techniques you have learned from this book, and see what sense emerges.

6 *If you recall nothing,* or can't make sense from the dreams you do remember, try again for no more than three consecutive nights, then take a break. Be aware that any anxiety you bring into this procedure may block your recall. Practise.

Problem Solving through Lucid Dreaming

Lucid dreamers have a great advantage when it comes to dream incubation. The moment you realise you are dreaming you can take control of the situation and bring in all the people and tools that you need to answer your question. You can speak to estranged lovers and hear their answers, talk to the boss about your chances of promotion, or experiment with the idea you had for that unusual function by staging it in your lucid dream. What you are essentially doing here is role-playing and looking at the possible outcomes. Even though you are consciously lucid in the dream, your subconscious and other dream input systems are in action too, so you can 'let the dream roll' and let the characters speak for themselves. This gives you access to knowledge of which you were not consciously aware before the dream.

In his book, *Exploring the World of Lucid Dreaming*, Stephen LaBerge quotes the inspiring experience of one dreamer who used to design new computer programs in his lucid dreams. He would take the 'problem' to bed and, when he became lucid, would flit over to his Sherlock Holmes-type parlour and invite Einstein around. Together they would sit and talk and write ideas down on a blackboard. A flow diagram would evolve as the dream progressed, and this dreamer programmed himself to wake up when he was satisfied with a new program. He would then jot the diagram down and try it out the next day. He reported that he found this method to be 99% accurate.

Imagine taking this approach a step further: bringing into your lucid dream all the computers or technology you do not have access to in waking life, or being able to kaleidoscope ten years worth of experiments and results into a 20 minute dream!

With that mind-boggling thought, I'll leave you to contemplate the enormity of your potential to truly 'Sleep on it ... and change your life.'

CHAPTER 19

Time Travel

The Reality of Time Travel

For decades now we have relegated time travel to the realms of science fiction and fantasy, and we love it! We have no real difficulty in comprehending the various sci-fi technologies and have built a pseudo-scientific knowledge about time travel from decades of following our space-age superheroes. Yet many people shudder at the thought of real time travel and scorn personal experiences with utmost sarcasm. I guess it is human nature to remain disbelieving until you have experienced something for yourself, just as much as it is human nature for others to believe anything they are told, no matter how fantastic, if it offers them hope. The truly open-minded attitude can be hard to find.

I have received far too many accounts of dreams which have later eventuated, from survey participants, private clients, radio contributors, friends and relatives, to have any doubt that we can and do often see parts of the future in our dreams. I am lucky enough to have also experienced this on several occasions.

A concept which seems ridiculous quickly reduces to the state of normality after personal experience. To precognitive dreamers, the gap between personal acceptance of a perfectly normal (for them) experience and the potential derision from others is too wide, and few are brave enough to risk losing their credibility in this scientifically conscious, rational world. We look over our shoulders and see, not too long ago, the persecution and humiliation that has befallen the outspoken. Yet we look ahead and realise that there is a crying need for people to open their minds to see what really is there. Clear vision and understanding of the universe should be our goal. We should be open to follow every lead, turn every corner and pass through every door in our quest to understand why we are here. Neither should we be held back by the technological boundaries of what can be scientifically investigated. What science may disprove through lack of tools or knowledge today, it may prove tomorrow. It often has.

> *My precognitive dreams have shown me that Einstein and his physicists may be correct and that time may be open-ended and circular with all events, past and future, happening simultaneously somewhere in space with my mind simply tuning in to the right frequency.*
>
> (Susan, sales representative)

Be assured, many people can and do dream of the future. Whether you choose to close your mind and wait for personal proof, or to allow yourself to look ahead to the 'what ifs' is your prerogative. This section of the book is concerned with dream interpretation, and it is important to realise that we can 'time travel', so we need to know how to tell which dreams are glimpses of the future, or of the past, and which need interpretation. Or is interpretation always valid, no matter whether the event has already occurred or is about to occur?

This chapter stays with the practical: how to sort the time travel dreams from the rest. You'll need to wait for Chapter 20 to learn more about the other dimensions of dreaming!

Precognitive Dreaming: Dreaming for Real

The following dreams were shown to be predictions of future events which occurred within 24 hours. In these cases, there is almost no time to question whether the dream was one needing interpretation or whether it was a preview of the day ahead:

I dreamed I was lying in bed reading the Sunday paper, as was my normal Sunday habit. My brother, who was dead, came into my room and said, 'Kate, my daughter, is getting married.' I had not seen her for some years, since she was a little girl. When I woke up and was reading the paper, there was a photo of Kate and her bridesmaids taken at their pre-wedding party!

(Carmela, tutor)

I remember as a small child dreaming of the small gift my father brought home from work one night. Mum was amazed when I woke and asked her to pass me the gift as I couldn't reach it off the shelf, let alone see it. I don't think she believed I had actually dreamed it would be there and that it was for me!

(Jayne S., home duties)

Part of this dream also occurred within 24 hours, although the final results needed more patience:

At a get together about two years ago, I met up with an acquaintance I hadn't seen for some time. By coincidence, the night before I'd had a dream about this woman's grown-up daughter. I've never actually met Kris but have known her mother casually for quite a while. I knew Kris had been married for about a year. Seeing her mother the dream popped back into my head, and without intending to I blurted out, 'Is Kris having a baby?'

My friend gave me a strange look and said no, her daughter already had a little girl who was six months old, and what had made me ask the question? I just laughed and told her I'd had a dream about Kris having a baby girl with blonde hair and the most delicate pale skin. That's what had struck me in the dream, how fair the baby was.

There were a few other people listening to the conversation and someone said that just proved you can't take dreams seriously because Kris's little girl had a mass of black hair and olive skin like her father. Anyway, when I arrived home later in the day the phone was ringing. It was my friend calling to say that her daughter was pregnant, had only just found out, and was keeping the news a secret until she and her husband had a chance to get over the shock. When the baby was born she phoned again, 'Well, she's arrived and guess what she looks like. All this blonde fuzz and the fairest skin you ever saw.'

(Mell, writer)

Precognitive dreamers often make their own observations over a period of time, so that they are able to distinguish between a precognitive dream and an 'ordinary' dream.

As with all my precognitive dreams and out-of-the-body dreams, these most often occur when I'm napping in the afternoon or the very early hours of the morning, or if I have been awake in the morning and dozed back off.

(Chiron, astrologer)

I have dreams and then I have what I call 'my dreams' which I know by the way I feel when I wake up, as if something has happened, or will happen. I feel really uneasy after a 'my dream' until I hear.

The first one I ever really took any notice of was about 40 years ago when a chap I was going out with at the time was with the Air Force in Korea. I was not overly concerned for his welfare because he was an aircraft mechanic and was based quite some distance from the war zone. In the dream there was fighting and two men were shot, a shed was burning and drums and things were strewn everywhere. Five men scattered in front of the shooting.

In my next letter from him, he related that he and two of his mates had had a lucky escape and the other two had been killed when a stray North Korean plane had strafed the base. Since he gave the date in the letter I was able to see that I had the dream when it was actually happening.

(Margaret, home duties)

Margaret's 'just knowing' feeling is common to many who dream precognitively, although perhaps we should look at the word 'precognitive' a little closer. All the examples so far have been instances where people have dreamed of something which has already been set in motion. Kate's photo was already in the paper, the shooting in Korea occurred around the time of Margaret's dream, and Kris was already pregnant (although the baby had not been born). The dreamers may have been picking up psychically (telepathically) the news of these future events from others.

In this next dream, Margaret describes the post-dream feelings which made her identify this 'my dream' as a precognitive dream. We don't know whether the actual events occurred just prior, at the same moment as, or after the dream, only that the dream took place during the night of the event. Note the more symbolic aspects of some parts of the dream (the coffin lid, for example).

About 20 years ago I had a very disturbing dream and when I woke up I felt quite strange. The dream kept coming back during the morning and I was so uneasy. When my husband came home for lunch he was rather quiet. A friend of his had been killed in Ipswich the previous night in a hit and run accident. His brother had been a regular customer of ours, so I knew him but had no idea what the other looked like. I described the man in my dream (quite different in looks from his brother) and my husband said this was him. I asked my husband who had told him and he said one of the Brad Prosser family when he was getting petrol. I asked if he had his little girl with him and the reply was yes. Then I related 'my dream' of the night before:

I dreamed I was walking around the Ipswich cemetery looking at headstones when Brad pulled up in his utility and got out with his little girl. We had a few words then walked among the graves and came to a newly dug open grave. As we were standing there a body sat up, said, 'Hello,' said a few words to Brad, raised his hand, waved and said, 'Goodbye, I won't be seeing you again.' He slid down into a coffin and pulled the lid closed on top of him. It started to drizzle with rain so we made our way back to our cars and left.

It turned out that it had been dark and misty when the fellow was killed.

(Margaret, home duties)

Amleh also reports waking with a strong sense of knowing when she has had a precognitive dream. Consider this:

I dreamed I was driving along in my own car with a truck in front of me. The truck braked and its brake lights lit up. I put my foot on the brake, but nothing happened. My foot and peddle went all the way down, but there was no more resistance. Then we drove on again and I was very wary now. Suddenly the truck stopped again and the dream repeated.

I believed the dream to be telling me that my brakes were failing, or were about to fail, and that I'd better check them out. I went to the garage, told the mechanic of my dream and told him to check my brakes. I did receive a wonderful derisive laugh and a pitying look from others.

In the afternoon, when I picked up the car, the reception was rather different. I nearly felt a form of reverence hanging around! A rubber hose, normally stiff and hardened, had been soft and dangerous. It could have collapsed in the next braking pattern when the vacuum was drawn through the tube. They replaced it for me and I was safe again.

(Amleh, receptionist)

Did Amleh foresee problems with her brakes which her waking action prevented? Was she already subliminally aware of her car problem, perhaps through subconsciously noticing a softness in her brakes? Or did the mechanics call her bluff and charge her for something that didn't need to be done? (The latter point was added to satisfy the cynics!)

When I was 32 weeks pregnant with my first child, I dreamed over and over again in the same night that my baby was born without much pain and passed to me clean and dressed in white and blue. I thought about it a lot when I woke and discussed it with my husband. I was still working at that time but felt compelled to pack my bag!

That night I went into labour and my baby boy was born. My first nurse of him was when he was 'clean and dressed'. The night he was born my father tells me he also had a dream of nursing a baby boy. They were not living close by and had no idea I was in labour.

(Jayne S., home duties)

Again, did Jayne tune into the future, or did she pick up subconsciously on the earliest stirring of labour? If so, how did she know the baby would be a boy, or know that he would be dressed before she had her first nurse of him? Notice here, as in Amleh's report, the compelling feeling that the dream was precognitive, since Jayne did pack her bag even though the baby was not expected for another eight weeks.

If many of the above dreams concerned events that had been physically set in motion, or which may have been sub-consciously picked up, perhaps they do not strictly come under the description 'time travel'. It was important to include these particular dreams in this chapter because these dreamers all described what it was that made them distinguish between a 'normal' dream and one which they knew would later occur (a psychic dream).

The following dream was experienced before the actual event was set in motion, with details that could not have been picked up telepathically within the same time dimension.

In 1940, on the last school day before the start of the Easter holidays, my teacher colleague asked me why I looked very absent and not happy at all. I told her I could not forget the dream I had the night before. I had dreamed I was at a cemetery standing next to the grave digger. Right before us were three open graves next to each other, and opposite these one grave only. There was a huge crowd of sad people. We could see more than one hearse approaching. My colleague thought I was silly to be upset by 'just a dream'.

On Good Friday, one of my inmates of my boarding house went with three friends to one of the most famous beaches on Java. In the afternoon we were informed that all four had drowned. Three bodies were recovered but the fourth was never found.

(Evelyn, home duties)

Other examples of longer term precognitive dreams are described in Chapter 6, Unusual Dream Experiences and Chapter 20.

It is always wise to be cautious about assuming a dream is precognitive in the long term. Quite a few people have frightened themselves because they have dreamed vividly of the death of their children, or other circumstances, when the dream was in fact symbolic of (for example) the loss, or death of their inner child through neglect. Until you have experienced the full impact of a 'real' precognitive dream, and then gained the personal experience to judge your precognitive dreams more precisely, assume a dream is symbolic. Take any action that would be sensible in case the dream is precognitive and then let it go. If you think your dream of your toddler getting run over by a truck is precognitive, for example, fence your garden then get on with life. If you think you have dreamed the lotto numbers, try them out. The idea is to be cautious and expect the dream to be symbolic unless it is proved otherwise.

Note Scotty's caution. He is a strong precognitive dreamer, and observes:

I've noticed a series of dreams over the last month or so with extremely powerful symbols. These dreams seem more powerful than the ones used to describe my own personal traumatic circumstances. They concern war, guerilla activity, murder, POW camps, devastated countryside, poor townships, armies, soldiers, refugees, escape scenes, caves and general despair. I gained an impression that these events will happen in two to five years and I don't know if they refer to my personal life, to future conflict in Australia or to economic depression.

(Scotty, petrol tanker driver)

As Scotty's experience shows, not only might we confuse the literal (world chaos) with the symbolic (present-day inner conflict and emotional upheaval), but we might also think we are dreaming of the world's future when we are dreaming of our personal future. Scotty will guard against any possible future despair for himself by being forewarned and taking any necessary action in his life now.

I often dream about things that later happen, although not in the way that I'd expect. After the event I say, 'So that's what the dream meant.'

(Kate, unemployed)

If you believe your dreams contain long-term predictions, write them down and give them to someone. Take any reasonable but very cautious action if you feel you must. Take care to interpret the dream symbolically in terms of what may occur in your own life unless you make positive changes. If your precognitive dream seems to show a great long-term future for you, note the clues and cautiously hasten it on.

If I dreamed something has happened, I feel sure I'm able to make it happen in real life.

(Kate, unemployed)

The Precognitive Dreamers' Discussion

Twenty dreamers from the dream survey who had strong experiences in precognitive, lucid or other unusual aspects of dreaming met at my house in mid-1993 to record a discussion. This was a great opportunity for these people who rarely had the chance to talk to other strong dreamers and it was also a heart-warming experience for me after several months of communicating through the mail and over the phone! Some of the quotes contained in this book were taken from that afternoon, but here (and in future chapters and Appendix A) is a small part of the discussion on precognitive dreaming.

Jane Anderson: 'How often do your precognitive dreams occur?'

Six people said they experienced precognitive dreams about once a fortnight while two people said once a week. Seven said their dreams were random.

My precognitive dreams about work usually happen within one or two days, but with other areas of my life it can take up to two weeks. I have a precognitive dream around once a fortnight.

(Scotty, petrol tanker driver)

Jane Anderson: 'How long does it take before your precognitive dreams come true?'

The common response was 24–48 hours.

I have two kinds. One, on the trivial level, happens within days, but the other on births and deaths can happen within months or years.

(Mell, writer)

Jane Anderson: 'How do you know which dreams are precognitive when you wake up?'

Experience.

(John, town planner)

Many shook their heads, still unable to pinpoint the difference at the moment of waking. Others were at a loss to *describe* the 'knowing' as they put it.

You've got to try to know by trying to take control the next night. This way you can go on for longer and ask more questions in the dream.

(Andrew, construction manager)

This opened up an inspiring discussion on lucid dreaming and other dimensions which is recounted in Appendix B, which is best consulted after reading Chapter 20.

Travelling into the Past

If we can travel forward in time in our dreams, then we can surely travel backwards.

Hypnotists have been able to regress thousands of people back to a time before their birth and then further back again to re-experience aspects of past lives. Many alternative practitioners achieve similar phenomena through applying different techniques. I do not have personal experience of this, but my husband has been privately regressed and consciously experienced (relived, in his opinion) several lives and times which proved to him, beyond doubt, that he has lived before. Do we experience past lives of our own, or do we experience past times, not necessarily lives we have lived, but see them through different eyes? Or do we enter a dream state, and put ourselves in a historical perspective through autosuggestion, a state which allows us to experience a dream which is symbolically relevant and immensely helpful to understanding our present-day relationships and challenges?

Various researchers have checked out details given through regression under hypnosis, and have traced historical details that the hypnotised person could not have known. Again the question is: were they tuned into their own past life, or into a past event, or into the surviving memory, spirit, or consciousness of a deceased person?

It may well be that thinking of life in terms of time at all is erroneous. Past, present and future may be the way we, with our limited perception, make sense of the world. Personally I lean towards an understanding of timelessness outside our day-to-day waking lives, but that will be discussed in Part Three of this book. In everyday language, if we can see the future in some of our dreams, we must surely be able to see the past too. That we can dream of the future is proved as time passes and the dreamed events occur. That we can dream of the past is more difficult to prove on an individual level, but consider the outlook of these past life dreamers. What do they perceive as the difference between a 'past life' dream and a 'normal' dream?

In Chiron's case, she dreamed of a shaman before she knew what a shaman was. For her, bringing back knowledge of something she did not carry in her conscious mind was proof enough.

When I was pregnant with my son, now five years old, I dreamed I was a shaman with the North American Indians. At the time of the dream I did not know anything about shamans. In the dream my elder daughter (in real life) had brought her baby boy to me. She had trouble feeding him and he wasn't well at all. My tepee was set up on a knoll away from the rest of the tribe. A few years after the dream I had a past life recall session where I 'discovered' I was a shaman in a past life.

(Chiron, astrologer)

It could be argued that we forget information, or that we store knowledge that we have seen on television, heard about or read, but which has bypassed conscious awareness and shot straight into the subconscious. Nevertheless, one approach towards distinguishing a past life dream is to do some research:

This felt like a past life dream. I was a crossbowman who had a hand chopped off for poaching in medieval times. I was wearing green-black leotards (like Robin Hood) and a black leather jerkin stitched in a diamond pattern and split at the sides. As I watched the official lopping off my hand, I was also studying myself. I was

Time Travel ☆

in my late 20s or early 30s with straight shoulder-length black hair. When I woke up I tried to draw the executioner's axe, but after three or four attempts I couldn't get it right, so I placed the biro in my left hand. I'm not left-handed. I closed my eyes and drew a perfect replica of the axe. I have since been to the local library and have placed the crossbows, costumes and that particular type of axe to around the 1350s to 1450s, in England, I think.

(Scotty, petrol tanker driver)

If we do travel back in time to relive the distant past, whether this is a physical journey of the soul, a tapping into everlasting consciousness of all that has ever happened in time (and all that ever will happen), or a replaying of some sort of cellular or spiritual memory, the important question for this chapter is: Should we apply dream interpretation principles to a dream which seems to be from our past?

If we have indeed lived many lives, why do we not dream of them more frequently? If we can tune into any aspect of the past, or tap into any 'past' consciousness, why do we rarely do this? My experience as a dream counsellor and researcher has been that any dream of the past has direct relevance to the dreamer's present life. If you have some problem to address it makes sense to go back to see the root cause of that problem. You may travel in your dreams back to your present-day early childhood to see where your block occurred, or you may travel back further in time to encounter some unresolved issue which is clearly still affecting your behaviour.

Since this chapter is concerned with dream interpretation, I therefore suggest that all dreams of the past are treated as symbolic and are interpreted using the tools you have acquired from this book. Ask yourself what you can learn from these experiences and how you can use this knowledge to improve your present life.

Further examples of past life dreaming are detailed in Chapter 20.

Summary

The best that precognitive dreamers can offer as a diagnostic tool for distinguishing time travel dreams from 'normal' dreams is a 'sense of knowing'. Over a period of time, individuals notice specific pointers, such as the best time of day to time travel, but these conclusions vary from person to person. The best advice appears to be to make your own observations.

If you travel in time, seeing the future or the past, keep a journal. As well as recording the date, time and details of your dream the next morning, write down whether you think it was a case of time travel or a 'normal' dream. Jot down notes to support your assumptions. Over a period of time, look back for hints of a pattern in your dreaming or in your waking thoughts and feelings about the nature of your dreams.

Be cautious about jumping to conclusions about possible precognitive dreams, but take reasonable care to protect your future or reasonable steps to enter the proverbial lotto coupon or to initiate possible changes for the better in your life. Above all, *always, always, always* consider the possible symbolic significance of your dreams, even if you are sure they refer to the past, or even if they do later come true. Whatever happens in your outer life, whether past, present or future, always has personal meaning on an inner level, if you care to see it.

CHAPTER 20

Housekeeping or Voyaging the Astral Plane?

Where Do We Really Go When We Dream?

Where do we really go when we dream? Do we travel the astral planes of dimensions beyond the physical universe, freed from the constraints of both physical body and time? Do we commune with the spirit world, interact with our living friends, share in learning and healing experiences, exchange notes with extraterrestrials, talk with God, Buddha or our Dreamtime ancestors? Do we then return to waking life with a dose of amnesia or a limited ability to comprehend the enormity of our travels, leaving us with inadequate impressions called 'dreams'?

Or do we journey the hills and valleys of the contours of our physical brains, mentally flicking the dust off old memories, cleaning out the crevices of useless behaviour patterns and processing and filing yesterday's experiences and thoughts? Deep in the computer-like centres of our brains, do we monitor the biophysical feedback systems to get a mental snapshot of our physical health while we check out the neurological wiring along the way?

Are our dreams the symbolic memory of our mind-body housekeeping, or are they remnants of a greater experience in another dimension: the 'astral plane'? Or are they both? Or are they the same thing?

The emphasis until now in Part Two of this book has been on how to interpret dreams in terms of the mind and body, so we cannot give justice to this question without first examining the case for the astral: the soul.

The phrases 'astral travel' and 'astral plane' are widely used in everyday language, but there appears to be much confusion and uncertainty about what these phenomena are, and whether they are 'real'. One person will say, 'I astral travel every night when I dream. That's what dreaming is!' while another will say, 'I've dreamed I've been all over the world, looked at the earth from the stars, had lucid and precognitive dreams, but I'm really looking forward to doing some astral travelling!'

This chapter is concerned with the question of the astral in dreams: is it 'real', imagined, or make-believe, and how does all of this fit in with dream interpretation?

Astral Travel and the Astral Plane: Towards a Definition

My twelve year old daughter looked over my shoulder at the computer screen and said, 'That's not how you spell *plain*!' It transpired that she had always envisaged the 'astral plane' as the 'astral *plain*', a kind of big, flat starry stretch of *land* somewhere off the planet earth. There has been much confusion with the terms 'astral travel' and 'astral plane'. According to *The Concise Oxford Dictionary*, 'astral', in this sense, means 'Relating to or arising from a supposed ethereal existence with oneself in life and surviving after death.' It gives 'ethereal', in this context, as 'heavenly, celestial', and 'plane', in astral terms, as 'level of attainment or knowledge'. Of course, 'plane' is also used to imply a different dimension or perspective of experience.

In simple language, I suggest the following definitions capture the flavour of the dictionary definitions:

Astral plane: A level or dimension of learning which is experienced by an immortal soul.

Astral travel: The process of experiencing the soul as a separate part of our being which is not constrained by the whereabouts of the physical body (place) or time.

Since astral travel, by this definition, is associated with freedom from the physical body, we need to look at the ways in which we do free ourselves from our bodies before we can consider which of these, if any, are astral experiences and how astral travelling does or does not relate to dream interpretation.

Freedom from the Physical Body

The Out-of-the-Body Experience (OBE)

Basically you have had an OBE if you have experienced the sensation of existing at a location outside your physical body. This may occur while your physical body is awake, asleep, unconscious, under anaesthesia, clinically dead or traumatised. In cases of severe physical trauma, the OBE is also known as a 'near-death experience' and may be accompanied by experiences of travelling through tunnels towards a white light, or of reaching the white light and conversing with other 'body-less' beings.

OBE reports range from a slight feeling of physical detachment from your body, through to experiencing yourself as a totally different 'entity' from the body which you can see lying on the bed, having complete freedom to go wherever you wish at whatever speed, perhaps even instantaneously. Somewhere between these two extremes is the 'anxious OBE' where you experience a separate existence from your physical body while remaining connected to it by a cord and a sense of time restriction ('If I stay away too long, I might not be able to get back in my body again').

Waking Life Freedoms

My OBE had a profound effect on me because I was fully conscious. I have experienced the sensation of being out of my body in my dreams, but this awake experience has allowed me to look at the OBE from a conscious, even rational, perspective. I have to confess that mine was a restrained experience, since I was so shocked that I frightened my physical body out of its deeply relaxed state and shot right back into it for fear of not being able to come back. I wasn't ready to give up my life yet! (That was how I perceived the experience: 'I might be dying, and I've got too much I want to do yet.')

I had been lying on my bed one mid-summer afternoon, after a half-hour meditation, and was just thinking about wriggling my toes and getting my body moving so I could get up. I was fully awake and conscious, but still had my eyes closed, and became aware of the sound of the blood rushing in my ears while my heart rate seemed to slow. My head then lifted from the bed, followed by my shoulders and then my chest. My head rose to about a foot off the bed and I remember being particularly aware of the height of my heart, a little closer to the bed but still outside my physical body. The half minute or so of amazement was soon ended by the sound of my soaring, panicky heart rate as I fell back quickly, instantly chiding myself for being so cowardly. I have since had this experience a few times, and I am most definitely not in, or anywhere near, a state of drowsiness or sleep. Neither is my body numbed so that my nerves have lost a sense of where my body is and have made a 'mistake' in calculating my position to be a foot above the bed.

(Jane Anderson)

Did I achieve a mental freedom from my body through detaching physical input and using the power of my thoughts to place the centre of my mind outside my body? Hardly, in this instance, because I was not seeking to do so. I had finished a meditation and was not consciously injecting any thoughts into disassociating myself from my body.

The power of creative visualisation is indeed strong, and I believe it is possible to achieve a mental detachment through sheer will. This has been demonstrated many times through hypnosis where people have undergone traumatic surgery (or just plain 'painful' dentistry) and felt no pain. The power of the mind to achieve pre-set goals through techniques such as hypnosis, creative visualisation and affirmations has become an

The Astral Plane ☆

acceptable part of life. All things are possible when the mind is fully activated, but, personally, I have concluded that my non-programmed conscious OBE was an experience of the soul: a part of myself which is neither physical nor mental. Furthermore, my soul contains the 'real' me, because, when the two were separate, I was 100% in the soul, sensing the body more as an overcoat which I had taken off.

Dreaming Life Freedoms

I could measure the 'realness' of my OBE (compared to my normal waking life) because I was awake and conscious. My waking life is something that happens to me while all my conscious senses are switched on. The OBE was a fully conscious experience, and my waking life is a conscious experience, so I could equate the two and say, 'Yes, that OBE was real.' In my dreams, unless I am lucid, I have no way of comparing my dream experiences to my waking life, because, in theory, my conscious 'reality indicator' is sleeping it off. I may wake up and say, 'That dream was so real!' I may carry memories and sensations of a 'real' dream around with me all day, just as certain that I have visited a place I once knew, hugged an old friend, or taken an instant overnight tour to Europe.

How bizarre. I have a conscious memory of a dream and its 'reality', yet I was not conscious at the time (unless I was lucid). So what is it that we bring back to waking memory? Are we more conscious than we realise while we dream? Does our subconscious pass on a summary of the dream to the conscious self shortly before waking? Does our conscious self have access to our subconscious dream experience with an ability to scan and extract information which may get a bit garbled in the translation between the dream experience and the language of the conscious self? How can we bring back into consciousness so much of our dreams if these are 'only' subconscious experiences? Is the dream state a bridge between consciousness and the subconscious—a way of accessing what is not conscious and bringing it into waking reality? Are dreams merely our subconscious experiences bubbling up to the surface into waking recognition, so that we can improve our lives through conscious understanding of previously buried thoughts and memories? Or are our dreams a communication bridge between our conscious selves and everything else that exists, physically, mentally and spiritually?

Consider this sleeping OBE and the events that followed for Joe in the days after the 'dream':

> *The most vivid experience I had was 26 years ago while I was in hospital in Brisbane. I remember clearly floating through the corridors of the hospital, moving out of the way of nurses coming towards me, visiting every ward, looking down at the patients in all the wards. A few days later, after I was allowed out of bed, I walked around and remembered everything I had seen and all the patients I recognised. In two of the wards where there had been someone in a bed who was not there now, I asked, giving descriptions. I was told that they had been discharged the day before. This convinced me that it was not a dream. At the time I did not know what had happened to me.*
>
> *(Joe, catering attendant)*

As Joe described, he was able to check his 'dream' OBE observations with his fully conscious, waking life observations, and find rational explanations for the differences. He had been out of his body and did not class this experience as a dream. What kind of freedom had he tasted during his dream time?

Freedom of the Mind or Freedom of the Soul?

In our dreams we appear to enjoy a freedom from our normal bodily constraints. I remember receiving a phone call on one of our ABC Brisbane dream talkback shows from a man who had been a paraplegic for a number of years following an accident. He described how he always had full use of his body in his dreams, an experience which was such a relief to express that his tears choked the end of his story, but his impact on the listeners, not to mention the ABC crew, was stunning. A friend of mine has relied on crutches to get around for decades, but often has dreams where he runs or walks without them. People who have become blind often still see in their dreams.

Is the brain still able to generate sensations such as movement or sight to match the dream theme in the absence of the physical input of moving muscles and limbs, or nerve impulses from the optic nerve, or are these sensory experiences gained on another level? Able-bodied dreamers do it all the time—with body unmoving and asleep—non-swimmers swim in their dreams and many of us fly, float or 'whoosh' along. We can even close our eyes and 'just be there'. We are transported in an instant from the middle of a Sydney city street to Amsterdam, or from December 1993 to May 1962, and it all appears perfectly normal. We may dream of going through the process of having an OBE, of looking down and seeing our separate body, or even of dying (a common dream) and then flying off to get on with something else.

In short, whether we remember actually leaving our physical body or not, our common dream experience is to get along fine without it, or to have a new power to make it do things that we just can't do in waking life. In these cases, are we *physically freed* from our bodies, like a detached soul gone walkabout (or flyabout), or are we *mentally freed* from our physical bodies, free within our mind and our imaginings to roam at will? Are our dreams wanderings of the soul or wanderings of the mind?

Astral Travel in Dreams

According to our simple definition (see earlier this chapter), astral travel is experiencing the *soul* as a separate part of our being, unrestrained by the physical body, in place or in time, in or out of dreams. To know whether we astral travel or not, we need to be able to distinguish between dreams stemming from the mind and dreams resulting from the soul which becomes freed from the body. Is this distinction possible?

John separates these two possibilities into 'dreams' (the mind) and 'astral travel' (the soul), and describes how he distinguishes between them:

Astral travelling, as I see and have experienced it, is distinct from dreaming because the subject and detail that I see is as I see it (usually) at some later stage in my life. The people I meet, their conversations and so on are as I meet and talk to them at some later stage. It is a distinct feeling of being 'out of the body' as opposed to being 'within the mind' which is more the location for a dream. I have travelled the astral with one of my old dogs, something that may raise an eyebrow or two, but I have heard of other people who have had similar journeys with other birds and animals.

(John, town planner)

Some relate 'astral travel' more to a combination of time travel and geographical travel as in Jasmine's experience:

Astral travel: I was in a walled city, dressed in the clothes of the day, probably hundreds of years ago, a sort of Middle East type city. We were all going about our business when I looked up to the turrets and saw soldiers coming over the walls. I called the alarm and ran down a side street, as did everyone else. As I passed a dark archway an arm stretched out, caught me and said, 'Come, we have been in this time long enough, we must move on.' That arm was so strong and comforting, although I did not see who it belonged to.

(Jasmine, teacher)

Others see astral travelling as the experience of being able to gain another perspective (learning) on life, presumably from an astral dimension (the astral plane)—the dimension of the soul:

My father died in 1965 and then in about 1972/73 I had an extensive period of dreaming and astral travelling. On one occasion

I was able to meet up with the spirit of my father and look on as he was helping other people in his new life. Later I came to realise that my physical body was in fact a vehicle in which other souls were able to find shelter for various periods of time.

(John, town planner)

So far it seems we can only distinguish between soul experiences and mind experiences on a personal level. Each dreamer may or may not have his or her own sense of 'knowing'.

Categories of Dreams?

If some of our dreams are soul experiences, while others are mental or physical experiences, would it be helpful to categorise dreams into different types? Many survey participants found it easier to deal with their own dream experiences by forming them into categories. Take John's dream categories, for example:

1. Relaxation. 2. Emotional. 3. Prophetic, either symbolic or literal. 4. Review of events. 5. Astral travel. 6. As a helper.

(John, town planner)

We each have our personal experiences, and you may wish to look back over your dreams to create a structure that makes sense to you. Throughout this book I have loosely indicated 'categories' when I have referred, for example, to 'precognitive dreams', 'lucid dreams', 'symbolic dreams', 'literal dreams', 'time travel dreams' and so on. It has been useful to use the English language in this way and to give some structure to aid rational discussion. It has not been my serious intent to offer a strict categorisation of types of dreams because I don't believe this to be the overall reality. My perspective, which will become clear in Part Three of this book, leans towards an acceptance that dreams are experiences which tend to occur at three different levels: the levels of the body (physical), the mind (psychological) and the soul (philosophical or spiritual—the immortal connection with the true meaning of life).

Astral Travel or a Meeting of Minds?

Take a dream such as Margaret's, and ask yourself if this was a meeting of minds or a meeting of souls. Or did one mind 'pick up' on the existence of the other, so that Margaret was 'reading' her ex-husband's mind? Or was it all coincidence? Or, or, or what? What is your opinion of the evidence?

One night I dreamed about my ex-husband, that he was really ill and had great difficulty breathing. He was trying to contact me in the dream, and I could see how ill he looked.

I tried to dismiss it as just part of the break up, but deep down I knew it was not an ordinary dream. It got too much for me in the days that passed. In the end I wrote to him and said I'd had one of 'my dreams' and he'd know what I meant. I asked him if he could let me know if he was okay. He turned up about ten days later and told me he'd been in an accident at work and had been overcome by toxic fumes. He had been very ill and was still having chest problems. My dream was on the night of the accident.

(Margaret, home duties)

Perhaps the feelings described in this next dream begin to point towards a distinction between a meeting of minds and a meeting of souls. Since the dream is also precognitive, it begs the question of which aspect is more capable of looking ahead to the future: the mind or the soul?

In the middle of a long, complex and very real dream, I sat down at a table in a restaurant and looked at the man sitting to my right. I instantly recognised him as an uncle I hadn't seen for about 30 years. I probably hadn't given him more than a passing thought for most of that time. This man had a different physical effect on me than the other dream characters. I would normally have been happy to see him, in or out of my dreams, but there was something unusual about this meeting. It was as if I had broken through into another reality, but a reality that was 'more real' than my waking life. My body swayed, my heart rate rose and I felt anxiety choke my throat. I tentatively checked it was him by using his name. He showed me a magazine and told me he was selling advertising at $40 a page. I thought this was very cheap, then the dream returned to its previous story-line.

A few weeks later I received a letter from my mother, who lives in Britain, to say this uncle had just died (about four weeks after my dream). I received her letter on the 40th day after my dream. On reflection I felt that he had communicated this to me in my 'dream' but that I had confused the original meaning and woke up with a symbolic 'near fit'. Symbolically he had 'advertised' that I would read about (magazine) him in 40 days ($40). Since then, I have had similar 'swaying reality' dreams which have been later verified, and I feel these are 'astral meetings' rather than 'mentally tuning in', an experience which I know well. This new type of 'dream' is helping me to distinguish personally between symbolism, meetings of the mind and meetings of the soul.

(Jane Anderson)

Why Visit the Astral Plane?

For those who have personal experience of, or have faith in, the existence of an immortal soul, it makes little sense to live waking life without reference to what the soul is learning. If we accept that it is useful to interpret our dreams on a psychological or physical level to give us insight into improving our waking lives, then the same philosophy must surely be applied to the spiritual aspects of our being. In this context, dreams can either be a way of communicating more directly with your soul, or the souls of others, or they can be used as a springboard to free the soul from the body to experience and learn more in astral dimensions. This higher plane of learning, I believe, is open to whoever wishes to take the journey. We may elevate our dream experiences to this level to discover more about ourselves, or we may choose to interact with others, perhaps on a healing level.

To understand whether we can take these astral experiences literally or whether we bring back a distorted picture and need to interpret them as dreams, it is instructive to look at the astral experiences of some of the survey dreamers.

Healing on the Astral Plane

Several of the survey dreamers feel that they participate in healing while they are asleep and that some of their remembered dreams are fragments of their healer-helper roles while asleep.

I see faces just before sleep and I have been told these are people (in spirit and of this world), who are in need of help. I can't be positive but I feel that some of the people are shock deaths whom I have asked to be allowed to assist in knowing they are dead. I feel they come back to let me know they are okay—one friend in particular who was killed earlier this year.

(Regina, executive assistant)

Many dreamers have the experience of tuning in to someone who needs help, but often they don't realise this until future events reveal the original cause of their dream:

My mother had dreams like mine. I remember as a child her saying she'd dreamed the old Scots man who lived next door to her mother was calling for her to come at 4 a.m. and he was distressed. In Grandma's next letter, she told how the old chap had died at 4 a.m. on the night of the dream. There were 320 miles distance between us.

(Margaret, home duties)

I had an afternoon nap on this day, so I was asleep between 1 p.m. and 1.38 p.m. In the dream the whole room was grey and empty. Suddenly I felt weightless as if there were no gravity. On my left hand side I saw a television set. There was no picture, only scratching sounds and 'scratch marks' appearing on the screen. I was frightened and called out, 'Who's there? Do you come in peace?'

Suddenly, close to my right ear was a loud but croaky whisper. A man's voice said, 'My name is Martin.' By this time I was aware of a deathly cold around my ear, like frostbite. I told him to speak up but he replied, 'I can't because of my throat.' I said, 'I can't hear you very well and besides, you're as cold as a corpse, a dead man.' Instantly I felt a 'whooshing' like being pulled backwards. I woke up and I recall my right ear was almost 'frozen'. I went to the bathroom to apply a warm towel when the phone rang. It was my ex-boyfriend to tell me that a friend of his, Martin, was dying of throat cancer. He died in hospital later that week.

(Eloise, unemployed receptionist)

It is possible that both of these dreamers have responded to the call for help, and that the memory of doing this has been obliterated by the morning light. If you have this kind of dream and are willing to be of spiritual assistance to others, you may wish to consider doing so. It is wise to realise that if you accept that communication with other spiritual beings (alive or dead) is possible, then you should perhaps also accept that among the well intentioned souls in need of direction and help are those who carry negativity, or who are destructive to themselves and others. Before dedicating yourself to being available as a helper on the astral plane, do whatever feels right to you in consideration of your beliefs to protect yourself from taking on any negativity from such souls. If you are completely blank on this, a good method is to mentally draw perfect (divine) white light down through the chakra at the crown of your head and let it fill your whole body. Let the white light spill out through your pores until it forms a protective covering or 'aura' around you. Mentally seal the outer layer against negativity, leaving gaps which allow only positivity to go through in either direction. Ask this divine source for protection and for guidance to help in a way that is for the highest good of all concerned. If you feel inadequately prepared for this, or feel unsure, read other literature on this subject, but use only that which feels right for you.

228

If all this seems totally way out to you, take a wide berth, but keep an open mind. As your dream experiences accumulate, you may well find yourself turning back to these pages one day. It would be totally irresponsible of me to allow this chapter to be published without including the above paragraph on spiritual protection.

Sharing Astral Plane Experiences

I lived with my sister when we were going to art school together. We often went astral travelling together and would write down our dreams the next morning. We'd do things like go from Sydney to the Blue Mountains where we were brought up. She would go and visit her friends and I would visit my children, then we'd link up before coming back. Through that one year of living together and dreaming together we became really close. We always know what the other is going through.

(Robyn, sculptor)

Casebook: Astral Travelling or Housekeeping?

The following dreams are presented to challenge you. Take each dream separately and ask yourself whether these are astral experiences (the soul) or housekeeping experiences (clearing out the mind and body) ... or somewhere between the two.

Dream 1 Future Perspective

As the dream begins, I am looking out across a barren landscape where everything is brown. There are no trees, shrubs or grass. Off to my right is a rocky headland which juts out to sea. A huge man is set into the cliff. There is a line across his head from which emanates a waterfall of tears. The river of tears flows down upon the desolate earth, but it is too late. I realise the enormity of the situation and look to the sea. Suddenly I am 40 feet under the water standing on the sandy bottom, but I can still breathe. The colours in the water are intense and crystal clear.

Three grey shapes approach quickly and I am afraid until I recognise them as dolphins. I am aware of their immense power and perfect mastery of their domain. A loud singing 'thought message' comes from them. 'Have faith, you will survive the age of destruction.' They veer away, still in formation and look right into my eyes. Such joy, wisdom and compassion. Immediately they break the surface, the dream finishes.

The part that intrigues me the most is the cliff man's dress: gold buckled shoes, brown breeches, brown coat and ruffle instead of a collar on his shirt. I also didn't know whether the dolphins meant me personally, or 'you' as a race of people.

(Robyn, sculptor)

Dream 2 Learning on the Astral

Introduction: *Do you feel that dreams are sometimes a way for your subconscious to cover up what people are doing in their sleep? I believe that some people are very active while sleeping (e.g. learning in other dimensions, giving or receiving healing, etc.) and that dreams are a coded form of what we are actually doing, hence the sometimes scrambled nature of dreams.*

(Serena, administration officer)

Dream: *I seemed to be in a place down on the Gold Coast where people were learning some sort of tarot. A man came in and I was mystified about him. I wanted to know all about him. He never said a word. Next thing I knew I was in a hospital situation and this mystery man was in a bed. I wanted to know more and they told me what was happening. He was having a vasectomy. Next thing I am in a learning situation in a museum type place, looking at all the things on the walls. Someone was with me all this time. The teachings on the wall were like a family tree with the word 'philosophy' at the centre. I remember asking the person with me if we were in a lift as I could feel us going down slowly, just like being in a lift.*

(Jayne A., home duties)

Dream 3 Cushioned on Air

If my dreams are ways of experiencing qualities of the inner me then I can find parallel situations and personalities to coincide with what I have imagined. Still, there are some other areas which I find hard to explain. I had a most unusual dream the other night which has been on my mind since then. After dreaming this particular dream I went on to dream various other things throughout the night but when I got up it was this one particular aspect which I just couldn't help but feel had been real. I'm sure we all dream things which appear lifelike, but this was so real that I would swear on a Bible it had actually occurred.

Basically I was overseas, projected into the future and a friend of mine from England, with whom years ago I felt I was in love, was there with me. We were looking at something and he began to hold me and show me varying degrees of affection. It was not a sexual dream, more a sensuous encounter that left me feeling as though I had honestly felt his presence.

It is as if we were in strange surroundings. I remember feeling very lightweight as if cushioned on air and it was definitely in the future tense. Even now, days later, I can still feel the warmth of his clothed body against mine. That's how real it was to me.

(Rowyn, student)

Dream 4 Twilight Cat

I know I was asleep when a voice said, 'Look above you', and I saw my white cat on the bedside cabinet. My reply was, 'I don't care as long as it doesn't jump on my head.' The cat came onto the bed, walked down the side of me and passed to my husband's side. I woke up and went to the toilet and about half an hour later, while still awake, the above events happened exactly.

(Jane, cook)

Dream 5 Reliving the Past

I am involved in family history research and particularly during the last six months I have been producing a detailed book. Photos are always greatly prized and sought. Then I had a 'dream':

I was sitting at the huge dining room table in my paternal grandmother's very old home. I was a child aged about eight to ten years and I was looking through an old photo album. I could smell the familiar odour of their much loved old house. My aunt, in her mid-20s, was coming and going through the room as the bedroom was off this room. All the furnishings and so on were totally accurate and my auntie's hairstyle and dress were totally accurate of the time 1948–50. She was telling me about the photos as she walked back and forth.

I do not have any impression at all that this was a dream, but an accurate re-occurrence of an incident that I have no conscious recollection of. I can only clearly remember one photo in the album.

A month later I rang an uncle, to whom I would not have spoken for more years than I can calculate, to ask if he had any of the old family photos that all disappeared when my aunt and grandmother moved to a new home. He didn't have any or know where any were, but during the course of the conversation he said my aunt had a lovely album with lots of photos a cousin had sent her from the Middle East during World War II, as well as family photos. I was very close to this particular aunt who died when she was only 33. I used to sleep with her and go through her things when we went to town.

On waking I had the emotional experience of having been in the presence of the persons involved and I did not intellectually accept that they were 'dreams'.

(Dorothy, retired teacher)

Dream 6 Lucid on the Astral

I dreamed I was at a girlfriend's house (although it was different to her actual home) and we were chatting, when I suddenly realised I had no recollection of getting there. I told June this and she laughed. I said, 'The last thing I remember is reading in bed and dozing off.' June thought I was mad. I knew if I was there in spirit I would be able to fly. So I told them to watch me as I walked down the end of the hall, rose up to the ceiling and flew back towards them. It scared the wits out of them!

After everything had calmed down, June and I went out to the back room for a cup of tea. I was touching June's hand saying, 'Look, my hand doesn't go through yours like it does in the movies.' Also I could feel my hand gripping the mug. More happened in this dream and then I found myself back in my body in bed looking at my bedside table and the things on it. I wasn't awake, this was still part of the dream. I went on to another dream from this point.

(Chiron, astrologer)

Dream 7 Aliens

I'd like to mention a dream I had when I was about ten years old, and it had so much impact that it has been stuck in my mind for all these years and the memory keeps coming up. In it my younger brother and I were sitting on the lounge room floor of the house we lived in at the time. We were playing a game of jacks, or something similar, when we suddenly saw what looked like a spaceship of about two feet in circumference, hovering just below the ceiling.

We looked at each other and froze as the spaceship hovered for, what seemed like, a few minutes. Then it slowly flew down to about a foot away from our heads and began letting off some kind of gas. I felt my consciousness fade and then the next thing I remember is waking up in a sweat with my heart pounding very fast.

Now, I'm not implying that we were captured by a UFO and I realise that this could possibly be a typical ten year old's dream, especially with all the spaceship and science fiction stories so readily available through books and television. But I mention this dream because it seemed so real and left me feeling strange for a while.

(Tara, medical typist)

Dream 8 The Lockerbie Air Disaster

I dreamed I was at a dance and I went out on to the back verandah and looked out of the window. A white circle appeared and my vision zoomed into it. I saw a large object burning in the middle of a field. People were coming from all directions, firefighters, police, etc. People were saying something about children and Christmas presents. This dream occurred in the early hours and I awoke around 10 a.m. (I had been out late at a Christmas party). I put the television on and

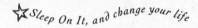

then saw what I had dreamed: the Lockerbie plane crash in Scotland.

(Chiron, astrologer)

Which Reality?

I have dreamed quite a lot of foreign cities and places where I am convinced, during the dream, that I am actually there. The amazing thing is that during the dream, I realise that it's only a dream and that I really am not in Paris or San Francisco and I am so disappointed that it's only a dream. Soon after this realisation I usually wake up feeling upset and disturbed.

(Kerry, student)

Does Kerry's experience capture the point where we discover that we have been deceived by our dreams? Or does she describe the moment we cross over from an astral reality into a waking reality, a transition which our waking mind finds hard to comprehend and, in the confusion, dismisses as irrational?

We are incredibly good at using rational thought to argue ourselves out of situations we don't understand:

In this dream I was speeding in my car and was pulled over by the police. At that point I realised I was dreaming and told the police they couldn't book me as this was only a dream. They didn't believe me, nor did the person I was with and eventually I was convinced it wasn't a dream and I paid the fine.

(Leigh S., mother)

I have also had an experience, at night in sleep hours, that I thought was real, but was so odd that I must have been dreaming: an alien dream.

(Amanda, astrologer)

Can we really ever be sure which is more 'real': our waking life, or other realities which we may access through our dreams?

The ins and outs of Dreaming

So we return to the original question: Are our dreams the symbolic memory of our mind-body housekeeping, or are they remnants of a greater experience in another dimension: the 'astral plane'?

My assessment of the evidence is that we have both housekeeping dreams and astral experiences.

The housekeeping dreams are largely concerned with tidying up aspects of the mind and body and can be viewed as experiences which are focused within the physical body, brain and subconscious mind. External physical effects such as light, thunder or a mosquito bite may have input at this level, perhaps appearing at the 'physical level' of your dreams. These dreams are largely symbolic. External 'power of the mind' effects such as telepathy, tuning into the thoughts or dreams of others, and perhaps some aspects of time travel may also come into this category.

The astral dreams are more concerned with the experiences of a detached soul and its learning and interactions in dimensions outside those of waking reality. I believe much of this experience is lost to waking memory, and that what we do bring back is often confused in the translation, surviving only as fragmentary symbolic dreams.

Dream interpretation. In practical terms, I believe it is best to consider all dreams, no matter whether you feel they are housekeeping dreams or astral experiences, as 'best fit' memories which are best understood through the application of the dream interpretation techniques you have learned in this book. I also believe that there is great value in looking at other aspects of life from the point of view of our first language: the language of dreams, but this idea is reserved until later in Part Three!

See Appendix B for an extract from The Precognitive Dreamers' Discussion on this subject.

The Astral Plane ☆

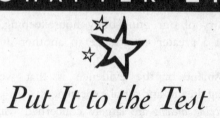

CHAPTER 21

Put It to the Test

I can't decide if my dreams are a symptom of my unhappiness or a cure for it.

(Polly, rose grower)

They are both symptom and cure Polly! The pleasure and joy you experience in your dreams is there to urge you forward: 'Come, taste this freedom,' they implore. Only you can make the choice. Do you continue to live with a gulf between unhappy days and beautiful nights, where the dreams are but symptoms of your unhappiness? Or do you read between the lines and see that, yes, a new life can indeed be yours if you are ready to drop the old and embrace the new, transforming the dream 'symptom' into the 'cure' you seek? Symptom or cure? The difference lies in the *action*.

Bring Back the Magic!

Now you have all the tools you need to interpret your dreams, but there is very little purpose in understanding your dreams if you don't act on them! The only way to bring back the real magic of the astral plane is to translate your dream experiences into a waking life action plan. Learn, learn, learn from your 'night school', wake up, interpret your lessons until you understand their practical application to waking life, then get on with your 'homework', or 'day work' as we should perhaps call it!

Cautiously test different approaches to your relationships, following the roles you played out successfully in your dreams. Take a step or two along a path suggested by a dream, or pay heed to a dream warning. Use something you have learned about yourself through a dream to work on attitude changes, or to fulfil a higher potential. Use each dream as a stepping stone to higher ground.

How Will I Know If my Interpretations are Correct?

Once you open yourself to your dreams, interpret them and start to pay serious attention to their meanings, you can expect your dream life to blossom. When you are ready, the dreams bring you all you need to know. Your dreams also give excellent feedback if you listen to them carefully. If your interpretation was a little off the mark, or your action was inappropriate, you are likely to experience a powerful dream which makes things clearer for you. This will be akin to a 'Wrong Way!' highway sign and you will understand the warning immediately! On the other hand, making a good decision based on a dream is often rewarded with a 'confirmation dream', which leaves you in no doubt about the action you have taken.

> *I first started to keep a journal and analyse when I was getting repetitive dreams. Once worked out, they haven't returned.*
> *(Regina, executive assistant)*

Recurring dreams disappear once you understand them and act to remove the blocks which cause them. Once a lesson has been absorbed and acted upon, it is no longer required. If you fall backwards at a later stage and slip into old behaviour patterns, an old recurring dream might reappear to alert you to the fact.

Some people dream in series, almost as if a new chapter is unfolded each night, with the same characters, same theme, but next scene. Unless these represent very long dreams broken over several nights, they tend to belong to a dreamer who is making progress in waking life. The dream scenes progress in line with the waking life advances. Day and night lead and feed each other, hand in hand.

The Value of Hindsight

How perfect our lives might have been had we had the benefit of 20/20 hindsight!

Keeping a dream journal may seem an onerous task, but if I haven't managed to persuade you to try it yet, consider its value as a tool of hindsight. Many people use a dream journal on a daily basis, writing, interpreting and moving on to the next page, never to glance back. It can be most instructive to read back a month, a year, or even a few years to follow the pattern of your dreams and the actions you decided upon. We see so much more clearly when we can look back with a more objective eye. Dreams that seemed difficult to understand a year ago because your comprehension was clouded by your emotional blocks at the time, can suddenly make sense. Flicking through the pages, a new wisdom often leaps from those past times. You suddenly notice that *this* dream contained good advice that you missed, or *that* dream obviously carried a warning of a future relationship difficulty which you later encountered.

While you and I may share many common dream themes, our dreams carry individual hallmarks, our own unique stamps. Just as one language dialect is distinct from another, so your dream language differs from mine. To intimately know ourselves, to catch every comment, every warning, every guideline, we need to study our own dreams with the benefit of hindsight.

Just Do It! Case Histories
1 Pack up and Leave
ACTION ON A SYMBOLIC DREAM
Background: *I loved living in my Sydney apartment. It was my first place on my own with my own special pieces around me and I*

had no intention of leaving after being there for five years. My work at that time was under liquidation. I didn't know which way was up, but I wasn't going to give up my apartment. I was going to fight and start again.

Dream: I kept dreaming that the muzzle of a gun was pointed at me, following me around my apartment.

Action: A friend said my dream seemed to say I was being threatened, that my lifestyle was going to change and that it was time to move on. Thinking about the dream I realised I was being forced out, but since the gun was never fired I had nothing to fear. I packed up and left Sydney after 12 years and moved back home to Queensland.

Result: My life since then has been very happy and a thousand times better.

(Coral, interior designer)

2 Working Relations

ACTION ON A LUCID DREAM

Background: In waking life I had an employer who controlled my very being. It really was unbelievable until I realised that I was repeating a part of the role of my marriage because my reaction to this man was how I reacted to my husband.

Dream: I continually dreamed I was in bed with this man and in one lucid dream I asked him why he did this and he answered he would do anything to keep me.

Action: I interpreted this to mean that in my job I was able to assert my rights without fear of dismissal. This I did and it worked. Although I then saw this man as weak, because of my spiritual development I determined to handle this situation with love and compassion, whereas in marriage I had desired escape and exercised resentment.

Result: It worked.

(Regina, executive assistant)

3 Transformation

ACTION ON A LITERAL DREAM

Background: *This was a very sad traumatic period in my life. It happened nearly ten years ago. I went to visit my brother who had inherited the family farm where I grew up. I had not seen him for some years, but his marriage had broken up and he was selling the farm, so my sister and I went for a last visit. We intended to stay for a week but stayed for two months as my brother had a nervous breakdown. I didn't want to leave him alone as he needed help.*
He eventually killed himself.

Dream: *I had dreamed that my mother (who was dead), my brother, my sister and I were standing on the front porch and the house was surrounded by black, murky water. My mother said to me, 'It's time to go now. There's nothing more you can do here.' I said, 'I'll have to pack', and she said, 'There's no time for that, you have to go now. Leave everything and go.'*

Action: *Two weeks later I left my house, my restaurant and everything that I owned and had worked all my life for. I went to Sydney with three suitcases, containing only clothes. I completely changed my life. The only person I knew in Sydney was my sister. I had no job and virtually no money as it was all tied up in the house and restaurant. I told my daughters they could live in the house and run the restaurant.*

Result: *I stayed in Sydney for nearly five years and when I came back home I changed my lifestyle again.*

(Carmela, tutor)

4 Resolution of the Past

ACTION ON A RECURRING DREAM

Background: *I dreamed for three days about an old boyfriend of mine. I'd accidentally met a friend of his which brought up a whole lot of memories, especially as I was not having a great time with my husband then. I was tired of dreaming of Trevor (the boyfriend), the same old dream, and then it changed.*

Dream: *Trevor started running after me, in the sense of courtship.*

Action: *I rang him and had a chat. He was astonished I'd rang and said he constantly asked after me and had not forgotten our last conversation on splitting up. I was able to release him from the 'hex' as it were, and told him I didn't always believe what I said back then.*

Result: *I have felt so much better since then and have no desire to make contact ever again. He no longer comes on the astral with me at night and I'm sure I have released him to get on with his life.*

(Frances, actor)

5 Waterscapes

ACTIONS ON UNIVERSAL SYMBOL DREAMS

Background: *Jutta was thinking about leaving her husband.*

Dream: *I had a dream where I was on a plane taking off from somewhere. My eight year old boy was supposed to be on it with me, and I thought he wasn't and asked the pilot to turn around. He was just beginning to do this when I realised that Allan was on the plane. The plane couldn't shift its position and went into accident mode. It landed on its belly in a field of cane. Looking out the window I could see all these bandits surrounding the plane. They were armed to the teeth with machine guns. Anyway, the door was opened, the sun was shining, the sky was beautifully blue and I felt so happy and totally fearless. I went out and stayed at a beautiful surf bay among friendly, active people.*

The dream shows Jutta's anxiety over whether her inner child (boy: relationship to the outer world, even though he appears as her own son) will be with her if she really does 'take off' and leave her marriage. In other words, will she be able to survive the challenge of the outer world alone? The confusion is shown by the plane crash. Her view of the future alone (view through window) is confronting and full of conflict, but the door opens (opportunity arises) to show quite a different future. The dream inspires hope of a bright future once she takes the risk and has her inner child on board with her.

Put It to the Test ☆

Action: *Very soon after that dream I left my husband.*
Result: *Jutta stayed away and moved to the coast.*

6 If Only I Had Listened To My Dreams

INACTION ON WARNING DREAMS

Background: *When I was 32, I was trying to recover from the break-up of a close relationship. We had been apart for almost a year when I met a man who seemed like 'all my dreams come true'.*

Dream 1: *I dreamed that the first man came to my house and was trying to tell me something. Whatever it was, we didn't agree. I realised that I was naked. I sent him away, but as I opened the door to let him out, three children came rushing into my house and down towards the back (living area) in a very noisy, disruptive fashion. The back of the house, which in real life was open to a garden, suddenly seemed to have been built into a rock face. There was no back exit. It was like a womb.*

Maeve was naked showing her vulnerability after her disagreement with her previous lover. Her vulnerability, the dream warns, may leave her open (door) to invasion: likely to get trapped.

Action: *None. The new relationship developed.*

Dream 2: *I was asleep in my bed and I saw a man outside my room (although that room had no windows to the area where he was). He was loitering at the entrance of the house as if he hoped I would let him in. It was night and I felt there was something wrong about the way he was there, as if he would bring trouble. I felt that there were presences there who were looking after my interests, who were trying to move him away.*

Action: *Because this dream contradicted everything I actually felt about the man in my dealings with him, and everything I hoped for, I ignored it. I did let him into my life and I married him after I became pregnant to him.*

Dream 3: *Prior to the wedding I dreamed I was walking through a* village setting on my way to the church. I had on a sort of wedding dress, but my feeling was that this walk among the people who had come out of their homes to see me was sort of impromptu and not really what I would have planned for myself. As we got closer, I realised that I didn't have a bouquet. My feeling was that some of the people in the procession looked down their noses at me. I panicked, but people started pulling flowers out of their front gardens to make into a sort of posy for me. The wedding went ahead, but I felt it was all very raggle-taggle and disorganised.

Action: None. The wedding went ahead as planned.

Result: In life the marriage turned out to be a disaster. He was a chronic liar. Nothing he had said about himself was true. His friends and family (what few there were of them) deliberately kept information from me. He was already married and had not obtained a divorce. Therefore our marriage was bigamous. His business dealings and educational qualifications were non-existent. He cheated money from people and was soon charged with fraud. At that point he explained that there had been some confusion in his dealings and that there had been no wrongdoing on his part, although he may have made an overly generous and poor business decision. The extent of his lies was only gradually uncovered by me, and the next dream occurred, I think, after the first visit from the fraud squad but before charges were laid.

Dream 4: He and I were running away from people in authority who were gaining on us. We started running down a hill. I felt that our pursuers were not really interested in me, so I rolled myself into a small ball and hid behind a log. I was hoping my husband would have the sense to do the same thing, but he kept running and they were gaining on him. Soon I was the only person 'in the picture'. I did not find out what happened to him.

Result: Many people helped me after I made the decision to leave my husband (who was in gaol). A very significant number were people who were previously unknown to me and whom I have not met since. They helped me when they saw that I was panicking.

Each gave me what they could. Some of the people from whom I expected assistance chose to make things difficult for me instead.

(Maeve, writer)

7 Making Peace with the Past

ACTION ON A TELEPATHIC OR PRECOGNITIVE DREAM

Background: *My father left us when I was very small and I hadn't seen him for years and years.*

Dream: *I dreamed that he wanted to see me or needed me.*

Action: *My mother would have been very hurt if I had gone, and anyway, he lived in Victoria and I in Queensland, so I wrote to him saying that there were no hard feelings on my part, and how sorry I was all those years not to have had a whole family.*

Result: *There was no answer to my letter and we found out two months later that he had since died after being very ill with emphysema.*

(Sandey, retired)

8 No Regrets

ACTION ON A SYMBOLIC CONFIRMATION DREAM

Background: *I had a strong psychic feeling about coming to the Gold Coast, and plans were under way to make the move to Queensland.*

Dream: *I was on the highway, when there was a ray of light over the Gold Coast, like a multi-coloured rainbow. There was a strong feeling associated with the dream.*

Action: *When I awoke the next morning I wrote in my journal that I knew I was coming to the right place. This dream really confirmed my decision to come to the Coast.*

(Yvonne, charity worker)

9 Love Conquers All

ACTION ON A TELEPATHIC OR PRECOGNITIVE DREAM

Background: *My husband is quite a bit older than me and I had* known him on a casual basis for years. I thought of him as a friend, and if anyone had told me that I would marry him, I would have laughed. He was unhappily married, but didn't believe in divorce. Our paths diverged for quite a long time then we met again. He told me he had been in love with me many years before, but I didn't take this seriously. At that time he was cantor at the church and I was in the choir. After driving home one night he kissed me and I was very angry and pushed him away. To this day I don't know why I was so enraged. I barely spoke to him for a year although I was impressed by the fact that he was always friendly and polite. I began to believe I was an idiot.

Dream: Then I dreamed he was sick and I was very upset. I awoke thinking, 'I believe I'm in love with him!'

Action: When I arrived for the next service I was told, 'Simon's not here, he's sick.' The following week I started being very friendly.

Result: The rest, as they say, is history.

(Fiona, retired medical secretary)

10 Sensing Danger

ACTION ON A PRECOGNITIVE WARNING DREAM

Background: I grew up on a property in western Queensland. One night I had a premonition dream.

Dream: I dreamed that I was shot in the stomach by a gun. I heard the gun go off, felt the impact and smelt the gun smoke. Then I put my hands to my stomach and felt the blood gushing out. It felt warm and it flowed over my fingers. I felt myself thinking, 'I'm dying, but I don't feel any pain.' The dream was frightening because it was so real.

Action 1: A few months after the dream, when I was sweeping the back verandah where the unloaded guns were stored, I felt the same fear as I had experienced in my dream. I felt this was strange because I had swept the verandah many times since the dream and hadn't felt anything. I stayed clear of the guns and soon forgot about it.

Result 1: That night my father went to the rifles on the verandah.

He occasionally used to shoot up in the air to scare away wild pigs if they got into the vegetable garden. Anyway, the next minute we could hear him yelling and he came and asked us if anyone had touched the guns. He said the 22 was loaded and if anyone had knocked it, it could have gone off.

Action 2: *About a year later I was with my brother when he was practising shooting old tin cans. When he was finished he unloaded the gun. As we were walking home we were talking and he had the gun pointed straight in front of him as he was describing something, rather than down to the ground which is the correct manner. We didn't worry on this one and only occasion because the gun was unloaded. However, when I walked in front of the gun I got the same feeling again as I had in the dream, but really strong. I couldn't breathe properly and I started to sweat. When he asked what was the matter I told him that the gun was loaded and to be very careful. He said I was silly because I saw him unload it.*

Result 2: *To prove it, he pointed the gun to the air and pulled the trigger. The gun went off. We both screamed.*

(Morag, research student)

CHAPTER 22

Summary:
Interpretation Guide

The Tree of Discovery (see pages 250–251) guides you towards interpreting your dreams according to the methods and insights you have acquired from the Magician on the Astral Plane.

Start at the base of the tree, where you awake from the dream and write it down. Select seven different coloured highlighter pens to highlight the separate branches, as shown:

Purple: Universal/shared symbols (Chapters 9 and 10)
Blue: Personal symbols (Chapter 11)
Pink: Feelings and emotions (Chapter 12)
Green: People (Chapter 15)
Yellow: Clichés, puns, 'telling words' (Chapter 13)
Dark red: Actions: active (Chapter 14)
Light red: Actions: passive (Chapter 14)

Refer back to the appropriate chapters until this becomes second nature!

Move higher in the tree to work on these branches and contemplate their meanings, dividing the branches into smaller twigs as you grow in understanding (Chapters 9–15).

Now let your twigs start to *bear leaves and fruits* as you begin to tie your learning together and embellish the meanings which are beginning to develop from your dream work (Chapters 16 and 18).

247

Move up to the growing tips of the tree to see if your dream came to a satisfactory conclusion. Were all actions carried out? Do you see resolution? Or did you miss the end of the dream and need to work up here in the top of the tree on filling in the blanks? (Chapter 17)

Did you fly away from the dream tree and reach *other realms*? Perhaps you time travelled, experienced precognitive or spiritual dreams or indulged in a trip around the astral? Spend time here in waking contemplation (Chapters 19 and 20)

Take the leap from the top of the tree: *Go and do it!* Put the dream learning into action to improve your life. Start slowly and watch your dreams for feedback (Chapter 21).

Later, from the distance (up in the sky, somewhere near the rainbow!), some way further down the track, look back through your dream journal with the benefit of hindsight.

The Tree of Discovery

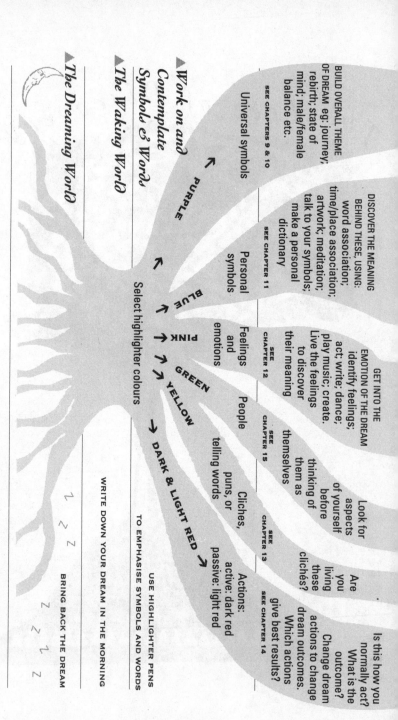

▲ Work on and Contemplate Symbols & Words

▲ The Waking World

▲ The Dreaming World

Select highlighter colours

PURPLE → Universal symbols

BUILD OVERALL THEME OF DREAM eg: journey; rebirth; state of mind; male/female balance etc.

SEE CHAPTERS 9 & 10

BLUE → Personal symbols

DISCOVER THE MEANING BEHIND THESE, USING: word association; time/place association; artwork; meditation; talk to your symbols; make a personal dictionary

SEE CHAPTER 11

PINK → Feelings and emotions

GET INTO THE EMOTION OF THE DREAM identify feelings; act; write; dance; play music; create. Live the feelings to discover their meaning

SEE CHAPTER 12

GREEN → People

Look for aspects of yourself thinking of them as themselves

SEE CHAPTER 15

YELLOW → Cliches, puns, or telling words

Are you living these cliches? Which cliches give best results?

SEE CHAPTER 13

DARK & LIGHT RED → Actions: active: dark red passive: light red

Change dream actions to change dream outcomes. Which actions give best results?

SEE CHAPTER 14

Is this how you normally act? What is the outcome? Change the outcome?

WRITE DOWN YOUR DREAM IN THE MORNING

USE HIGHLIGHTER PENS TO EMPHASISE SYMBOLS AND WORDS

BRING BACK THE DREAM

▲ *Enlightenment through Hindsight*

Record all your dreams, waking life events, thoughts and feelings
. . . and look back over them a few months later

Know yourself in hindsight!

▲ *Take Action*
CH 21

DO IT! DO IT! DO IT!

Slowly at first,
look for feedback in your dreams

▲ *Other Realm Dreams*
CH 19 & 20

★ ★★ ★★ time travel, precognitive dreams; astral travel, spiritual dreams . . .

Always look for meaning on an inner level too:
interpret your dream for deeper meaning

Past dreams: how do these relate to your present challenges? **Future dreams:** how can these help you now?

▲ *Find Resolution in the Dream*
CH 17

Did your dream have a satisfactory ending? Are all actions carried through? Did you miss the end of your dream?

To find resolution:
relax & re-enter the dream;
folded paper method; dream incubation;
create a new ending; meditate; day dream

▲ *Embellish your Understanding So Far*
CH 16 & 18

Write about your feelings

Go back for more/dream incubation

Meditate

Write a story version or poem, myth, or fairytale

Create your dream in art, dance, music

251

PART THREE

PHYSIOLOGY
PSYCHOLOGY
AND
PHILOSOPHY

Dreaming the Holy Grail

Dreaming the Holy Grail

Eyes shut
Tight
Floating.
Sideways I see
repeated
Repeated
All of them: Me.

A mirror
A mirror
Reflected
Yet, no ...
Open the door
Expand
And Just Go!

Look back
And ponder
The tiniest place
A speck of a planet
From up here,
In space.

Push through
Loud heart beating
Beside all else pale:
Sshhh!
I am dreaming
The Holy Grail!

CHAPTER 23

Physiology:
The Body and the Physical Causes of Dreaming

Is It All in the Head?

A small child I know told his mother that his dreams came from his pillow. Later he decided he saw the pictures inside his head. Throughout human kind's existence, beliefs and theories about the origins of dreams have been as diverse as the human race itself, but few dispute that the dream experience seems to be captured and replayed from somewhere inside the mind or brain.

   Some see the mind as being just another word for the brain, one and the same thing, so that the mind becomes something explicable in terms of brain biochemicals. Science has certainly shown the brain to be, at least in part, an incredibly sophisticated biochemical computer capable of directing and controlling the entire physical processes of human life from conception to death. Some 90% of the brain remains unmapped or apparently functionless. These areas may contain 'back-up facilities' in case of brain damage, be our 'unused potential', be obsolete or serve us in ways which are beyond our current level of understanding. So much about the brain and the human mind is unknown. Can we really comprehend the latent power of an iceberg purely by mapping the details of its tip?

Should we see the mind as a brain equivalent, our dreams as biochemically generated and ourselves as amazingly awesome cybernetic machines? Or should we look beyond the present limitations of scientific observation and rational experimentation and scan the metaphysical horizon for a more holistic, intuitive understanding of our existence ... and of the source and meaning of our dreams?

The Scientific Brain Work Begins

Although the centuries have been filled with conjecture and philosophising over the role of the mind or brain in dreaming, very little was achieved in hard brain science terms until 1953 when the Chicago based sleep scientist, Nathaniel Kleitman, was accompanied by his student, Eugene Aserinsky, as they observed sleeping babies. Aserinsky noticed bursts of rapid eye movements (REMs), discernible below the infants' closed eyelids, which seemed to appear at regular intervals and he wondered what this eye activity signified. The two scientists attached EEG type machines to the eyelids of sleeping adults as well as EEG machines to monitor their brain wave patterns throughout the night as they slept. When they compared the print-outs, they saw a correlation between the REMs and a specific brain wave pattern. There before them, in ink traces on paper, lay the burning question: Could these eye movements and brain wave patterns be related to dreaming, and if they were, could they be used to pinpoint exactly when their volunteers were dreaming? With such a 'dream indicator' tool, science would at last be set to answer the big questions: how many dreams do we have each night, how long do they last, what happens to our bodies while we dream, what is happening to our brains, what, how, why, when?!

The definitive test was simple. Aserinsky and Kleitman woke people up at various critical points during the night and asked them if they were dreaming, and, if they were, to describe their dream. People were woken in REM and in 'non REM' (now known as NREM) periods. The two researchers found that 80% of REM wakings were associated with recall of vivid, detailed dreams, compared to only 7% of NREM wakenings. In scientific terms, this was more than enough evidence to conclude that REM sleep was probably indicative of vivid dreaming. They continued to work in this field, as did others, to refine their findings and further research the relationship between dreaming and the brain. The results of several decades of this work are summarised in the next section.

Physiology and the Dreaming Brain Today

The Sleep Cycle

All mammals have sleep cycles which become obvious when their brain waves and REMs are measured during sleep. As humans, we fall firstly into a very light sleep known as stage 1, which lasts about five minutes, where the brain waves are very similar to our waking state. At this point, as we are just drifting off to sleep, we may experience 'hypnagogic' images: flashing, 'slide show' images which may or may not be 'true' dreams. We do not have REMs during this hypnagogic sleep which science has described as 'random images accompanied by thought'.

As time progresses we fall through stages 2 and 3 and finally enter stage 4, where sleep is said to be 'deep' because the brain waves resemble those observed in a coma. After some time, maybe as long as half an hour or so in stage 4, we then come up through stages 3 and 2 and, as we enter into stage 1, our rapid eye movements start and so, apparently, does our first dream. This whole cycle, from falling asleep to experiencing the first dream of the night, takes around 90 minutes for human beings and less for creatures with smaller brain stems. The correlation between the width of the brain stem and the length of the sleep cycle does seem to suggest an underlying physiological mechanism to the pattern of sleeping and dreaming.

We generally stay in this first dream state for five or ten minutes, before going through the cycle again, although we tend to spend less and less time in the deep stage 4 sleep, and sometimes miss it out altogether after the first cycle. The second time we emerge into stage 1 for our next dream, we tend to stay there for around twenty minutes. As the night continues, so do the cycles, but we commonly spend less time in stages 3 and 4 and more time in stages 1 and 2 as morning approaches. Although the time in each stage varies, the overall length of each cycle remains around 90 minutes, so for an eight hour sleep, we generally experience four or five stage 1 dream state periods, each longer than the previous. This is why experimenting with setting an alarm clock at roughly 90 minute periods during the night can help you to recall your dreams, since the chances are high that you will be rudely awoken in the middle of a dream with the experience fresh in your mind.

These cycles do vary from individual to individual, but we generally spend about 12% of a seven to eight hour sleep in deep stage 4, about 50% in stage 2 and roughly 25% in stage 1, the dream state stage. Whether we dream throughout this period is unknown

NREM SLEEP: THE 'NON-DREAM' STATE

People woken from NREM sleep do report some kind of mental activity. This ranges from vague thinking, or a persistent, night-long single thought to a non-visual dream. Some people report visual dreams during this period, but they are rarely of the vivid intensity experienced in the REM periods. In general, NREM experiences tend to be more like chewing the cud than seeing the action.

This period of less exciting dreams, or perhaps of dreamless sleep (depending on your definition of dreaming!), has been tentatively identified with the process of physical renewal. Increased growth hormone is released into the circulatory system by the brain during stages 3 and 4 of NREM sleep. This is the hormone largely responsible for growth and repair of body tissues. People who exercise in the afternoon or those who produce too much thyroid hormone (which, like exercise, causes a high metabolism) spend more time in these stages of sleep. People with thyroid deficiency (who produce no natural thyroid hormones) do not experience stage 3 and 4 of the sleep cycle, but when they are injected with the hormone, the normal cycle is restored. These kinds of observations have led scientists to propose the NREM phases of our sleep are periods of physical regeneration and growth.

So what is the purpose of our REM dreaming sleep?

REM SLEEP: THE 'DREAM STATE'

Some researchers call this REM dream state 'paradoxical sleep' because we are harder to wake while we are in stage 1, yet, according to our brain wave patterns, we are only sleeping lightly. As well as the rapid eye movements, which often seem to correspond with what we are dreaming of watching, scientists have detected small movements of the inner ear which they believe may be related to 'hearing' in our dreams. Our pulse rates fluctuate as does our blood pressure and rate of respiration. The brain consumes more oxygen while we dream and males tend to have full or partial erections during most stage 1 sleep. It is believed that women may secrete vaginal fluids during this stage too.

During all this activity, our major muscles remain flaccid, with only minor twitches breaking through. A part of the brain (pons) switches off the signals which are normally sent to the muscles to make them move. This body paralysis, or 'sleep paralysis' as it is known, is a safety mechanism to stop us acting out our dreams. French researcher, Michel Jouvet, found that making a surgical cut in this area of cats' brains resulted in the cats 'acting' in their REM periods as if they were awake. They would suddenly move as if enraged, afraid or in pursuit, often making the experimenters recoil in surprise! Jouvet was left to conclude that they were acting out their dreams, and that the pons normally protects against this. Sleepwalking and sleeptalking do not occur in stage 1, the dream state, and we tend to turn over or move about in bed in stage 2. We do indeed appear to be 'riveted' to the action during dream time!

In sleep laboratory studies, lucid dreamers have been asked to perform actions in their dreams such as singing, counting or holding their breath as soon as they realise they are dreaming. The results showed that when a lucid dreamer dreams of holding his breath, he also does so with his physical body. The brain cortex is divided into two hemispheres. The left (in 95% of right-handed people and in more than 70% of left-handed people) deals with rational functions (what we have called male, or Yang qualities) such as counting, whereas the right (female, Yin) deals with the more creative functions such as singing. When a lucid dreamer counts, the measured brain waves show the left brain is involved in the dream action, whereas when he sings, the emphasis shifts to the right brain. All of this is true, of course, for people who know they are dreaming. Whether it is valid to assume the same physical responses follow our non-lucid dream experiences is another question.

Newborn babies and congenitally blind people also have REM periods during sleep, even though they have not 'seen' anything in the waking world. While people with strong beliefs in non-brain dream sources would probably see this as a physiological response to whatever is causing the dream (a side-effect of the brain's experience of the dream), scientists tend to view this observation as suggestive of a physiological cause of dreaming. The thinking goes: 'Whatever physiological mechanism is responsible for the eye movements must also be responsible for the sensation of dreaming.' The scientific notion is further supported by a series of experiments performed by Michel Jouvet in 1959 and by William Dement in 1960.

Dement allowed people normal hours of sleep, but woke them up every time their REMs started. So, they had plenty of NREM sleep, but, supposedly, no dreams or REM sleep. The more his volunteers were deprived of dreaming, the more they attempted to make up for lost time. Their sleep cycles would change and, as the deprivation continued, they would fall straight into REM sleep without going though the other sleep stages first. After only a couple of days of dream deprivation they would be fatigued, irritable and often have slight memory loss. The next night of undisturbed sleep would be filled with more than the normal amount of REM sleep and they would awaken refreshed again. The 'control' volunteers who were awoken just as often, but in NREM periods so they still dreamed, were unaffected. REM sleep and dreaming, he concluded, had physiological purpose and both were necessary for mental stability.

Jouvet found that he could manipulate REM periods and dreaming in cats through injection of chemicals such as acetylcholine. When nerves send electrical impulses to and from the brain, they have to 'jump' the coded impulses across the gaps (synapses) between one nerve fibre and the next. This is done by releasing chemical molecules such as acetylcholine from the nerve tip which flow across to the receiving end of the next nerve cell in the chain and attach themselves there temporarily. This causes that second nerve fibre to generate the required electrical impulse which carries the message further on its journey to the brain for decoding or action. These communication molecules are known as 'neurotransmitters'. What Jouvet discovered, then, was that dreaming is probably switched on or off by the balance of chemicals in the nervous system. The sleep and dreaming cycle is now believed to be controlled by a kind of continuous competition between excitatory nerve chemicals and inhibitory nerve chemicals.

Many scientists see the study of the dreaming brain as the key to understanding mental illness (presumably in biochemical form), since many of the signs of mental disease, such as hallucinations, bizarre thoughts, disorientation, amnesia and delusions, are the common stuff of dreams. This was the motivation behind much of the earlier work with LSD and other hallucinogenic drugs which apparently switched on a dreamlike state without switching off consciousness.

In the month or two before birth, babies spend up to 80% of

their total sleep time in REM sleep and this is also known to be a time of fast brain growth. Senile people spend less time in REM, and their brain size is also known to shrink. Mentally defective people have reduced REM sleep periods. These observations suggest a correlation between REM sleep and brain growth which is, perhaps, necessary for learning or laying down memory.

Summary

There seems little doubt that sleeping and dreaming are necessary for our health, both physical and mental, and that the dream state may well be a bodily phase during which various brain and nervous system regulatory functions are carried out, but we are still left with the question of the source of dreams. Many see the dreaming brain as totally turned in on itself, generating its own sensory perceptions and creating its own dreams, but science shines no light here. This idea is like a television or radio that turns itself on, creates its own programs from its electronic insides, screens them, then turns itself off again. Much of this may be true, but I wonder what proportion of our dreams invisibly fly in on the wind, much like television or radio signals, generated by some distant source and requiring only that the brain be tuned in at the right frequency?

The Brain and Perception of Alternative Realities

The experimental observations with lucid dreamers who counted or sang their way through their lucid dreams under the eagle eyes of brain monitors (see above section) suggest that the brain (or, at least, the forebrain) is activated as if the dream is actually happening. It appears that the brain cannot distinguish between a dreamed and a 'waking' event, and that we are, perhaps, only protected from acting out this alternative reality by the pons area's sleep paralysis phenomenon.

It seems paradoxical that these assumptions about the brain's commitment to the reality of the dream have been based on observations on lucid dreamers who obviously do retain an objective awareness of the brain's apparent delusion! Is this lucid consciousness of the dream located in the brain, the mind, the soul or elsewhere?

Consider the Colorado experiment where Dr J. Stoyva fitted volunteers with spectacles which turned the world upside down. They had to wear the glasses for several days, and, during that time, they gradually saw the world the right way up again. The brain could not match the incoming visual information with other incoming information (such as touch or sound), or with its 'internal model' of what the world should be like, so it simply changed its perception and turned the images upside down again. When the volunteers' spectacles were taken off, guess what? They immediately saw the world upside down again, this time with their own 'bare' eyes. Within a short time, the brain adjusted by inverting the incoming messages to make everything fit in with the expected view.

This is, in fact, what happens after birth. The physics of the eye is much like the physics of the camera. The retina, at the back of the eye, is like the photographic film in the camera, and the world's image appears inverted on this screen. The message sent to the baby's brain is one of an inverted world. Trial and error soon gives feedback to the brain that what it sees is not, apparently, what it feels, hears or moves around in. The brain turns the image around accordingly.

So it is seen, from our earliest days, that our brain works to alter incoming messages about its sensory environment if they do not fit in with its expectations. The great magicians and illusionists rely on the brain's stubbornness in seeing what it expects to see, rather than what it actually does see! Such is the art of deception. We cannot necessarily trust the brain with what it deciphers and concludes about the waking realities of our environment. It does an incredibly good job, but it does not always get the picture right. It may perceive alternative realities that are not there at all. Just as often, though, it may apply rational restraint, and cause us to discount its genuine experience of dimensions beyond those of waking life. Can we, then, ever trust our neurophysiological wiring to distinguish between 'real' and 'unreal'?

Perceptions of the Outer and Inner Worlds

In active waking life the brain is generally occupied with the external world. It makes evolutionary survival sense to be 'tuned in' to the dangers around us while we are moving around our environment, vulnerable to attack or accident, or to be on the alert for signs of food, water or suitable mates. We see, hear, touch, taste and smell our way around our environment in search of survival and self-protection. We may tune in to other helpful cues about our external world through telepathic communication or, perhaps, a sensitivity to electromagnetic and other fluctuations around us.

If the external world becomes boring, or we feel safe and in less need of environmental surveillance, we often turn our attention inwards, monitoring thoughts, creatively juggling words, mentally painting pictures, daydreamingly having conversations with ourselves or others or engaging in wishful flights of fancy. Perhaps we drum up a more exciting, dangerous inner world to balance a boring outer reality, or indulge in a little negative self-talk, ruining our self-esteem and setting ourselves up for negative experiences with our outer world. We may later manifest some of these inner wanderings as novels, poems, paintings or low confidence, but while we are indulging in a little daydreaming, we are aware that it is 'not real'.

So what happens at night, when we sleep, to cause us to lose our sense of 'reality' and to live the dream as if it is real? Does the dream state feel real because there is little external input to measure it against? Does it feel real because the brain is adjusting the dream sensations to a 'best fit' scenario and translating them as being 'real'? Does the dream feel real because it is an alternative reality? Is there a waking reality and a dream reality and are these both equally real? Does the brain mediate between the two realities, or does it just fail in its analysis and perceptions of its sleeping activities?

Science Explains ... Or Does It?

Science: Sleep paralysis, the process by which the brain inhibits large muscle movements during REM sleep to prevent us from the physical dangers of acting out our dreams, can cause experiences such as Marina's:

Sometimes in the morning, my mind seems awake but I just can't function. I have an intense sense of peril, that if I do not wake I will die. The fear is very upsetting even some time after waking properly. I have tried to yell to someone to wake me up. Using all my strength the most I have managed is a half audible grunt or moan. I am completely helpless during this dream.

(Marina, student)

Science: Hypnagogic images are often seen as we drift into sleep. Described as a pictorial consciousness, they are comprised of consciously perceived random images or thoughts which can last up to ten minutes. Some scientists call these 'dreamlets', but they are not classed as true dreams because they are not accompanied by REMs.

It used to happen that as I was falling asleep, or was just very relaxed, I would have constantly changing images flashing through my mind, similar to a fast slide show. At the time I could describe each picture in great detail.

(Hannah, home duties)

I can watch these 'slide show images' and pinpoint the exact moment where consciousness gives way to a dream. I watch the images while checking on my level of consciousness by constantly trying to recall the previous 'slide' while viewing the next. This is easy for a few moments, then I pass through what seems like a minute of knowing I am trying to recall the last image but of being unable to do so. (It's like waking up knowing you've had a dream, but having no idea what it was!) The exciting thing is the moment of consciousness where you realise that the images change from individual slides into motion picture quality accompanied by sound and other senses. (You can use this moment to launch into a lucid dream.) This is often the point where your body 'jumps' or 'falls' as you let go into physical sleep. This regular personal experience has shown me that I often fall into normal dreaming immediately I fall asleep.

(Jane Anderson)

If my sleeping and dreaming experiences do not fit what science has proved, who is wrong? I may acknowledge hypnagogic sleep as being accompanied by a different type of brain wave pattern from later periods of dreaming, but if the images I see seem to me to be exactly like the kind of dreams I have through the night, why on earth would I want to dismiss them as 'random images accompanied by thinking'?

The dream survey research has shown that people can and do experience apparently 'normal' dreams within the first 15 to 20 minutes of sleep.

This dream lasted only a few moments. I remember looking at the bedside clock. It was six minutes past midnight and I awoke at 23 minutes past midnight.

(Joe, catering attendant)

Several people on the survey especially noticed dreams during short afternoon naps, and, in many cases these also had psychic or telepathic elements. One afternoon I dreamed I was lying on a beach in the sun, when four boys suddenly rushed up the beach carrying a huge black whale-like shape raised on their shoulders, in coffin bearing style, except they were running and making a noise. As they passed me they dropped the thing which made a resounding thump as it landed very close to my ear. I opened my eyes (in the dream) and saw the thing was made of matted grass. Later, when I woke, I told the dream to my husband who had been out for a cycle while I slept. It turned out that a big truck had surprised him by roaring too close and knocked him off his bike onto the verge of long grass.

Science: When the brain is still in dream state but the eyes are open, the brain may confuse which images it 'sees' are internal (from the dream) and which are external (the view in front of the open eyes). In many cases, the dream images can appear to be superimposed upon the waking scene, so that presences may appear before the dreamer's open eyes. Scientifically referred to as 'hypnopompic hallucinations', these phenomena are described as extensions of dreaming into waking, and may occur because the dreaming process is slow to switch off. This is David's experience:

> *One of my recurring nightmares involved steel or timber beams. I would dream that the beams would enter the room approximately two-thirds of the height of the room in the air and float across the ceiling before plunging at great speed at my head. I generally always awoke just prior to the final lunge. Often I would be awake and physically watch the beam float across the room. Sometimes I got up to ensure it would not hit me. A similar experience would be waking to see a presence. As it got closer I would often get up to turn the light on to assure myself the room was empty. Once awake I couldn't turn my back on it, I had to watch it all the time.*
>
> *(David, surveyor)*

Science can explain waking psychic phenomena, whether they be visual, auditory or whatever, as dreamlike hallucinations perceived as being in the waking world simply because the subject's eyes are open.

This certainly does not deny the clairvoyant, clairaudient or clairsentient experience which, in my experience, is an inner perception of an alternative reality. As far as the waking dream is concerned, two possibilities remain. One is the scientific view that the hallucination is the slowly disappearing dream, while the other is that the dream was a psychic experience which the waking dreamer has seen with her inner eye, but which she momentarily perceives as external in the transition to waking. In either case it is important to interpret the experience firstly as a dream to look for any relevant inner meaning.

Science: External stimuli are incorporated into REM sleep in about half the times they are presented, and are occasionally incorporated into NREM sleep. The external stimuli do not cause the dream, but they do work their way into the ongoing dream.

> *As a child I dreamed I was being kidnapped by guerillas and driven in a car rather like my father's to a cliff or waterfall and being tossed over the edge. I woke when I hit the floor after falling out of bed.*
>
> *(Geoff, priest)*

Dreaming About the Physical Condition of the Body

Hippocrates (around the 4th century BC), the father of medicine and a prominent dream interpreter of the Ancient Grecian Asclepian temples (see Chapter 18), made a special study of dreams which indicated physical disease. These were called 'prodromic' dreams (Greek for 'running before'). Aristotle (383–322 BC) explained the prodromic dream as being small symptoms of an impending illness that are perceptible to the sleeper, but perhaps imperceptible once the person is awake and involved in outer activities.

My research survey results uncovered many examples of dreams which picked up on physical symptoms, for example:

> *I broke my arm and wrist and it was in plaster. Just prior to having the plaster removed, I dreamed I was in hospital undergoing the removal of the plaster to find a deformed hand and wrist. I woke up, but a few days later I had the plaster removed to find the wrist deformed, as in the dream.*
>
> *(Martha, retired)*

> *My mother dreamed that the stomach discomforts she had been experiencing were caused by swallowing a silver threepenny bit in*

her childhood (which she never did). She had been having a lot of digestive disturbances and was booked in to have a gastroscopy. That day I picked up a free health magazine from the health food shop and I noticed an article about the sort of indigestion sweets which my mother lives off. The article said these tablets contain aluminium which can cause severe digestive disturbances. I gave Mum the article and said, 'There's the silver threepenny bit of your dreams: aluminium metal in your stomach!' The moral of the story was that she stopped taking the sweets and now she's well again.

(Amanda, astrologer)

My daughter, who is age seven, has a recurring dream which mostly comes up when she is sick. In the dream there are coloured balls of different sizes and colours which come and bowl her down.

(Rochelle, home duties)

Have you ever experienced, when you are really tired, unwell or in need of a boost of energy, a vision of coloured 'balls' coming towards you when you close your eyes? The colours can be quite enlightening, and it has been my experience, along with others', that different colours impart different energies that are needed for balance. Purple, for example, brings a psychic or spiritual balance while yellow tops up the flagging intellect. Red gives physical energy and enthusiasm while blue brings peace and healing. You've got to experience it to know it! Children commonly report the coloured ball phenomena, and knowing what colours they see can give guidance as to what they need in their daily life. Scientifically, colours are just visible wavelengths of light energy and energy always dissipates from one form into another, so the experience is not that bizarre!

I have been suffering from frequent migraines for about two months. I dream of an 'aura' on the night preceding the migraine. Predicting a migraine can't help me avoid it, I don't think, but it would help me plan or cancel my day's activities.

(Jayne S., home duties)

One morning, several months after receiving this letter, I was reading a scientific paper on lucid dreaming and out-of-the-body experiences, when I came to a single paragraph suggesting a possible connection between susceptibility to migraines and frequency of lucid dreaming. At that moment, my telephone rang, and Jayne S. came on the line and I was able to ask the question. Yes, she *is* a lucid dreamer!

This chapter has skimmed the surface of the physiology of dreaming, but it still poses the basic question: are we physical, mechanical dream machines, or is there, quite literally, more to dreaming than meets the eye?

CHAPTER 24

Psychology:

The Mind and the Psychological
Causes of Dreaming

The last chapter looked at the physical biomechanics of the dreaming brain and various possible physical causes behind dreaming and our perception of reality. The brain, many scientists believe, may be the source of our dreams, so that all dreams are the result of biochemical fluctuations, sensory input and self-generated neural impulses which are scrambled together and then sorted into a final composite dream based on the brain's previous experience of the world. At the other physical extreme, the brain may be seen as a sophisticated mediator device, biochemically equipped to capture, code and translate incoming sensory information from any level of body, mind or soul and present it to the conscious waking memory as dream recall. Science, it was argued, has been able to describe some physiological aspects of how the brain controls sleeping and dreaming, and it has been able to theorise on how the brain compares and perceives its external and internal sensory worlds, but it has not been able to elucidate the source of all of our dreams.

Whether you think that all dreams will eventually be explained in physiological terms, or whether you feel they connect us to a wider spiritual reality, the fact remains that we tend to see our daily problems, concerns or thoughts reflected in our dreams. This book has shown that careful observation and interpretation of our dreams can and do lead us towards self-knowledge and provide us with the tools for meaningful development of our full potential. Surely this is where we leave physiological science and enter the realm of psychology: the study of the human mind and behaviour in given circumstances?

Much of this book has focused on what our dreams can tell us about our behaviour patterns and attitudes towards ourselves and others. This chapter takes a brief overview of the history of dream psychology, and the 'mental' or emotional causes of dreaming.

According to the Ancients

The word 'psychology' was not used until the late 19th century, but what was the view of the ancients on dreaming and the human mind? Much of the ancient and classical focus was on the philosophy of dreams, which is presented in the next chapter, but were allusions made to the existence of 'mental' causes or aspects of dreaming?

The earliest records of dreams still in existence are probably those of the Ancient Egyptians, recorded in hieroglyphs some 4000 years ago, but information on dreams dating back to around 5000 BC was believed to be stored in the oldest known library, the Assurbanipal Library in Nineveh, belonging to Assurbanipal, the Assyrian King (668–627 BC). Clay tablets dating back to this period, presumably from this library, have survived into modern times. This archival material was believed to have been consulted by Artemidorus, a Greek physician living in Rome in the 2nd century AD, when he wrote his dream interpretation book *Oneirocritica*. This is the most complete treatise on dreams which has survived from the ancient world. It combined all that was known from Greek, Assyrian and Egyptian realms and went on to lay the foundation for dream interpretation for the next 1500 years or so! In fact, the 24th English edition of this manual was published in 1740. Artemidorus's work shows seeds of early psychology, but first, let's return to Ancient Greece.

Heraclitus was a Greek philosopher (*c.*535–*c.*475 BC) who stated that each man retreats in sleep into a world of his own. Here, perhaps, was one of the earliest allusions to the inner dream world, the world of the mind, of the psyche. Plato (427?–347 BC) saw a 'lawless and wild beast of nature which peers out in sleep'. Again this could be interpreted as an insight into psychology, the observation of our less socially acceptable mental inclinations breaking through to express themselves in sleep. Plato himself regarded our dreaming comfort with incest, murder and sacrilege to be due to our release from the rule of reason in sleep. This, he believed, freed the other two elements of the 'soul', namely anger and desire, to have full reign.

Bridging the Gap: Artemidorus

As we have seen above, Artemidorus took all that was ancient in dream interpretation, represented it, researched it, added to it, and published it in a form which became a credible point of reference for some 1500 years. In his words: 'I have done no other by day and by night but meditate and spend my spirit in the judgement and interpretation of dreams.' The result of his dedication was to see two classes of dreams. The first class were somnium dreams, which contained references to the future and were often highly symbolic. For these, he created a dream interpretation dictionary. The second class were insomnium dreams, which Artemidorus saw as the product of everyday life (much like this book's concept of 'housekeeping dreams') that reflected the dreamer's current physical and mental state.

He realised the usefulness of dream interpretation, writing 'Dreams and visions are infused into men for their advantage and instruction', and saw the key to understanding dreams lying in the conscious associations they evoked. This emphasis on personal association was summarised as 'The rules of dreaming are not general and therefore cannot satisfy all persons, but often, according to times and persona, they admit of various interpretations.' His 'body and mind' analysis of the insomnium dreams included looking at a range of physical and psychological aspects such as how the dreamer spent his days, the conditions of his sleep, his occupation and name, the dreamer's associations to the dream, the appearance of word plays and puns in the dream content and so on. In many ways, Artemidorus bridged the gap between the ancient and modern worlds of dream interpretation and his interpretation methods certainly reflect the beginnings of dream psychology.

The Birth of Psychoanalysis: Freud

Sigmund Freud (1856–1939), who was trained in both medicine and neurology, practised in Vienna as a neurologist with a special interest in the treatment of mental disorders, in particular, hysteria. He noticed that when he let his patients talk, they would often lead themselves from subject to subject by a process of association, and would frequently come round to the origin of their neuroses by themselves. Their neurotic symptoms commonly disappeared after this, particularly when some painful memory and its associated emotions came to light. He concluded that their physical or mental symptoms (headaches, rashes, phobias, delusions, etc.) were the result of these unconscious emotions which the patient had been repressing. The repressed emotions were letting off steam as neuroses instead. Once the repressed emotions were acknowledged, they no longer needed an outlet, and the patient recovered.

Freud also observed that his patients often mentioned their dreams and that this frequently led, by association, to the 'cause' of the neurosis. Freud saw these dreams as expressions of his patients' innermost repressed wishes. Putting it altogether, Freud concluded that his patients' unconscious repressed emotions manifested as mental and physical neuroses by day and as wish fulfilment dreams by night. In this way, Freud saw analysis of the dream as the Royal Road to the Unconscious, a previously untrodden path.

In studying dreams closer still, Freud developed the theory that the unconscious contains a part of the psyche which he called the 'id', a collection of inherited instinctive impulses (such as infantile sexuality), which we tend to restrain while we are awake. He believed the id was released from waking censorship during sleep and would break through into our dreams in an attempt to express itself in ways which the waking ego would not permit. Now, since the dreamer would not approve of such behaviour, Freud postulated that the dreamer tries to suppress the id and disguise the dream to make it more acceptable. This Disguise-Censorship Principle, according to Freud, is why dreams seem bizarre. Instead of dreaming of a penis, for example, we censor it and dream of a symbolic penis disguised, perhaps, as a pen, or a pole or any other long, thin, pointed shape. Since Freud believed most of his patients' repressed desires were sexual, a large proportion of his dream symbols were too. Freud saw added benefits for the dreamer to disguise his or her real instincts in symbolic form, because this gentler dream would not awaken the dreamer in self-disgust. This became known as his Dream as the Guardian of Sleep principle.

Freud called the original, unadulterated dream that the id tried to express the 'latent dream', and the censored version which actually resulted, the 'manifest' dream. Since the dreamer obviously couldn't face the uncensored latent dream, Freud calculated that the dreamer needed a professional interpreter to explain the true meaning of the manifest dream. In this way, Freudian analysis was in danger of imposing a professional interpretation on a patient. Freud was aware of this and ad-vocated the importance of finding out the patients' personal associations to their dreams. He also noted visual and verbal puns in dreams but perhaps laid greatest emphasis on inter-preting through dream symbols. Freud was later criticised by several of his more prominent students for being too dogmatic and rigid in this approach.

Freud published *The Interpretation of Dreams* in 1900 after a decade of personal research including much self-analysis. This was a courageous step for a doctor to take and Freud risked ridicule. It took eight years to sell 600 copies, but the book finally became a classic, marking the beginnings of both the scientific acceptance of dreams and the birth of psychoanalysis. From this point psychiatry and neurology went their separate ways until the Aserinsky and Kleitman discoveries (see Chapter 23) on the physiology of dreaming in the 1950s.

In later decades, Freudian psychoanalysts were perhaps perceived as being preoccupied with sexual repression, rigid symbolism, imposed interpretation and an apparent need to relate every dream back to childhood trauma. In many ways this tight attitude finally caused a public move away from Freudian analysis and towards a more subjective, dreamer-focused psychology.

Transparent or Mystical?: Jung

Swiss-born Carl Gustav Jung (1875–1961) greatly admired Freud, his teacher and mentor, but gradually experienced a different vision of dreams and their relationship to the dreamer's mind. Trained in medicine and neurology like his teacher, Jung formally broke away from the Freudian method in 1914 and spent a lifetime building an alternative psychology.

His basic contention with Freud was that he did not see the dream as a disguise but as 'transparently meaningful' in itself. He saw the dream not as concealing the dreamer's unconscious, but as revealing and expressing it. Neither did he agree with Freud's concept of infantile sexuality, nor with his idea that the dream always pointed to the past, to a trauma or to a childhood repression. Instead Jung saw the dream as expressing something about the dreamer's present life. If today's anxieties or challenges were hooked up in some way to a past memory or trauma, he argued, then yes, the dream might well show how the past has influenced the dreamer's present outlook. Just as often, though, Jung realised that dreams reveal our potential, and act to inspire us to achieve a greater future. This forward looking, almost spiritual outlook moved Jung even further away from the Freudian view.

Jung dismissed Freud's blanket approach to symbolism by reinstating the importance of personal symbols alongside the universal. Like Freud he studied myths and legends, but whereas Freud saw mythological characters as representative of, perhaps, one's parents, Jung saw them as aspects of the dreamer. He developed this theory of 'archetypes' to show how the role model strangers in our dreams represent the parts of ourselves that need to be integrated into the Self. For example, Jung saw the dark, shadowy, perhaps 'evil' figure in our dreams as symbolic of repressed aspects of our personality which we disown, and he saw God in a dream as symbolic of our future, integrated, whole Self. Heroes, monsters, angels and devils all played their part, he believed, in introducing the dreamer to the various facets of her personality which needed to be owned and brought into integration to achieve wholeness. Dreams, he saw, might sometimes be seen as compensatory, as the dreamer's inner drive towards integration resulted in 'balancing' dreams.

Jung saw within each person the need to balance the male (animus) and female (anima) qualities. He underlined the importance of watching the activities of the male and female strangers in our dreams as pointers to achieving a better inner balance. He perceived people known to us who appear in our dreams to be representing themselves, and only strangers to symbolise parts of our inner selves.

Jung argued that all people throughout the world have a common understanding of these archetypes and other universal symbols which surface in our dreams simply because we are freed, through the dream state, to experience a universal language, unrestricted by the rational confines of waking thought. This shared understanding was expressed by Jung as a shared 'collective unconscious', a kind of 'shared mind' or collective memory. This collective unconscious could also, he believed, be accessed as a source of wisdom.

Whereas Freud used dreams and psychoanalysis to investigate and, hopefully, cure neurotic patients, Jung's approach was to see dreams as the expression of an inner drive in all people, mentally healthy or unhealthy, which could be tapped by the conscious mind to bring the dreamer a sense of wholeness and potential. He suggested that a greater picture should be obtained by looking at series of dreams, rather than individual dreams, to get a balanced view of the dreamer's mind and progress over a period of time. He believed the only correct interpretation was the one which made sense to the dreamer, so the dreamer should meditate on his dream and its symbols, or perhaps converse with the dream characters. Above all he believed he had no method of dream interpretation, but that dreams should be interpreted in the way that was most helpful to each particular dreamer. I have huge admiration for Jung and his pioneering work, especially in his choice of focus in seeing the hidden treasures rather than the buried past traumas in dreams. I also applaud his endeavour to hand dream interpretation back into the capable hands of the dreamers themselves, but I sympathise with those who argue that Jung's highly intuitive grasp of collective unconscious symbolism is beyond their reach. I wonder if Jung would agree with my humble advice to 'have faith and stick in there' because, in the end, what looks mystical to the uninformed is simply a working knowledge of another language: the language of dreams.

An Apology!

The 20th century has seen mighty contributions in the fields of psychology and psychiatry, and I apologise for the huge omissions I have made in confining my modern-day overview to Freud and Jung and for the omissions I have made in attempting to summarise each man's lifetime work in a few meagre paragraphs. The purpose of this chapter has been to illustrate the range of possibilities in approaching dreams as manifestations of that elusive quality, the human mind.

New Age Psychology?

It would also be inappropriate to leave this chapter without mentioning the enormous popularity of psychology in the general media today. The literate man or woman on the street is versed with at least a spattering of an insight into psychology and a deep appreciation of the power of the mind, even though they may be hard put to answer the question: What is mind?

The New Age has also brought a new dimension to popular psychology through a blurring of the perception of the difference between the mind and the soul. With its licence to drop rationality, the New Age brings as many questions as it attempts to answer. Does mind die with the physical body, or does it survive as a mental energy, a lasting memory, or an eternally accessible file still capable of generating thought somewhere in an expanded collective unconscious? Would a surviving, eternal mind negate the purpose of a soul? Can mind escape the clutches of time? Is the mind a separate entity from the soul? Can the soul survive without the mind? Does the soul, or the mind, carry an indelible imprint of its past mental and emotional experiences, a time bomb ready to pop up in a dream in a future life, or to roam the astral dimension, accessible to the dreams of you or me?

Yes, you've got it. With the New Age came the suspense of reason. Anything is possible, and, although perhaps beyond the proof of science or the application of psychology, with a leap of faith, it probably is.

CHAPTER 25

Philosophy:
The Soul and the Spiritual
Causes of Dreaming

Gus

After ten years of close working relationships, there came a rift in our family and my father-in-law chose to isolate himself from us. He had a lot of anger and frustration in the last years of his life, brought on mainly by his own actions and reactions to previous events. The consequence of all this, and developing cancer of the larynx, caused him to end his life in the December of 1979.

My dream was extremely vivid this night. Gus (as we called him) came and took back every single item he'd ever given us during our lives together. I sensed bad feelings, bordering on evil or hatred, emanating from him and directed towards us. Almost like a greedy, grasping kid, he was grabbing back what he'd given freely before. (We had been aware of the manipulative power of Gus's gifts, so had purposely accepted so little anyway, which made this dream all the more curious.)

At five o'clock the next morning, after my dream, the phone rang with one of Gus's daughters informing us that Gus had died. My dream left me with a heaviness and sadness for many months. At that time we had no problem dealing with Gus's death. My anguish

280

*was for him and why he had left so much unresolved when he so
carefully was able to plan his own time to leave this earth.*

*A few months later I awoke one morning feeling completely at
peace with his death. In a dream I was on the lower part of a hill.
Walking in the distance I saw a figure. As I drew nearer, the back of
this person gave me a sense of recognition. Slowly he turned half
around and said, 'Don't worry any more. I'm okay now. It's all
right.' This person was Gus. It was like a dark cloud had been lifted
from my being.*

(Nette, potter)

Did Nette tune into Gus's mental state at the moment of his
suicide and, as time passed, come to terms with her anguish for
him? Did she then see this reflected in a 'psychologically
caused' dream which allowed her to have faith in peace after
death? Did she meet his surviving mind which had progressed
in understanding since his death? Did she communicate with
his spirit or soul in the dream dimension? Or did his spirit
communicate with Nette's sleeping mind, reassuring her
through a dream?

This book has been dotted with examples of dreams that
appear to be beyond physiological or psychological cause (see
Chapters 6, 19 and 20), but what do we mean by 'spirit' or
'soul'? According to the *Concise Oxford Dictionary*, 'spirit' is
another word for 'soul', and generally means 'the intelligent,
non-physical part of a person' or 'a rational or intelligent being
without a material body'. The soul is defined as 'the spiritual or
immaterial part of a human being, often regarded as immortal',
although, in an everyday sense, it is also 'the moral or
emotional or intellectual nature of a person or animal'.

As these definitions show, there is much blurring between our
concepts of body, mind and soul. Is the soul a non-physical part
of the body that dies with us? Is it another word for the mind,
dying also with the physical body? If the mind can survive
physical death, does this mean it is not 'mind' but 'soul'? Or
does the mind, that 'seat of consciousness, thought and volition'

Philosophy ♈

or 'intellectual powers' or 'memory' (all from the *Concise Oxford Dictionary*), have a physical component that dies with the body, liberating its immortal component as a soul? Or is terminology irrelevant, an aberration of a rational language which should bow down to our much wider grasp of 'reality' through our deeply intuitive, and primal, language of dreams?

Talking to Dad

My father died unexpectedly in 1980, aged 70 years. I loved him particularly deeply and we had always been mates. I was living in Adelaide when he died and it had been 12 months since I'd been over to visit my parents, although I kept in constant contact. He was also the devoted father figure to my daughter after I divorced when she was 18 months old. For ten years I had been quietly bitter and angry that he died, because he had worked extremely hard as a farmer since he was eight years old and had few fruits from his labour, and also because he was the only person in the world who unconditionally loved me. He was the only person in the world I unconditionally loved too.

Nearly two years ago he spoke to me in a dream. The dream situation was as I had often seen him, sitting on a log in the bush, physically accurate and familiar down to the detail of his clothes. He told me I had to stop being sad and angry about his death, that he was fine and that I too was fine. He told me that we were always together still and some day I'd join him. (I don't believe in God, the other side, etc., so I have no idea where he meant.) He spoke to me but I only kept saying 'Dad'.

When I became aware that he was going to go, I tried to reach him to put my arms around him and kiss him, but there was an invisible force in the air around him that I knew I couldn't reach through. He said simply that he was sorry I couldn't touch him. When I awoke crying (as he faded) I said to my partner, who was woken by my crying, 'I've been talking to Dad.'

After the dream I was left with a sense of peace and acceptance, and knowledge that somehow Dad still has awareness of me and how I am.

(Dorothy, retired teacher)

Perspectives of History and Philosophy

Let's glance through just a few of the multitude of windows which history, philosophy, religion and quantum physics have opened on realities beyond the one we perceive in waking life.

The Ancient Egyptians

According to the earliest dream records still in existence, the Egyptian hieroglyphs of almost 4000 years ago, the Egyptians believed the gods revealed themselves through people's dreams, but did not think the soul could leave the sleeping body. Theirs was more a belief that people could perceive more through their dreams than they could with their waking senses. Perhaps they were right. It is possible that waking life, with all its anxieties and concerns for safety and survival, drowns out the more subtly sensitive areas of the mind which are free to receive input during sleep, when input from the external waking world is toned down.

India: 1000 BC

In India, around 1000 BC, the Brihadarmyaka-Upanishad records the belief that we live in two states (realities), 'one in this world, the other in the other world, and, as a third, an intermediate state, the state of sleep. When in that interim state he sees both these states together, the one here in this world, and the other in the other world.' 'Dreamless sleep' was seen as the highest state where man seeks unity with space-time infinity, whereas waking life was perceived as a lesser state. The intermediate dream state allowed man closer knowledge of his inner self, a position from which he was better able to view both worlds. In modern terms, this belief sees the dream state as a mediator between the conscious and the unconscious.

The Roaming Soul

Hindu and Chinese Buddhists see the soul as roaming at will during sleep, able to communicate with spirits, the dream being the memory form (albeit perhaps inaccurate) of this experience.

Illusory Worlds: the Path to Nirvana

Tibetan Buddhism, throughout the ages, has taught the value of lucid dreaming. While lucid, Buddhism argues, you can manipulate the illusory dream world and use this learning, while awake, to manipulate the equally illusory waking life. The illusion that we are individuals in a real world is overcome, according to Buddhism, through reaching a state of Nirvana. This can be done by practising meditation while lucid. This procedure, in modern form, means realising you are lucid and then gradually removing all dream sensations until you are left with only ... Nirvana. Tibetan Buddhism, it seems, sees the physical body and the mind as illusory, and the soul as 'existing' only in unity with infinity.

Awakening from the Great Dream

The Chinese sage Chuang-tzu (around 350 BC) described our inability to know illusion from 'reality' thus: 'While men are dreaming, they do not perceive that it is a dream. Some will even have a dream within a dream, and only when they awake they know it was all a dream. And so, when the great awakening comes upon us, we shall know this life to be a great dream. Fools believe themselves to be awake now.'

The Rationality of Extrasensory Perception

The Greek philosopher Democritus (*c.*460–*c.*370 BC) thought that people and objects were able to emanate some essence that could penetrate the dreamer's body (like telepathy) and enter her consciousness. In this way, he saw dreams as, in part, impressions formed from increased sensory awareness during sleep, a function of the brain or mind, but not of the soul.

Rationalising the Precognitive Dream

Aristotle (384–322 BC) philosophised that the great variety and number of dreams we experience are bound to result in some which later occur in the waking world, so that we look back and call them precognitive dreams. He also saw that we often take inspiration or an idea from a dream and put it into action in waking life, making the dream come 'true'.

Heaven and Hell

Saint Thomas Aquinas (13th century AD) wrote that there were two types of dream: the first type emanated from within (the body and mind) while the second category were received from without, be that from heavenly or demonic sources. Common to many religious beliefs, and certainly evident in the Bible, is the notion of 'good' or 'true' dreams and 'evil' or 'false' dreams, with little guidance as to how to distinguish between the two!

Soul and Dream as a Universal Key

Descartes (1596–1650) perceived of a separate soul which resided in the pineal body: the third eye. He believed that dreams contained the key to universal wisdom.

Quantum Physics and the Search for Spiritual Reality

The purpose of this chapter is to look for possible spiritual causes for some of our dreams. Perhaps this is the wrong approach. The possibility exists that our waking life is but a dream, an illusion, and that the 'true' reality lies outside our waking perception, perhaps in the dream, or perhaps beyond. Instead of questioning the reality of our dream spiritual experiences, perhaps we should turn the question around and ask whether we can be sure about our waking world reality. Could the spiritual experiences we recall from our dreams be the residual memories of our true reality, not in the waking world, but in a wider dimension?

Quantum physics has begun to push us out of our comfortable security about our waking world. This branch of science, born in the late 1920s, challenges our every notion of reality. At a subatomic level, according to Heisenberg's Uncertainty Principle, we can never really be sure about the behaviour of subatomic particles. In very simplistic terms, sometimes they are there, and sometimes they are not, and these appearances and disappearances are unpredictable. On the whole, enough subatomic particles tend to be 'in place' enough of the time, to make 'matter' appear to be present and subject to the laws of physics which we have observed over the centuries. No-one really expects all the subatomic particles to 'disappear' at the same moment, but if they did, 'matter' could reasonably be expected to momentarily appear or disappear before our eyes. The branch of science known as 'Quantum Cosmology', which theorises on the spontaneous generation of universes, is based on such observations.

Not only can science now argue the case for appearing and disappearing universes, but, through Einstein's Theory of Relativity, it also questions our everyday concept of time. Paul Davies, in his excellent book *The Mind of God*, points out that absolute universal time, as scientifically described by Newton, works out well for us on a day-to-day level. However, he argues, if we were to start moving about faster than the speed of light, our concept of time would change; it would no longer work for us.

In the same way, I suggest, when we move from waking reality into dreaming reality, we come under the influence of a different set of conditions: different laws, different realities. I believe it is possible that many of our 'time travel' dream experiences occur because we are released from our waking reality's limited perception of time. Freed from the boundaries of waking time and matter while asleep, our reality expands.

While on the subject of time travel, past lives, future lives, parallel lives, immortality and other areas snubbed by the 'rational scientist in the street', quantum science has argued that, at least in principle, a multitude of parallel universes containing a multitude of parallel selves, could, theoretically exist. The basic thinking is this: every subatomic particle faces uncertainty; it can be here, there, appear, disappear, act this way, act that way and so on. It is arguable scientifically that all possibilities for each particle can occur. These multiple possibilities build an ever increasing existence of independent parallel realities. You, as a person, would also be replicated, split into every possible action or inaction, living in a multitude of parallel 'lives'. According to this theory, well supported by a number of quantum physicists and philosophers, each parallel copy of yourself would feel complete and would live in ignorance of the others.

The theory's critics suggest we *would* be aware of our other parallel selves, and therefore discount the concept.

Wait a minute though. Don't we meet an awareness of other aspects of ourselves through our dreams? Don't we see ourselves in sometimes slightly different surroundings during astral travel? When, in our impoverished 'time orientated' waking state, we talk of glimpsing past lives or having precognitive dreams, are we instead bringing back a conscious memory of a link with one or other of our parallel selves?

Where would all this leave God, souls and spirits? Parallel universes could survive as a purely physical, self-generated phenomenon or as a God-inspired set of parallel experiences designed for our ultimate learning. If we ever arrive at a point where science can reach out and identify the certain existence of alternative realities, then we may be faced with a startling possibility: rather than science being at the opposite extreme from mystical or religious experience, it may find itself 'back at the beginning', completing the circle of ultimate knowledge. Science, through quantum physics and metaphysics, may fuse with mystical experience to complete our understanding of the world, of dreams, of psychic phenomena, of alternative realities and maybe, even, of God.

Dream Channel

I believe that many areas covered in my dream state are merely extensions of my inner self, but I know without doubt that there are people there talking to me, wanting something from me which, at present, I am unable to give. Recently I had the strange sensation of someone calling to me while I slept. I knew I was asleep and remember thinking how relaxed and receptive I was. There was a woman calling me by name, asking me to help her. Then she said something like, 'We've got through … Rowyn, can you hear me? … hurry, the channel is open … Rowyn, you may have to help us get through … try hard … Rowyn?'

I felt a little fear and hesitated to respond. I remember taking time to consider what I should do. Of course, I had no idea what I was supposed to be doing and eventually stretched out and decided fate would decide. Then, as quickly as the voice had come, it was gone and I knew most certainly that I was on my own. I was 100% relaxed and felt warm and content, although nothing had transpired. I felt both relieved and a little disappointed that it had ended so abruptly.

(Rowyn, student)

Dreaming the Holy Grail: The Dreamer Holds the Key

In the end, it is perhaps only the dreamer who knows whether his or her dream was out of the ordinary, came from a spiritual source, gave reassurance, hope, peace or a glimpse into another world. Whether these spiritual dreams are communications with the deceased, with our parallel selves, with heavenly hosts, with God, or with all of these and more, it is their hauntingly inspirational ability to radically change our outlook on life and to give meaning where emptiness rattled before that stands above everything else.

Changed Perception of Life

The dream I had in 1991 helped me change my perception and attitude towards life. However, the dream that warned of my impending darkness occurred just prior to this, in April 1991:

I was a passenger in a car travelling across a bridge. The driver, a young male, leaned over the side of the car to try to touch the water below the bridge (an impossibility in real life). In doing so the car overbalanced and we fell into the river, inside the car. I remembered that my husband had said if something like this were ever to happen I should hold my breath until the car reached the bottom, wait for the water to fill the car and then swim out. However, the river was exceptionally deep, and even before the car hit the bottom I knew I couldn't hold my breath long enough. Then everything went completely black.

This dream really worried me as I had learned from dream interpretation workshops how significant deep, dark water was. It was shortly after this that I fell into a very deep depression.

The story of my illness is long and involved so I shall cut it short. I hit rock bottom and felt life was emotionally and mentally too painful to continue. I was at the bottom of a dark and dangerous pit with no way out. I couldn't work or think rationally, or be on my own without panicking. I couldn't eat, I cried continually and I thought I was losing my sanity. I couldn't sleep so I had no relief from my own personal hell. I firmly believed I would never recover and suicide (as death was not readily forthcoming) was the only answer.

I did get professional help and was taking medication when I began having some broken sleep. I began dreaming of my father-in-law (to whom I had been very close) who had died in 1984. I believe somehow he helped me through this period. Then I had my dream in May 1991.

In the dream I lay flat on my back with an impenetrable conglomerate of cobweb-like substance immediately above my face and body like a cloud mass imprisoning me between it and the solid base on which I lay. I knew I could not move in any direction except through this mass. I tried to puncture it until I was exhausted, but to no avail. When I regained strength, I tried again and again. This went on for what seemed like forever!

I tried to cut myself out with a knife, slashing and slashing but the conglomerate simply rushed back into place like a knife cutting through water. At some stage I found myself more as an observer and I realised that a hole appeared in the mass and I knew that I must have pierced the cobwebs.

To my amazement I noticed the beautiful blue of the sky as the hole *enlarged. It was the most wonderful sight and I felt marvellous!*

Up until this dream (even though I was on medication and I was having therapy) I was still depressed and suicidal. It was not until my dream and the realisation I would pull through that I became more positive. I still had my ups and downs, and in the down moments I forced myself to remember my dream, and this would help pick me up again. This dream gave me the courage and strength to work on myself. I often find myself feeling an overwhelming gratitude, for I believe I have almost come to terms (I am still working on this) with a very deep-seated fear which was programmed into my subconscious at a very young age. This fear had surfaced in 1974, haunting me at different periods in those 17 years, culminating in the experience above.

(Pearl, secretary)

If our search for the spiritual meaning of life is a search for that which transcends the physical and the mortal, perhaps dreams give us our best chance of finding an answer. Through dreams we may reach our personal conclusions about our spiritual nature based on dream experiences which the human brain will perhaps never be able to translate. As Alex, one of the dream survey lucid dreamers put it:

It is possible that the key [to the meaning of life] *exists, but is only discovered, comprehended and understood in the dimension of dreaming, and that it's not possible to bring 'it' into the physical universe, even conceptually.*

(Alex, clerk)

If he is right, and I suspect he is, then we should acknowledge the spiritual influences that may shape our dream memories from time to time.

CHAPTER 26

Levels of Dreaming:
The Body, Mind and Soul of It All!

Was That a Physical, Psychological or Spiritual Dream?

Now for the thunderbolt! Having spent the last three chapters individually appraising the physical, psychological and spiritual causes of dreams, I don't believe it is valid to consider these as *separate* from each other at all.

It was necessary to examine dreams from each angle, to acknowledge the contribution of science, psychology, history, religion, mysticism and philosophy, but this can be likened to an extraterrestrial visitor trying to understand the earth with only a telescope, a microscope, a subatomic particle accelerator, a stethoscope, an EEG print out of a frog's brain waves, a volume of Chaucer, an astrology chart, a scratched record of an operatic performance and a fossilised termite nest. Gradually, if we examine something from a sufficient number of angles, we begin to see the pieces fitting together to form a whole picture.

So it is with life and dreams. There comes a point where the physical body, through the nervous system and the brain, seems to overlap with the mind; yet the mind, with its power to effect changes in the physical world, becomes confused with the physical body, or even with physical matter itself. Is it the mind which transcends time, or is that the soul? And is that the spirit which breathes life into the baby, that inspires the suicidal to decide to live, that speaks through dreams, or is that the mind? The distinctions are blurred because the body, mind and soul are all part, in my opinion, of the human whole.

A Personal View

This is my view, largely based on my dreams:

I believe we are part of a greater and timeless reality, one which we experience vividly while we sleep, but of which we bring back only a tiny, distorted fragment recorded in our memory as a dream. Our waking life binds us, in my belief, within the constraint of time and space, possibly because this enables us to experience cause and effect. With practice and dedication I believe it is possible to break through the illusion of waking life and see the greater reality beyond, not only through our dreams but also with our eyes open. My personal experience tells me that human life is not a remarkably chancy quirk of physics, but that it does have ultimate meaning. My brain and intellect is still trying to catch up with this intuitive knowledge! If I keep it open, it may surprise me one day.

My experience tells me that I am probably not a distinct and different individual to you, but that we overlap and influence each other all the time. I am as much a part of you as you are a part of me, since we probably share the full range of human and spiritual experience through an infinite number of parallel waking realities, each individually bound by time and space, but each accessible through our timeless, spaceless dreams. While I may express that paragraph in a different way in another parallel reality, in yet another I may fail to gather the courage to write the book at all. In another I may be making a far better job of it! Whatever I have done, am doing or will do on which ever level, I believe my every action reverberates and influences all the others. Somehow, on all these levels, my ultimate mission, like yours, is to liberate my soul through the learning experience created by time-space restrictions.

I see the power of the human mind as an incredible moulding force which interacts with everything that appears to be physical. I believe that the mind, once it releases its hold on rationality, frees the soul to return to its timeless dimension.

I see the body, mind and soul in waking life as closely bound and interacting. Our thoughts about ourselves shape the way we hold our bodies, the way we grow, our health or lack of it, how tall or short, how beautiful, how plain, how charismatic we appear or how and when we age. The state of the body reflects the state of the mind. I wish I had more control over mine!

I believe that every experience is recorded at a physical, mental and spiritual level, and, since I see our dreams as experience of a wider reality, I believe our dream experiences filter through at each level too. Thus, in my opinion, what we see as the physical, psychological or spiritual causes of dreams are just different manifestations of the same experience.

For example, I may have the misfortune to find myself in a disagreement with someone. I may feel angry (psychological) which makes my skin flush (physical), yet some truth about myself may evolve because of the anger, in which case I may experience a spiritual learning.

Accessing the Body, Mind and Soul through Dream Interpretation

The same philosophy can be applied to a dream. If a dream is a memory of an experience in a greater reality, it too will carry physical, psychological and spiritual imprints into my waking human memory. The dream experience may be a bit garbled, but once I have applied my dream interpretation techniques, I should begin to see its meaning. It is most likely that I will perceive its meaning as being physical one day, psychological the next, and maybe spiritual the following week, depending on my attitude and clarity, but if I were to examine the dream closely, I might see that the dream applied to each of these areas of my waking life at the same time.

When I am asked to interpret someone else's dream, I find this much clearer. It's always much easier to see in from a distance! I can usually see physical, psychological and spiritual meaning captured in the one dream, as if the true meaning hangs, suspended at three levels, inextricably entwined. In order to offer an interpretation that makes sense to the dreamer, I usually choose to help them interpret on one level only.

In interpreting your dream I might see that you will understand your dream better today if I explain it to you on a physical level and suggest you get your blood pressure checked. On another day I might have interpreted the same dream on a psychological level and showed you why you get angry in certain situations. At another time I might have illustrated the spiritual aspects of the same dream, pointing you in a direction which might enlighten your learning about the purpose of experiencing anger in your life, and how to use this to break through into new ground. These interpretations of the same dream might all be correct, but you might understand one explanation more than another, or you might see more clearly how to take effective action from the psychological point of view rather than the spiritual.

So it is with your own dream interpretations. Look at each dream and try out the interpretation techniques given in this book. Then stand back and see the physical, psychological and spiritual connotations according to your personal understanding of life. Go for the one which makes most sense to you, and then consider how you can take action on it to improve your life.

CHAPTER 27

Synchronicity:
Got the Message?

To Hold a Dream in your Hands

Imagine bringing something physical back from a dream!

> *I dreamed, or astral travelled, flying around the caravan park. I slowly drifted towards the hills where I started to fly down into the trees and found a clearing. I walked around and through a marijuana plantation. I remember picking a leaf in the dream. Next thing I knew it was morning and I awoke to find a marijuana leaf in my hand. I told a friend about the dream later that day. He was sceptical but agreed to come with me for a look. I was able to find my way from the dream and found it to be just like the dream. I have not been able to bring anything back from astral travelling before or since that time.*
>
> *(Ian, unemployed chef)*

Like many others, Andrew (see Appendix B) has set himself the task of bringing back something from one of his lucid dreams. We often bring experiences back from our dreams that later become physical realities, such as ideas for a business, words for a poem, colours and images for a surrealist painting, spiritual learning or truths that change our lives, or a lingering warmth from being with an old friend that physically lasts all day.

What if, instead of making your dream happen, and instead of waking with something in your hand, that dream object actually appears the next day?

The Gold Leaf Bedroom

I thought I'd woken up in my own room after having a really vivid dream. I'm going through the dream, trying to recall it, lying there in the pitch black. I stretched and my feet touched the footboard. I thought, 'Oh, that's strange, I haven't got a footboard on my bed.' Then I realised I was lucid and I thought, 'Great, now I'll go and follow the rules in the lucid dreaming book. I can make anything happen that I want to happen.' So I said, 'Lights on!', and they did. They came on very gradually and I saw I was in a huge chamber with gold leaf on the walls, the bed and everywhere. It was a beautiful bedroom.

Anyway, a couple of weeks later a truck driver at work, who I didn't think would be interested in dreams, leaped out of his truck and right out of the blue said, 'Would you like to borrow a book?' Well, a couple of months earlier I had lent him a Playboy, *so I was expecting to see a girlie book as we had never discussed dreams. The book he lent me turned out to be on Tibet! Right on the middle page was a bedroom similar to the one in my dream. I won't say it was the same bedroom. I don't think dreams are intended to be absolutely perfectly right, but it was so similar: the gold leaf, the bed and so on. It happened to be the bedroom of the 13th Dalai Lama of Tibet.*

That's what I'm going through now. I think there's more to life than coincidence on many occasions. You have to work out what is not coincidence and what is somehow trying to tell you or warn you of something.

(Alex, clerk)

The Book of My Dreams!

I dreamed I was telling my sister's fortune through palmistry. The next day someone offered me a palmistry book on loan. I hadn't mentioned the subject to her.

(Carly, home duties)

Gemstone and Diamond Rings

I dreamed I was packing bare essentials to go on an expedition to Antarctica, when I opened my drawer and saw two beautiful gemstone rings, each a slightly different, but unusual colour, and each with a specific diamond setting. Apparently these were my mother's rings, but she didn't have the courage to wear them. Someone was shouting at me to hurry up and get ready but I decided to take my time and told Mum that if she didn't have the guts to wear her rings I would wear them until she was ready to take them back. By now my fingers could hardly bend for all the rings I threaded onto them, and I decided not to go to Antarctica after all.

The day after the dream a friend visited me, and it intrigued me to see that she was wearing earrings of the same colour, design and style as one of the rings in my dream. I thought I must have subconsciously noticed them in previous meetings with this girl, although it didn't escape my attention that her birthday was the same as my mother's (though a different year). I thought nothing more about it until the following day when I was visited by Lainey, a lady on the dream survey, whom I had not yet met in person. She wore the other ring.

I had only half-heartedly thought about my dream until the experience of seeing the two rings and noticing the 'coincidence' of the birth dates. The effect of all this was to send me back to the dream, since the daytime events were clearly showing that I had not credited my dream with the importance that it, and I, both deserved.

When I interpreted my original dream I saw that I had been feeling under pressure to conform to the demands of others and was feeling 'frozen out' by it all. I saw shades of my mother in this response and determined, in the dream, not to take the same attitude. If my mother didn't have the courage to let her own light shine, then I didn't have to be tarred with the same brush. In the dream, my mother represented the mother aspect of myself, and I won the struggle between acting as my mother would have done, giving away her rings and her power, and taking back my power and charge of my own situation. Realising this I had no further need for retreating to the emotional ice and snow of Antarctica!

As a result of the daytime synchronicity and my closer attention to my dream, I changed my attitude.

(Jane Anderson)

Notice that in each of these cases, the dreamer was sufficiently inspired by the daytime coincidence to take an action or change an attitude. Are these simply examples of precognitive dreaming, where we see waking life objects or events beforehand in our dreams? Are these just coincidences? Do we make these objects physically manifest in our waking life just because we have powerfully dreamed about them? Did God or some higher being place the object there to alert us to the dream, or to something else?

When this happens again and again, do we reach a point where regular manifestation of our dreams moves beyond coincidence?

Synchronicity: Beyond Coincidence

Coincidence is 'a remarkable concurrence of events or circumstances without apparent causal connection' (*Concise Oxford Dictionary*). Carl Jung labelled the phenomenon of being presented with an overabundance of *meaningful* coincidence, either in everyday life or relating to dreams, as 'synchronicity'. The difference between coincidence and synchronicity, at this level, lies in the meaningfulness of it all. The more meaning the coincidence seems to have, the more it becomes a synchronicity.

Meaningfulness implies purpose, and purpose implies the existence of a motivating force: a cause. Today the word synchronicity has come to imply a coincidence of grand and purposeful design, perhaps presented by God, a higher being or the universe itself in order to enlighten the observer in some way.

During the research period for this book, I was receiving completed questionnaires, letters and phone calls continuously for some nine months, and I noticed that these would often arrive in batches of themes. One week the emphasis might lie with precognitive dreams, for example, whereas the next week every communication might relate to lucid dreaming. I noticed that phone calls to my radio talkback segment often focused on the topics I was mulling over for the next chapter. An example of how specific this synchronicity tends to be was given in Chapter 23, which described the phone call I received from Jayne S., a lucid dreamer and migraine sufferer, at the exact minute I was reading about the possible relationship between migraines and lucid dreaming. (Jayne had phoned me only once or twice that year.)

A man who later became a contributor to the dream survey came to one of my dream lectures in 1992, more interested in accessing other dimensions of the mind than in dream interpretation. He arrived early and went into a bookshop where he happened to see a book on dreams. He flicked it open and saw an entry on the symbolic meaning of insects in dreams. It was the only symbol he read. During my lecture, as he recounted the story later, I talked about dream interpretation books and used one example to illustrate my point: insects. This remained in his mind, and he has since spent an extraordinary synchronicity-packed year.

Synchronicity: Linking the Inner and Outer Worlds

When the outer world produces a synchronicity with the inner world, whether the world of waking thought or the dream world, the observer often experiences a sense of meaningful continuity between his outer and inner worlds. When my waking life shows synchronicities to my dreaming life, barriers between the two realities crumble.

My dream reality and waking reality seem to be merging. I might think of something and wonder, was it from a dream or from waking reality?

(Serena, administration officer)

Synchronicity shows me that my dream and waking lives are both part of the one overall reality, and that this universal reality is one of design and meaning, speckled with signs and symbols for my further guidance.

Practical Guidance

Living, moving and breathing in a world of human earthly experience, as we are, how can we put daytime synchronicity to our dreams to practical use?

Look out for signs in your waking life which connect with your dreams, and use these to add to the overall picture. If objects or situations arise that seem connected beyond co-incidence with your dreams, look more closely at how you interpreted your dream. Concentrate on the symbol which appeared in waking life, and make that the focal symbol of your dream interpretation. A symbol from your dream encountered in a positive way in waking life (like my gemstone and diamond rings, for example) may be there as a signpost, a confirmation to 'follow your dream', a great elbow nudge to interpret the dream seriously, or perhaps even a message from God.

What about the less desirable synchronicities? If you had dreamed of a car crash, for example, this might have been symbolic of losing your motivation or losing control over your life. If, a day or so later, you crash your car in waking life, perhaps the dream message is spilling out into your waking life to get more immediate recognition. Synchronicity becomes a waking dream shouting in your ear, playing dramatically in front of your eyes, physically and emotionally affecting your waking life until you finally get the message. If this happens to you, try treating the waking life situation as a dream, looking at the main symbols (for example, 'car' and 'crash'), and interpreting it as if it were a dream. Then look for the message behind the 'dream'/daytime experience, and consider what action you could take to improve your life.

If such events in our waking life are sometimes spillovers from unheard dreams, just as a diseased physical body can be a manifestation of an ignored dream too, then where does this leave the apparently precognitive dream? Do we see the 'future' in a dream because we roam timeless realms in our dreams, because we experience similar events in our parallel lives which resonate with us in our dreams, or because we have ignored the original dream and needed a waking life revision lesson? I feel all these possibilities occur, and I personally enjoy seeing the 'positive' synchronicities that might cause me to recognise a precognitive dream and feel good about the direction I am taking. At the same time though, I think it is ultimately wise to heed the deeper messages behind our more 'negative' dreams, to give us time to take early action and avoid a symbolic or literal waking life reminder.

Synchronicity and Quantum Physics ...
The 'Science' of God?

In the subatomic world of quantum physics, pairs of particles are observed to 'behave' according to the whereabouts and condition of their subatomic particle 'partners'. If particle behaviour were totally predictable, there would be nothing amazing in this statement. Remember, though, that in quantum physics (see Chapter 25, Philosophy: The Soul and the Spiritual Causes of Dreaming) everything seems to be indeterminate, or, at least, it defies description according to classical physics. A subatomic particle may appear, disappear, be in one place, in several places or not be at all, apparently at random. Yet, at the same time, pairs of particles, even if separated by any distance (be that metres, kilometres or light years apart), behave simultaneously as if they are connected or in instant communication with each other, with no need for time to send a signal.

Imagine, then, this web, this inextricably balanced, simultaneously inter-communicating, yet somewhat unpredictable, unity of subatomic particles that make up this universe, and possibly other universes too. All forms of energy are related to all other forms of energy. What happens here affects what happens over there, simultaneously. If I do this, how does that affect you?

Just as I perceive my body, mind and soul to be different levels of the same energy, so I perceive my waking reality and my dream reality to be different dimensions of the same whole. Your waking and dreaming realities are interdependent with mine as we live and dream our apparently individual ways towards the ultimate experience: liberation from time and space and a return to the freedom of unity.

APPENDIX A

Meet the Rest of the Survey Participants

Age, Education and Occupation

The survey dreamers range in age from 10 to 82 (10–20 years 10.6%; 21–30 years 20.6%; 31–40 years 23.1%; 41–50 years 24.4%; 51–60 years 13.1%; 61–85 years 6.3%). In geographical location they are scattered from the far north of Queensland down to Melbourne in the south and across to Perth in the west, and also include a couple of participants living overseas. Not all were born Australian, with input from America, South Africa, the Philippines, Eastern Europe, the United Kingdom, New Zealand and other areas of the world.

The survey dreamers' occupations span a wide range, from writers to sales people, from artists to company directors, film producers, actors, pensioners, teachers (6.3%) and students (11.8%). They vary from home-based parents (16.8%) to the unemployed (10%), the retired (4.4%), health professionals (5%), computer experts, researchers of economics, researchers of land management, bank officers and barpeople. They came forward from secretary to petrol tanker driver, cabinet maker to cook, psychiatric nurse to astrologer, town planner to parish priest, from architect to lecturer and landscape gardener to tax consultant. In short, they are a diverse group!

Of the survey dreamers, 31.9% are tertiary educated (college or university), with an additional 9.4% having attended a further education course, while 6% were still at school.

Marital Status

Married 40.6%; Single 35%; Divorced 11.3%; De facto 5.6%; Widowed 4.4%; Separated 2.5%

Religion

No religion 36.8%; Anglican, Presbyterian or Protestant 24.4%; Catholic 17.5%; 'Open', 'New Age', 'Love', 'Oneness', 'Universal' etc. 7.5%; Spiritualist 6.3%; Single individuals representing other religions★ 5.6%; Buddhist 1.9%

★*Quaker, Pentecostal, Methodist, Church of Ireland, Orthodox.*

Source of Dreams

In response to the question 'Where do you believe your dreams come from?' 17.5% said they didn't know or left this blank. While 21.3% wrote the single word 'subconscious', most offered a short list of possible sources.

Health

Of the survey dreamers, 30.6% rate their health as excellent, while 10% consider themselves to be fair and 2.5% assess their condition as poor or very poor. When it comes to alcohol, 5.1% drink 15–21 glasses a week, while 2.5% take more than this.

High stress ('very' and 'extreme') accounts for 14.4% of the dreamers, while 28.8% feel they are 'mildly' or 'rarely' (21.9%) stressed.

Coping with Problems

Meditating on a specific problem to seek a solution was favoured by 12.5%, whereas 10.6% look for guidance either through prayer or through other metaphysical sources. A solid 16.3% stoically stated that they coped with their problems by 'solving them', while smaller percentages read books, exercised, kept themselves busy, drank alcohol, listened to music, wrote their worries down or went for a walk. The self-confessed worriers accounted for 9.4% of the survey, while 13% either ignored their problems or positively worked at relaxing and letting go, knowing that it would 'sort itself out' later.

Sleeping and Waking Routines

Of the survey dreamers, 28.1% fall asleep in 5–15 minutes, while 24.4% drop off in somewhere between 15 and 30 minutes. Lying awake for an hour or more is common for 12.5%.

The dreamers sleep from 4 to 10 hours, and while 22.5% don't usually wake up during the night, 25% regularly wake three or more times before morning. Even so, only 5.6% describe themselves as 'restless' sleepers; 'light' sleepers accounting for 20%.

People were asked to tick the waking patterns that generally applied to them, so most picked several categories.

The majority wake up naturally or are woken by others; 28.8% rely on an alarm clock. Almost a third get up as soon as they wake up; 67.5% generally lie in bed for some time. Just under another third go back to sleep again, while 16.9% have great difficulty waking up the first time round. Thinking about their dreams before jumping into the day is favoured by 68.1% and 25% also plan the day before climbing out of bed.

Understanding their Dreams

Of their dreams, they estimated they understood:
None 4.6%; A few 22.8%; Several 19.5%; About half 15%; More than half 9.8%; Most 24.4%; All 3.9%.

Appendix A

The Precognitive Dreamers' Discussion

Introduced to you already in Chapter 19, this group of survey precognitive dreamers met in June 1993. Parts of the discussion are presented below for your further thought!

On Being Lucid:

I tend to remember dreams better now than I can remember what happened to me yesterday! I'm not so interested in the interpretation of dreams, perhaps that's waiting for me, but I'm really trying to understand what it is that's inside my mind.

(Alex, clerk)

This may sound a bit way out, but having access to all my senses in a lucid dream, I want to come back with something material. I always want to get to bed quickly to get on with it. Daytime is boring compared to this! I don't think you can separate daytime life from dreams. Dreams are an extension of daytime life. I think you should try your best because it helps you to grow. I think you're supposed to do that.

(Andrew, construction manager)

Have you asked anyone in the dream if you may have something? You must request. You must reach a level before you are allowed to bring something back.

(Tania, tax consultant)

You are looking for proof that the dreams are real, to reassure yourself.

(John, town planner)

No. I don't need to prove to anyone else that my dream is real. I know it's real. I just want to experiment. I want to go as far as I can until the time is finished.

(Andrew, construction manager)

Lucid dreams can also be escapism.

(Tania, tax consultant)

I think mine can be. I lucid dream when I've been having a scary dream and I am trying to escape so I start doing the kinds of things they do in Die Hard II.

(Jayne S., home duties)

Have you ever found yourself, in a dream, conscious, being warned that you are in someone else's dream?

(Tania, tax consultant)

Yes, commonly. I have many times resolved personal problems with other people through dreams. Resolution is made and when I meet that person again later, the past has been cleared. No hard feelings remain and we move on from there.

(John, town planner)

I was trespassing in someone else's dream and I was told to get out. I was met by a man who explained that I shouldn't be there and I had to drive behind him in his four-wheel drive to get out. We drove on a highway through a miniature city or community with miniature skyscrapers. It was absolutely fantastic. I got out of my car and was invited into a room, but again this man followed me and told me I was in the wrong place and I had to get out. He told me to walk ten steps in the other direction to go through my door. I stepped out and

watched the dream going on. I was watching someone else's dream.
                                                    (Tania, tax consultant).

On Time:

If you're open minded enough to believe that all dimensions of time exist simultaneously you can pick out anything at will. And that's it.
                                        (Eloise, unemployed receptionist)

I feel we're bound up in time in our waking life but our dream state gives us the opportunity to explore other realms.
                                                    (Chiron, astrologer)

Physically and mentally you're locked into a segment of time and space in your waking life, whereas in your dreaming period you are released. You can choose to go and do, observe, correct whatever you want, but you have to make that choice. You have to be willing to make that choice. That is where you walk from your dark room into your bright light. You're conscious, you know you're dreaming and you know you're doing something.
                                                    (Tania, tax consultant)

On Learning in Dreams:

Does anyone have any experience of learning at a place, where you are taught or something is explained to you in the dream? When you wake up it doesn't seem significant, but within a short period of time it comes up and you actually draw on the whole knowledge without even realising that you've got the knowledge?
                                                    (Tania, tax consultant)

I go to a classroom in my dreams. I see myself float in. One night I went to bed really late and by the time I got into the dream everyone was waiting for me! They said, 'Where have you been?'
                                                (Michealla, natural therapist)

I have had the experience of going into the great halls of learning, and you can ask to do that.
                                                (Voice unrecognised on tape)

Has anyone gone to an actual library in a dream in search for something?
(Tania, tax consultant)

I went to a library and walked around. The librarian said, 'You've got to have this book' and gave me a title. The next day, when I woke up, I went to the book store to see if they had it and bought it. It's probably one of my favourite books now: The Way of the Peaceful Warrior.
(Isabelle, legal secretary)

Sometimes you are given titles of books in dreams because there's something in them to open the door to the next stage.
(Tania, tax consultant)

I had a dream where I was shown three huge old books, one entitled Beginners, one Intermediate and one Advanced. I went straight for the Advanced, but was told I had to read all three, starting with Beginners! I did, but when I woke up I had no recollection of what I had learned. In another dream I died and went to a 'holding place' where I was given a leather book with my surname on it, which seemed to be a Book of Karma or a Life Plan. I sat down and read it cover to cover, but have no memory of the contents.
(Jane Anderson)

Maybe I shouldn't look at my library dreams as being about work then, but as being more than that.
(Jaquelyn, librarian)

Which Reality?

Perhaps as we get older our dreams are a way of allowing us to continue to have a full life. That's why I'm so rapt with lucid dreaming. At one stage, since I believe in euthanasia, I convinced myself that I would commit suicide when I became useless. Now I'm lucid dreaming I don't think I will. I feel that dreaming is an aspect of my life which is now improving. As my physical life is starting to deteriorate, my lucid dreaming life is just starting to explode.
(Alex, clerk)

So it's the slow slide from one reality to another?

(Jane Anderson)

That's how I feel about astral travel. As a child I wanted to travel and would read over atlases. I haven't had the opportunity to travel so now I do it in my dreams.

(Chiron, astrologer)

And you do often see a lot more than you would in a photo or a book.

(Tania, tax consultant)

It's just as real.

(Jaquelyn, librarian)

If it's real to you, you don't have to prove that to anyone. If it felt real to you and it was an experience which changed your life for the better in some way, it was real.

(Jane Anderson)

BIBLIOGRAPHY

Capra, Fritjof. *The Tao of Physics*, Fontana Paperbacks, London, 1989.

Crisp, Tony. *Dream Dictionary*, Optima Macdonald, London, 1990.

Davies, Paul. *The Mind of God*, Penguin Books, 1992.

Faraday, Ann. *Dream Power*, Berkley Books, 1984.

Gackenbach, Jayne & LaBerge, Stephen (eds). *Conscious Mind, Sleeping Brain—Perspectives on Lucid Dreaming*, Plenum Press, New York & London, 1988.

Hayward, Susan. *A Guide for the Advanced Soul*, In-Tune Books, Avalon, Australia, 1984.

Hobson, J. Allan. *The Dreaming Brain*, Basic Books, 1988.

Kaplan Williams, Strephon. *The Dreamwork Manual*, The Aquarian Press, London, 1984.

Kennett, Frances. *How to Read your Dreams*, Marshall Cavendish, 1975.

LaBerge, Stephen & Rheingold, Howard. *Exploring the World of Lucid Dreaming*, Ballantine Books, New York, 1990.

MacKenzie, Norman. *Dreams & Dreaming*, Bloomsbury Books, London, 1989.

Your Innermost Thoughts Revealed: Dreams: Hidden Meanings & Secrets, Tophi Books, Ramboro London, 1987.

INDEX

Guide to Good Dreaming, and 63

high detail dreamers and 37

recurring 15, 31, 49–51, 103, 114, 158

see also hypnopompic hallucinations

Nirvana 284

non-visual dreams 14, 41, 42, 43–4

noses 92

NREM sleep 256–7, 258–9, 260, 261, 268

nurses 173

OBE *see* out-of-body experiences

observing 148–9, 150

occupation 25, 303

odours *see* smells

offices 88

Oneirocritica 272

open-plan houses 85–6

ornaments 90

out-of-body experiences 16, 31, 37, 52, 131, 218–22 *see also* astral travel

outdoor locations 19–20, 36

outer world 264, 299–300

overburdened and stressed 110–11

pain 44

paintings 122, 134

palaces 85

paradoxical sleep *see* REM sleep

parallel realities 286–7, 292

parks 77

passages 88, 137, 138, 142

passive action 144, 145, 148–51

past 111–12, 157, 161–3, 212–14, 231–2

Paula 137–8

Pearl

on changed perception 288–90

on falling & being trapped 76–7

on problem solving 193–5

people

acting as themselves 157, 160, 161

aspects of self in 160–1

checklist of 174–6

identity of 156–7

known entities 156, 157–65, 174–5

past life 156, 161–3

survey dreamers and 36, 155–6

see also deceased people; elderly people; presences; relatives; strangers; yourself

perception

of alternative realities 262–4

of outer/inner worlds 264

perfume 46, 47

personal symbols 119–26, 247, 274, 275, 276

personality aspects 170–1

Peta 114–15

phallic symbols 100, 275

Philippa 112

philosophy 66, 280–90

physical exercise 25, 31, 32, 37, 38, 65

physical warnings 114–15

physiology 255–70, 274, 291, 294

pictorial conciousness *see* hypnagogic sleep

pigs 101

stress
    detail and 37, 38
    frequency and 32
    Guide to Good Dreaming and
        64
    High Frequency Dreamer and
        31
    Ms Survey Dreamer and 26
    nightmares and 51
    overburdening and 110–11
Stuart
    on emotional hangovers 128
    on his feminine side 167–8
studies 88
study
    detail and 37
    Guide to Good Dreaming and
        65
    High Frequency Dreamers and
        31
    nightmares and 50
subatomic particles 286, 301
subconscious 25, 39, 48, 127,
    145, 186, 305
sugar 42, 64
suicide 280, 281
summer 83
sun/sunshine 80, 83
supplements see health
    supplements
survey see Dream Survey
Susan 203
swans 99
swimming 19, 80, 109, 130, 145
swimming pools 76, 109
symbols 35, 36, 45, 69–102,
    119–26, 136–42, 147, 161,
    162–3, 164, 173, 174, 200,
    239, 244, 247, 275, 276–7,
    300

synchronicity 295–302

tables 89
Tai Chi 32, 64
Talmud 103
Tania
    on learning 308, 309
    on lucid dreams 30, 307–8
    on time 308
tanks 76
Tantric philosophy 101
Tara
    on aliens 233
    on strangers 165
taste 41, 42, 46
tea 32, 50, 64
teachers 173
teeth 91
telepathy 47, 157, 159, 206,
    244, 264, 266
television
    detail and 39
    Guide to Good Dreaming and
        65
    hours of viewing 12, 26
    nightmares and 51
    recall and 33
    symbolism of 90, 183, 227
television script method 188
temperature 44
temples, healing 196, 197
termites 98
texture 44
third eye 285
third parties 149
thought messages 230
throat 92
thunder and lightning 81
thyroid hormones 259
tidal waves 82, 104–5, 142